do not go gentle

do not go gentle

my search for miracles in a cynical time

ann hood

picador USA   new york

www.picadorusa.com

Picador® is a U.S. registered trademark and is used by St. Martin's Press under license from Pan Books Limited.

For information on Picador USA Reading Group Guides, as well as ordering, please contact the Trade Marketing department at St. Martin's Press.
Phone: 1-800-221-7945 extension 763
Fax: 212-677-7456
E-mail: trademarketing@stmartins.com

Book design by Victoria Kuskowski

Material from this book originally appeared, in slightly different form, in *DoubleTake* magazine, *Parenting* magazine, *Italian Americana*, *Bon Appétit*, *O, The Oprah Magazine*, and *Tin House* magazine.

Grateful acknowledgment is given for permission to quote from "Do Not Go Gentle into That Good Night" by Dylan Thomas from *The Poems of Dylan Thomas*. Copyright © 1952 by Dylan Thomas. Reprinted by permission of New Directions Publishing Corp. Excerpts from "Part II: Day In and Day Out" are from *The Habit of Being: Letters of Flannery O'Connor*, edited by Sally Fitzgerald. Copyright © 1979 by Regina O'Connor. Reprinted by permission of Farrar, Straus and Giroux, LLC.

Frontispiece and all photographs, except as noted, are courtesy of the author. Captions and credits appear on pages 261–263.

Library of Congress Cataloging-in-Publication Data

Hood, Ann.
    Do not go gentle : my search for miracles in a cynical time / Ann Hood.
        p. cm.
    ISBN 0-312-24259-X (hc)
    ISBN 0-312-28313-X (pbk)
    1. Hood, Ann. 2. Catholic women—United States—Biography.
  3. Women novelists, American—20th century—Biography.
  I. Title.

BX4705.H6346 A3 2000
282'.092—dc21   00-034702
[B]

First Picador USA Paperback Edition: November 2001

10 9 8 7 6 5 4 3 2 1

for my father

prologue

Do not go gentle into that good night,
Rage, rage against the dying of the light.
—DYLAN THOMAS

EVER SINCE I STARTED to write professionally, I would tell my parents the plots and characters I had dreamed up. My mother always listened attentively, then said, "That sounds like a good story." She'd wait a minute and then add, "Next time, why don't you write about the family. Why don't you write about my sister Ann, and how she fell in love so young and died so tragically? Or about Nonna and the things she could do, that no one can explain?" Then she would sigh. "There are so many things right here," she'd say.

I always smiled and told her that was a good idea. But I didn't really believe it was a good idea.

I grew up Catholic in an Italian-American family in a small mill town in Rhode Island. At the heart of my family lay an unwavering faith in the power of things larger than ourselves. Sometimes this faith took the shape of traditions and superstitions brought over from the Old Country with my great-grandmother at the turn of the century. Sometimes it reflected beliefs of the Catholic Church, of which we were members and believers in its doctrine. And sometimes this faith's roots lay in family, in the strength and closeness that comes from a shared history, a shared home, a love that has no greater match.

Despite the usual falling away from faith that one suffers as time and experience intrude, I mostly held on to the same strong faith that my great-grandmother and grandmother and mother passed on to me. That faith gave me strength and hope and optimism. It kept me from loneliness and even despair. It was a faith that allowed me to believe in possibility, in goodness, and in miracles.

Then, on a beautiful September day in 1996, a series of events began that put my faith to a test. One day, in the midst of those events, as my father lay sick in the hospital, he took my hand and looked me right in the eye.

"What's all this supposed to mean?" he asked me.

"What?"

He shrugged. "All of it," he said.

We sat quietly for a moment, then he said, "You're a writer. When this is all done, figure it out and tell the world this story."

I did not know that by taking my father's advice to tell this story, I would also do what my mother had suggested for years: tell all of our stories. W. R. Inge wrote that every person makes two journeys in life. The outer journey is full of various incidents and milestones as we pass through our youth and middle age. The second is the inner journey, a spiritual Odyssey, with a secret history all its own. This is the story of my spiritual Odyssey.

1

the dream

THE DAY MY FATHER was diagnosed with inoperable lung cancer, I decided to go and find him a miracle. My family had already spent a good part of that autumn of 1996 chasing medical options, and what we discovered was not hopeful. Given our odds, a miracle cure did not seem too far-fetched. Eight years earlier, my father had given up smoking after forty years of two packs a day, and he had promptly been diagnosed with emphysema. Despite yearly bouts of pneumonia and periodic shortness of breath, he was a robust sixty-seven-year-old. Robust enough to take care of my young son Sam and, since he had retired, to cook and clean the house he and my mother had lived in for their forty-five years of marriage, while my sixty-five-year-old mother continued to work at the job she loved.

The house has been in my mother's family for three generations. It is a hybrid of styles and designs: The panelled walls and aluminum siding arrived in the sixties, but the pear and fig trees that grow in the backyard were planted by my great-grandmother at the turn of the century. It was her husband who dug the dirt cellar to store his homemade wine. Now that cellar holds everything from the steamer trunks my great-grandparents used when they moved to Rhode Island from Italy to my brother's long-ago-abandoned surfboard and my own Barbie nestled in her moldy lavender case.

We are a superstitious family, skeptical of medicine and believers in omens, potions, and the power of prayer. The week the first X ray showed a spot on my father's lung, three of us had dreams that could only be read as portentous. I dreamed of my maternal grandmother, Mama Rose.

I had good reason to distrust my grandmother. Mama Rose stood four feet ten and had ten children, twenty-one grandchildren, and flaming red hair until the day she died at the age of seventy-eight. She liked Elvis Presley, the "Old Country"—a small village in southern Italy—*As the World Turns*, and going into the woods to collect wild mushrooms. What she didn't like was me. This wouldn't have been a problem except that she lived with my family and so every day became a battleground for us.

Although my parents had technically bought our house from her back in 1964, Mama Rose never really let it go. She had, after all, lived there since she was two, except for three years in Italy recovering from a bout of scarlet fever. Despite her limited time in the "Old Country," Mama Rose acquired a thick Italian accent sprinkled with mispronounced words, her favorite being "Jesus Crest!" As an only child, the small three-bedroom house had suited her fine as she grew up. Until the day she died she had the same bedroom she'd had as a girl. The only changes were in her roommates: her husband, Tony; after he died her youngest daughter, June; and after June got married and our family moved in, me.

Already slightly afraid of her, I begged for a different bedroom. "Where do you want to go?" my mother would ask me, exasperated. My father was in the navy and after moving us back to Rhode Island was promptly shipped off to Cuba, an assignment that did not allow families. My mother had to find room for herself, my ten-year-old brother, and me, who was five. Upstairs, my great-grandmother was still in the room she'd occupied for the last sixty years. My mother moved back into her old bedroom, the same one she'd shared with her five sisters. And my brother was in the tiny former storage room that my three uncles shared as children.

"Of course," Mama Rose offered, "you could sleep there." "There" was a beat-up green couch in the kitchen that Auntie June had slept on until after her father died and she moved in with Mama Rose. To me, that couch held nightmares and ghosts. My strongest memory of it was when I was three and my Uncle Brownie died. Mama Rose lay there all day screaming and pulling her hair. I eyed the green couch and mumbled, "No thanks."

The nightmares came anyway. As I tried to sleep in Mama Rose's bed, the voices of my mother, grandmother, great-grandmother, and visiting aunts in the kitchen right outside the door told stories into the night. The stories were about children who spontaneously burst into flames, babies born with gills, and bad women in our neighborhood who put curses on people or visited them while they slept, sucking on their skin until bruises appeared. There were other women too, the poor women of the neighborhood who, unable to afford proper gifts to celebrate new babies or weddings, paid their visits at night as vapor.

Before everyone went to bed, they traded stories about the ghosts of Uncle Brownie and Auntie Ann, my namesake who had died years earlier at the age of twenty-three while having her wisdom teeth removed. Auntie Ann usually came to them in the form of a beautiful bird. But Uncle Brownie appeared as a full-fledged ghost, wandering around our house whistling happily, kissing foreheads, and smiling as he flew out the window.

Finally everyone would go home and Mama Rose would come to bed. Already terrified, I'd press my trembling self close to her. "Jesus Crest," she'd say, "move over. I can't believe this girl. She doesn't give me any room." Then she would shove me to my side of the bed where I stayed, wide-eyed, waiting to spontaneously combust or for Uncle Brownie to put his cold ghost lips against my head. Most nights, after I finally fell asleep, I would wake up Mama Rose by letting out a blood-curdling scream. "Jesus Crest," she'd say. "You almost gave me a heart attack. What is wrong with this girl anyway?"

When left to baby-sit my brother, younger cousin, and me, Mama Rose fried thick steaks for them and a hamburger patty for me. "I want a steak, too," I would say. "That is steak," she'd tell me. "Now shut up and eat." "This is a hamburger," I'd insist, while my brother chewed his steak, moaning with exaggerated pleasure. I would wait up for my parents and then list my grandmother's infractions: there was the hamburger patty, the way she let my brother watch the movie *The Bridge Over the River Kwai* instead of my beloved *Mary Tyler Moore Show*, and how she held my cousin on her lap and told me there wasn't room for two. Mama Rose listened to my complaints, shook her head, and said, "That girl has a tongue she can wipe her ass with. She tells stories."

Why Mama Rose didn't like me was always a mystery. Perhaps, as my mother suggested, I was too much like her. As a child, Mama Rose had been pretty and smart and sassy. Aging was not something she did gracefully. "She didn't like having a pretty little girl around getting attention," my mother speculated. Too, as the family matriarch after her mother died, no one questioned her decisions or pronouncements. Except me. I would, in my way, badger her. Why don't we all still live in Italy? Why did you have so many children? Why did you choose the man you married? Why do we have macaroni every Wednesday? Mama Rose would stand at the kitchen stove frying meatballs, making spaghetti sauce—gravy, she called it—and answering my questions, until finally she'd scream, "Look what you made me do! I put in sugar instead of salt! Jesus Crest! Shut your mouth already. Get out of here before I go crazy, before I have a heart attack!"

But where do you go when you don't have a room of your own? I would pick up a book and read at the kitchen table. And when that book was finished, I would write my own stories about a little girl with a mean grandmother, or a little girl chased by ghosts, or a little girl who travels back in time and meets another little girl who adores her and turns out to be the modern girl's grandmother as a child. Then my grandmother would appear in her gravy-splattered apron and shout, "Get out of my sight! You're driving me crazy!" "You're driving me crazy!" I would yell back. "I hate you!" "Good," she'd say. "Now let me watch my story." She would go into the living room and turn on *As the World Turns*. As soon as it finished, she would put in a call to Angelo, her bookie, and play numbers based on dreams the family had had. Number 240 meant a dream about a dead person, 248 a dream in which a dead person talked. If the dead person told you a number, it negated 248 and Mama Rose played the number the dead person gave her. "What was your dream?" I'd ask after she placed her bet. "You again! Talking again! Shut up and leave me alone!"

Once, crying in the living room after a particularly big battle of wills, I overheard my mother and grandmother talking. "Ann thinks I don't love her as much as I do some of the others," Mama Rose said. "And she's right." I had sensed it all along, but having the proof of my suspicions only made me feel worse, and it only made me try harder to please her. Nothing worked. Not asking what Bob Hughes and the shrew Lisa from her soap opera were up to, not sitting through hours of Lawrence Welk with her, not listening to her stories about the Old Country.

We settled into an uneasy relationship. Mostly, we tried to ignore each other. With my brother away at college and my great-grandmother dead, we suddenly had rooms to spare, and I was able to move into my own room upstairs. But I still had nightmares that sent me out of bed and roaming the house. It was then, late at night, that Mama Rose and I often met. She would burst out of her room as I sat at the kitchen table, all the lights blazing, sipping milk. "What's wrong with this girl?" she'd say. "You're going to give me a heart attack." She questioned me about my dreams to determine if there was a number to play or a prophesy hidden within them. Most of the time she deemed them worthless. "I'm old and I'm tired," she'd tell me, disgusted that not even my dreams were worth her time. "Go to bed. Go."

I entered adolescence, made friends, had dates, worked on school plays and the school newspaper, which all kept me busy and out of the house. Mama Rose complained that I spent too much time on the phone. "That girl, all she does is talk talk talk." She complained that my friends were all noisy. "I can't even hear my story on TV." When I sat outside the house in the car with a date for too long she came out to the front steps and yelled, "Get in here, you puttana! All the neighbors are looking!" She stayed there until, embarrassed and reluctant, I went inside. "Puttana!" she told me as I pushed past her. "Whore!"

When I went away to college, my nightmares stopped. On Christmas break of my freshman year, I stood at the stove with Mama Rose as she made meatballs and gravy. She told me a story about a girl who used to live up the hill who had claws like a lobster instead of hands. She told me about the woman who could tell true love by looking into a candle flame. Hoping for peace between us, I asked her how she made meatballs. She shrugged. I asked her about having babies: Did it hurt? How long did it take? Was it always the same? "Jesus Crest!" she yelled. "You and that tongue. Talk talk talk. Leave me alone." Hurt, I went upstairs and read until it was time to meet my father for lunch. While we were eating at a restaurant, my grandmother finished making a gallon of gravy, sat down in her chair, and died.

YEARS LATER, SHE CAME to me in my dreams—like Saint Rosalia, the patron saint of Palermo, my grandmother's unintentional namesake. Rosalia withdrew into a cave in 1159 when she was fifteen years old. Five hundred years later, when Palermo was in the grips of the Black Death, she appeared in a dream to a hunter napping on the mountainside and revealed the location of her bones. The archbishop found the bones right where Rosalia had described, and they were proven to be hers. When they were returned to Palermo and placed in a silver urn in the cathedral, the plague abated.

My Rose, however, never brought me truth or helped me to avert disaster. Always somber, dressed in black and wearing the hat she saved for special occasions, she would pretend to make up to me all the things she'd done when she was alive. An irrepressible gambler in life, in death she brought me numbers to play. Eagerly, I bought lottery tickets: 6-15-21-12. Each time, I lost by a single digit. "She's still torturing me," I complained to my cousin Gina. Gina was one of my grandmother's favorites because Gina's father had died when she was only two, and a dead parent immediately elevated your status. That same cousin got numbers in her dreams and always won.

Then came the night in late summer of 1996, twenty years after Mama Rose died, when she came to me again in a dream. This time she took my hand and led me through hospital corridors. She held on tight. "Listen," she told me. "There's a spot on your father's lung. He needs to see a doctor." She whisked me past an Indian doctor who was shaking his head outside a hospital room. "He's a fighter," the doctor told me. "But there's nothing else we can do." My grandmother gave me a number: 410. Then she did something remarkable and completely out of character. She hugged me. "Go," she said.

That same night, my cousin Gina—who had grown up next door to us with my father stepping in as a surrogate parent—dreamed of our Great-Uncle Rum. My father dreamed of his father for the first time since he died in 1957. All of these ghosts had one thing in common;

they were happy. The night after we had these dreams, everyone gathered at my house to celebrate my mother's sixty-fifth birthday. Like most daughters, I worked hard to please my mother, and I often felt that I fell short of her expectations. But this time everything seemed exactly right.

My husband and I were renting a large Victorian house on the East Side of Providence, just a few blocks from Brown University. We already had a three-and-a-half-year-old son, and I was in my ninth month of pregnancy with what we had learned was a daughter who we were going to name Grace. That very day we had visited my midwife and discovered I was already two centimeters dilated. The baby, she predicted, would probably be born before her October 1 due date.

The anticipation of the new baby added to our celebration. However, my uneasiness with the dream I'd had the night before kept getting in my way, even as Sam and I shopped on Federal Hill, Providence's Little Italy, that afternoon for the birthday dinner. The thing about that dream was how clear it remained, even all these hours later. And how that number—410—stayed with me. As I chose fresh mozzarella, prosciutto, two kinds of salami, my mind kept working over the details of the dream: the Indian doctor, the hospital hallway, Mama Rose's urgency.

At six o'clock, everyone was seated in the high-ceilinged, red-walled dining room. Our table, an old one I had bought on sale years earlier at Pier One Imports, was disguised under a thick cream-colored lace tablecloth. Candles flickered. Gina poured wine. Everything would be perfect if I could only stop myself from glancing at my father as if I could actually find, if I looked hard enough, a tumor growing in his lungs. Even with emphysema, he remained strong. By now we had all grown used to the inhalers he carried and used frequently, to his shortness of breath. To my eyes that night, he was tall and blond and handsome—the way I had always seen my dad.

My mother was happy to finally acquire some new grandchildren now that her only granddaughter, Melissa, was twenty-two, out of college, and working in Houston. Both of my parents spoiled Sam, and they looked forward to doing the same with Grace. Now Sam climbed onto my mother's lap, eating the antipasto from her platter. He ran over to hug Pa, his special name for my dad. The main course of farfelle with prosciutto and peas was a hit, and I thought I had pleased my mom on her sixty-fifth birthday: She was a picky eater but I had managed to cook food she liked, which for an Italian family is a true triumph; I was about to give her a new granddaughter; and even the tapes my father and I gave her to play in her new car were exactly what she wanted— Patsy Cline, Simon and Garfunkel, Tennessee Ernie Ford singing gospel music. My father had chosen them all, easily, and I was struck by how well he knew her. It was too easy to attribute that to their forty-five years of marriage. I've seen couples who, after as many years, still remain strangers. But my parents knew each other and readily pointed out the other's foibles, successes, loves, and dislikes. Many conversations with my father began, "Now you know what Mom thinks . . ." I didn't always know, but he did.

Sam and I had baked my mother a cake and decorated it with her favorite thing—clowns. By the time I served it, our party had grown in number. My mother- and father-in-law had joined us, and so had aunts and uncles and more cousins. This is always how my family has parties—the larger the better. For me, who had already gone through one divorce and had had my share of emotional and financial catastrophes, this night stood as a real accomplishment. I knew that my parents were both seeing me as finally settled and happy. And in many ways I was starting to see myself that way, too.

But then Gina mentioned the dream she'd had the night before about Uncle Rum.

"Isn't that funny?" my father said as he fed Sam a mouthful of cake. "I dreamed about my father last night. You know, I haven't dreamed of him since he died in—when did he die?"

"Fifty-seven," my mother said without missing a beat.

"No kidding," my father said, pausing. "My father's been dead almost forty years and he seemed as real as if I saw him every day."

I sat, a smile frozen on my face. Here was my family spread out before me. Around me there was the laughter and shouting and general noise that I grew up knowing. But I felt separate from all of it. My dream had been longer, more elaborate. In a family that believed that dreams could prophesize the future, my dream foretold the worst tragedy I could imagine.

"Well," my father was saying, "I'm glad to know they're all happy. Rum and Charlie Hood."

"I had a dream too. I dreamed about Mama Rose," I managed to say, unable to take my eyes off my father's face.

Could it be that I was already beginning the process of memorizing my father? His eyes the blue of a summer sky. The indentation on his forehead from a long-ago run-in with a tin can in a game of kick the can. His Hood ears, long with fleshy lobes that grew droopier over time. His pale blond hair with the receding hairline that appeared when he was nineteen and never receded any further. The faded tattoo of an eagle in front of a setting sun on his left forearm. Over the years, I had watched that tattoo fade from a bright blue and hot red to dull smudges of color.

Everyone was looking at me now.

"Busy ghosts," someone said.

"Mama Rose brought me a number," I told them, as close as I could come to revealing anything about the journey she took me on.

"Hell," my father said, laughing. "If she gave you a number we know it's no good. Tell us what it is so none of us play it."

Gina was a firm believer in all the superstition and tradition with which we had been raised. I could see the worry in her face.

"What do you think it means?" she asked.

I studied my family's faces around me—open, expectant. I could not tell them what I was beginning to believe was true. My father was going to die.

"Nothing," I lied. "I don't think it means anything at all."

A FEW DAYS AFTER my mother's birthday dinner my father developed a fever as the two of us ate souvlaki at the annual Greek Festival. Rhode Island, with its rich immigrant history, has a large supply of festivals. There are festivals for saints that are held at churches and there are festivals for all of the different ethnic groups. In West Warwick, the town where I grew up and where my parents still lived, many different immigrants had settled during the nineteenth century when the mills there flourished. Even now the Polish population still holds a festival where you can get homemade pierogi and kielbasa, and the Portuguese community has a festival—the La-La, it's popularly called—every Labor Day. As a child, I remember the La-La as the event that kept our family dog in the hall closet, hiding from the barrage of fireworks that exploded all weekend.

My father and I always went to the festivals together. We were each other's best dates. We both liked to drink good beer, eat good food, and watch crowds. We could spend hours doing those things together, and often did, commenting on the people around us.

"Now why do you suppose," he'd say, "that a woman would wear those colors? I can see wearing lime green like that. I can see the orange. I like orange just fine. Hell, I can even see wearing lemon yellow. But why do you suppose she'd put them all together like that and wear them at the same time?"

Then we'd speculate, creating a life or a series of circumstances that made sense. Satisfied, he'd pose the next problem.

"Why do you suppose that man who looks like a bird is with that lady who looks like a camel? Now there's nothing wrong with looking like a bird. . . ."

Our favorite festival was the German Oktoberfest each fall. Just the year before the two of us had taken Sam along. We found a seat close enough to the oompah band for Sam to watch, and we tasted all the different brews and ate bratwurst and sauerkraut. My mother was not partial to beer drinking or exotic dishes. On the trips to Europe we made over the years, she never took to any of the cuisine, while my father happily ate raw herring, rabbit stew, and frogs' legs.

The Greek Festival was held in early September at the Greek Orthodox Church in Cranston. Even when I lived in New York, I somehow managed to get home around this time of year. We had a long history at this festival. We always got the souvlaki plate, beer, and a platter of pastries to nibble while we watched the folk dancers spin and twirl. Last year Sam had joined the dancers dressed in traditional costumes, clapping his hands and imitating them.

Maybe it was my dream that led me this year to leave Sam behind.

"I feel funny going without my buddy," my father said when I picked him up.

He drove a small red pickup truck and he loved taking it everywhere. Tonight he asked if I'd mind driving. That now familiar ache in my chest appeared again.

"Are you sick?" I asked as we drove west along Route 37.

"I'm not feeling that great," he surprised me by answering.

Nervously I glanced at him. Was it the light from the streetlamps that made his complexion seem so waxy, I wondered? I reached over and touched his forehead.

"You're warm," I said.

"Knock it off or we won't go," my father said. "I mean it. You worry too much. It drives me crazy."

I swallowed back my fears as best I could.

When we arrived at the church, all of the parking lots were full. "Let's forget it and go home," my father said too readily.

I chewed my bottom lip to keep myself from blurting my growing concerns. "Come on," I said, circling again, "it's the Greek Festival. We have to go."

Out of the corner of my eye, I saw him shake his head.

"You know what?" I said, when still no parking spaces opened up. "I'll drop you off here and I'll go and park and meet you inside."

For years now we'd grown used to how my father, always the one to drop us off at the door, could no longer make the walk across a shopping mall or restaurant parking lot.

"Why, you can't do that!" he said. "Look at you!"

Although it was true that I was fully pregnant, and had complained to him earlier that now that the baby had "dropped" it was difficult to walk, it somehow seemed more important that we go and eat our souvlaki, as if this festival could cancel out any bad health or bad news.

"It's not that far a walk," I said.

"This is terrible," my father muttered, fumbling with the door handle. "Making you walk all that way."

"No problem!" I said, trying my best to sound cheery.

Once inside, though, it was even worse. My father didn't drink any of his beer, and only picked at his dinner.

"Next year we'll take Sam," I said. "We can't even have fun without him anymore."

I recognized how forced the smile my father gave me was.

In front of us, the folk dancers gathered. Their costumes were colorful, richly embroidered, and garishly happy.

"We've seen this before," my father finally said. "Let's get you that rice pudding you like and go."

It was so like my father to remember that I loved the creamy homemade rice pudding, dusted with cinnamon, that we had at the end of each Greek Festival. His thoughtfulness never stopped amazing me. "Oh here," he'd often say, "I saw this and thought of you." Sometimes it was a small thing—the kind of pen I like to write with or a bag of Tootsie Pops. But other times they were unforgettable things, like the Christmas before my first novel was published. All that fall my father said to me, "You're the star of the family." Then he'd chuckle. I knew he was up to something, but with my father it was impossible to guess what it might be. That Christmas he presented me with a certificate from the International Star Registry. As of December 25, 1986, the star formerly known as Cassiopeia Ra 2h 39m 43sd 58 43' would now be known as Ann Hood.

We left the Greek Festival, me wobbling pregnantly and clutching two Styrofoam containers of rice pudding, my father unable to walk even a few steps without stopping to catch his breath, his forehead still hot to the touch. "I'm taking you to the hospital," I said. I was convinced, as we walked slowly into the emergency room at Kent County Hospital, that he had another bout of pneumonia.

The emergency room and its procedures had become familiar to us since my father was first diagnosed with emphysema back in 1988. My father had smoked for so long that he couldn't even remember exactly when he'd first started. "I was a kid," he'd say and shake his head sadly. "If I had it to do over, that's the one thing I'd change. I would never have smoked at all." As it was, he smoked several packs a day until, in 1967, he lost his voice and did not get it back. The doctor prepared him for the worst: throat cancer. His own father, my grandfather Charlie Hood, had had throat cancer and had to have his voice box removed. Now my father faced the same fate.

When the tests turned out negative, the doctor told him, "You're one lucky bastard. Since you got scared enough to quit smoking, why not stop anyway?"

That began a twenty-year cycle of quitting smoking and then starting up again. Once my father quit for three years, only to start again when my cousin's husband was killed in an auto accident in Europe. The pattern became a familiar one. My father tried everything, from cold turkey to hypnosis. But once hard times hit, he reached for his cigarettes again. Then, in 1988, I became pregnant for the first time. I had been married to my first husband for about five months when I learned that, much to my surprise, I was pregnant.

I drove the three and a half hours from New York to Rhode Island to give my parents the news. My father was the happiest. He loved children, and he had always wanted a house full of his own. Grandchildren, he decided, were even better. As soon as I told him I was pregnant, he put out the cigarette he was smoking and threw out the rest.

"I want to make sure I'm around to play with my grandkids," he said.

Even though I miscarried a few days later, he never smoked again.

So it was ironic that on a vacation I took with my parents to San Francisco, my father told me he had been growing increasingly short of breath. I remember standing on Geary Street, waiting for the bus that would take us to the Cliff House for brunch. It was a glorious Sunday, with a sky the blue that only California skies have. The three of us loved San Francisco and had vacationed there several times together. On this day, we saw the bus approaching and had to hurry to the stop not to miss it. But my father could not hurry. Something was wrong.

In 1982, my thirty-year-old brother died in an accident, and ever since then I had been especially sensitive to anything that threatened our fragile family even more. I shivered, despite the warm sun.

"He's going to get it checked when we get home," my mother told me, patting my leg and looking out the window of the bus. "He promised."

I could only manage a nod.

Not long after we got home from that trip, my father called to tell me he had a touch of emphysema. I knew better. Emphysema wasn't like a cold. You didn't get a touch of it. You had it and it was, ultimately, fatal. But all of us played along. Over the next eight years, the word

do not go gentle | 19

emphysema was never spoken. Instead, my father explained that he had asthma. He acquired several different inhalers, and his puffing on them became routine to us. He still climbed the stairs to the second floor of my parents' house without too much difficulty. He worked in the yard, played with my son, did most things. We could, for a while, pretend.

But when someone is slowly suffocating to death, it becomes more and more difficult to ignore. There is the heavier reliance on those inhalers, for example. There are more frequent trips to the emergency room for steroids or oxygen. Pneumonia strikes more often and becomes harder to treat.

Now here we were again, in the emergency room, my father breathing better with the oxygen and steroids they gave him. They took a chest X ray.

"I don't see any pneumonia," the ER doctor told us. "But with emphysema like you've got, it's hard to tell."

He prescribed antibiotics and sent us home.

"I already feel better," my father said.

I glanced over at him again. His cheeks were rosy now. Steroids can do that, giving the illusion of good health. He was more alert and hungry for that rice pudding that sat in a bag between us. There was no reason to dampen his good spirits and bring up the doctor's words about emphysema. Instead, I reached across the seat and held his hand the rest of the way home, along the same roads he had taken my mother to the hospital the day I was born.

the diagnosis

THE X RAY THEY took that night in the emergency room was sent to my father's regular doctor. I arrived at my parents' house the next morning with a bag of bagels. My father and I always brought each other breakfast, doughnuts, muffins, Danish pastry. We liked to sit together over what he called "coffee and" and talk away the morning.

I will always remember this morning in detail because I have come to think of it as the true beginning of the real nightmare that was to follow. My father stood at the back door of the house. When I got out of the car in my black maternity shorts and striped top, holding the bag of bagels, he stepped onto the back porch. He had built that porch himself and painted it my mother's favorite color, red. It was a sunny September day. A beautiful day, really.

My father was wearing a blue plaid flannel shirt, and when he stepped outside, I stopped walking, stopped right at the bottom of the steps, and looked up at him. Even now I do not know what made me pause there; my father always came outside to greet me, just as he always stood on the porch, waving, as I drove away. I stopped and looked up at him and he said the words that changed my life.

"The X ray showed something," he said dismissively. "They need to do a few more tests."

I remember swallowing hard, but not being able to dislodge the lump in my throat. I remember telling myself to stay calm, and how my legs grew heavier as I climbed the stairs and followed my father inside. When you walk in the back door of the house, you enter the pantry, a small room that always smells of equal parts coffee and Comet cleanser. From the pantry, you walk into the kitchen. My mother always decorates the kitchen to match the season. At the end of summer, it's often decked out for a picnic, with a red plaid tablecloth on the table and cheery red curtains on the two windows. It is hard to have the discussion we were about to have in such a cheerful room.

"Is it pneumonia they saw in the X ray?" I asked as I set out bagels and cream cheese.

"She said a widening."

"Widening? Or whitening?"

"I don't know," he said, fixing his coffee: cream, two sugars.

In the bright sunny kitchen, he looked healthy, despite how we'd spent a good part of the night before.

"Here," he said. "I wrote it down." He put on his glasses and read from a scrap of paper. "I need to go next week and get a CAT scan and a sonogram—"

The words buzzed uncomfortably in my ears. "You have a spot on your lung," I managed to say.

"Now that's not what she said," he told me. "Don't go putting words in everyone's mouth. She said a whitening."

"Or widening," I reminded him.

"I'm fine," he told me. Then he said one of his favorite lines: "Never had more or wanted less."

I smiled at him, then robotlike went upstairs to my old bedroom. It still looked exactly as I had left it: the yellow-and-white gingham curtains and matching bedspread, the antique white furniture with the gold trim, shelves that held mementoes from long ago—my TWA flight attendant graduation class photograph, a picture taken on a high school trip to Bermuda, a papier-mâché Don Quixote my mother and I bought on a day trip to a Mexican border town. I picked up the phone and called information for the number of my father's doctor. Then, with my father moving about downstairs, whistling happily, I called his doctor.

"Oh, yes," she said, "it's a spot of some kind. A former smoker with emphysema, of course we suspect the worst. Pray to God it's something else."

I thanked her and hung up. Then I sat there, on the edge of my girlhood bed, with sunlight streaming in the window and my father whistling in the background.

Until he called up to me: "Do you want any of these bagels?"

"Coming," I said, snapping out of my stunned daze.

I walked downstairs where my father sat at the red checkered covered table, a smear of cream cheese on his chin. When he ate, he always spilled or smeared, much to my mother's chagrin. I reached over and wiped his chin with my fingertip. He had a heart-shaped face, just like mine.

"What were you doing up there?" he asked me.

I did not want to let go of him, so I climbed onto his lap, all of my pregnant self fitting easily.

"I was looking for something," I said, holding on tight.

AFTER HIS FIRST CAT scan, my father had a consultation with his doctor. My mother, Gina, and I accompanied him, huddling together in the same office I'd had my tonsils looked at as a child and my college bout with mononucleosis diagnosed. My father's doctor had bought our old family doctor's practice and inherited a good many of Dr. Racioppi's patients, although there was a large group, of which my mother was a member, who followed Dr. Racioppi from one part-time job to another, grateful that his "retirement" was only a partial one.

My father, however, chose to stay on with the husband-and-wife team who had taken over. Usually my father saw the wife; she had been the one to read the ER X ray and find the spot. But it was her husband we saw when we showed up en masse for the consultation.

"I must be frank," he said. "You probably have lung cancer."

My father nodded and thanked him for his honesty while I sat, a notebook and pen in hand, unable to write or speak. Gina's friend, whose father had survived prostate cancer, had given her this one piece of advice: Write down everything the doctor says. I could not get myself to write this down, however.

"I'm sorry," the doctor said.

My father's lungs hung on the wall in front of us, his emphysema making Swiss cheese of them, the spot indeed a whiteness in the middle.

do not go gentle | 25

The doctor marvelled at his wife's astuteness in even seeing the spot at all. "I would have missed it," he said more than once. "She's amazing."

This triggered a question that had been on my mind since the beginning: My father had had pneumonia just a few months earlier, had had as many as four X rays in the past year. Why was this spot never detected?

The doctor shrugged. "I would have missed it even now." He gave us the name of a local pulmonary specialist and stood for us to leave. When he shook my father's hand good-bye, he gripped his shoulder as well, a gesture I saw repeated so often over the next few months that I began to wonder if it was taught in medical school, the farewell handshake to a terminally ill patient. Even though no one had said it, I was convinced early on that was what my father was.

Although my father took a wait-and-see attitude from the start, I could not stop from thinking the worst. My dream of a few weeks earlier kept returning to me, its detail vivid. If I kept my father away from Indian doctors, could I save him? I thought ridiculously at one point. The number 410, I decided, was the number of days my father had left. Mama Rose had come to prepare me for my father's impending death. I calculated from the day of the dream and landed on October 19, 1997.

My cousin and I argued for finding the best pulmonary specialist around. Forget these local doctors and this small community hospital, we said. We're fighting something big here. We need the biggest and the best. I saw my father glance at my mother warily.

"You are fighting, aren't you?" I asked. How often had I read about people surviving against all odds because they had a fighting spirit? Without that, surely he wouldn't make it.

"You're damn right," my father said. "I'm not ready to die."

"But he could have just some scarring on his lung," my mother said.

"We have to wait and see," my father added.

It was my turn to glance at Gina. The doctor had sounded so certain. But here was the beginning of the false hopes that get you through a terminal illness. When we had asked the doctor if anything other than lung cancer was possible, he'd struggled to come up with answers. "Scarring?" he'd said finally, doubtfully. "TB?"

I couldn't wait and see. I needed to fix my father. The first person I called was my husband's physician, a widely regarded gastrointestinal specialist. He gave me the name of the doctor he considered the best. Then I called a friend who was a nurse, and my sister-in-law, a locally trained doctor. The same name came up each time. Without hesitating, I made an appointment with Dr. Meyer.

ITALIANS FIND SIGNS EVERYWHERE. A song you danced to with an old love, played on a radio, can warn you of a phone call from him. A crossword puzzle answer could give you a deeper answer you seek. Seeing a license plate similar to the license plate of an estranged friend could mean that person is reentering your life. So it was that when we visited Dr. Meyer that first time, we found signs. First, his office was located right near Sam's school.

"Isn't this something?" my father said cheerfully as we walked into the office. "You never go to a place and then everything is there."

A good sign.

When we entered Dr. Meyer's office my mother and I both gasped. He was a dead ringer for my ex-husband. A bad sign? I wondered.

As if she'd read my mind, my mother patted my hand. "It's good that he looks like him," she said. "Familiar. Nice."

I wanted to go along with her interpretation but the doctor's seeming edginess made me wonder. He took my father's history, his face animated when he got the dates of my father's navy service.

"You were exposed to asbestos," he said, writing.

"Probably," my father said.

Somehow the doctor made this sound like a good thing, but my father's diagnosis was becoming more and more definite to me.

The results of a breathing test came back poor.

"You'd have trouble with a big surgery," the doctor said.

"He needs surgery?" my mother asked quickly.

"Now I didn't say that," the doctor said.

By the time we left, he had said very little. The only thing he was certain of was that my father had swallowed a button, probably as a little boy, and it was lodged in his lungs; and there was, most definitely, a spot in the mediastinum. My father had a schedule of tests. There was the strong possibility of lung cancer. But, at our prodding, this doctor also came up with a tuberculosis theory. There was so much in the blanks he left for us to fill in that I found it difficult to walk. When he said good-bye, the doctor looked right in my father's eyes, shook his hand, and gripped his shoulder.

"Why do you suppose they all do that?" my father said. "The next guy is probably going to kiss me good-bye."

EACH TEST CAME BACK negative. Our hopes began to soar. Even mine. It was completely possible that my dream—that all of our dreams that night of September 4—had been just coincidence. Instead of ghosts rallying to foretell my father's death, we had each simply dreamed of ghosts. Lymphoma was ruled out. So was TB. The next test was a bronchoscopy to have a look at the bronchial tubes. And, my mother hastened to add, the doctor did not believe he would find cancer there.

None of us understood that everything was being eliminated to make room for the diagnosis all the doctors believed my father had. Instead, we took hope from each clear test. On September 24, he would have the bronchoscopy. If that was negative, there was only one test left to have.

I woke at six that morning in labor. My labor for Sam had been induced, but I still recognized exactly what was going on. As my husband left for work, I asked him if I knew where to reach him. He paused in our bedroom doorway.

"Is something happening?" he asked me.

"Uh-huh."

The next person I told was my father.

"Don't panic," I began when I called him.

"Are you in the hospital?"

"No, no. I'm at home. The pains are still pretty far apart."

"What did the midwife say?"

"I called you first," I said.

"Call her. I'm on my way."

By the time he showed up, I had visited my midwife, who confirmed that I was definitely ready to have the baby. She sent me back home to eat some lunch and wait for the contractions to be three minutes apart. My father brought a big pot of my favorite Italian-style stew, with cubes of beef that fell apart at the touch of a fork, chunks of carrots and potatoes, and a red broth. He brought a loaf of bread for dipping, which was the necessary accompaniment. Feeding me was one of my father's favorite things. After I'd had an amniocentesis that spring, he spent the afternoon cooking for me so I could stay in bed. When I was ordered to gain more weight during this pregnancy, he had arrived at my door with a dozen cartons of Ben and Jerry's ice cream.

Now I sat with my father and ate his homemade stew, dipping in hunks of bakery-fresh bread. "It's F. Scott Fitzgerald's hundredth birthday," I told him as he paced with excitement and worry.

"I just think you should be in the hospital instead of sitting here eating stew and talking about F. Scott Fitzgerald," he said. He stopped pacing and laughed. "You might think I was the one having the baby," he said.

Then I asked him the impossible. "You aren't going to die, are you?"

"I sure as hell hope not," he said, laughing.

A contraction tore across my belly and I leaned over to ease it. As soon as I could I asked him again.

"I'm serious," I said. "I need you."

"Honey," he told me, "I'm not going anywhere."

LATER THAT AFTERNOON, MY father was in one hospital having a bronchoscopy while I lay across town in another hospital giving birth to Grace. My husband and I had opted to deliver her in the Alternative Birthing Center instead of upstairs in labor and delivery. The birthing rooms in the ABC, as it's called, looked more like Marriott hotel rooms than rooms in a hospital. While my father had a scope put down his throat so the doctor could look at his bronchial tubes, I sat in a Jacuzzi sipping ice water and doing my breathing exercises.

On their way home from the Miriam Hospital, my parents drove right past Women and Infants, where I was in labor.

"Let's check on Ann," my mother said, and they abruptly got off the highway and found their way through the lower-floor labyrinth to the

ABC. Confused by the layout, they took a seat in the waiting room with its soft drinks and TV and flowered sofas, unaware that on the other side of the door I was on a king-sized bed delivering Grace.

At one point, my mother heard me yell in pain. She dropped the magazine she was glancing at and said, "Hood, Ann is right in the next room."

"Don't be ridiculous," he said. "She's somewhere down that hall having the baby."

But the next time they heard me groaning, he was convinced too. "You're right," he said. "She's right here."

The next thing they heard was the midwife announcing that Grace was born.

In the midst of the worst of my labor, I was certain that I heard my parents' voices. Once Grace was safely delivered, I called to them. "Come on in," I said, "and meet Grace."

It is part of my family's lore that when I was finally born after my mother endured thirty-six hours of hard labor, the doctor did the unthinkable for 1956: He brought me unwashed and naked to my waiting father. "Here she is," Dr. Racioppi told him. "Now go home."

Whenever my father told this story, he added, "And you were the most beautiful thing I'd ever laid eyes on."

Now all these years later, my father—who hadn't seen his own son until he was already several months old and had first viewed Sam through the nursery's Plexiglas window—saw Grace before she was even one minute old, all bloody and naked.

He couldn't stop gazing at her. "You know," he said finally, "I haven't seen a baby this beautiful since Dr. Racioppi brought you to me forty years ago."

In that moment, when my father met his granddaughter, I believed that God would not deprive her of knowing him.

A few nights later, back at home again, my father and I had a Friday night together. He brought a spaghetti-and-meatball dinner, then sat with Sam and Grace and me as we watched Mary Poppins in my bed. From the rocking chair across the room, my father had a poor view of the television, but a perfect view of the three of us. Eventually, Sam fell asleep on one side of me, and Grace fell asleep in my arms.

"Ann and her babies," I heard him say softly as I too began to drift off. "What a beautiful sight."

THE FINAL TEST WAS, of course, the biopsy. My mother, Gina, and I—holding newborn Grace—took my father to Miriam Hospital in Providence and then went to get breakfast. We had grown optimistic with each new disease eliminated. We shopped in the hospital gift shop, and agreed it was the best one so far. I breast-fed Grace.

Then my mother said, "This is taking a long time, isn't it?"

It was, but we refused to return to the fears all of this had stirred in us. Gina spotted the anesthesia nurse and approached her.

"How's Mr. Hood?" Gina asked.

Was it my imagination, or did the nurse in the pink flowered uniform avert her eyes?

"He did fine for me," she said.

"So he's okay?"

"He did fine," the nurse said again.

I was not yet used to the euphemisms medical staff used. In her words I heard *he is fine*, and relaxed.

Finally, the surgeon we hardly knew shouted across the hospital waiting room: "Where are the Woods?" I stood, cradling my newborn daughter. "Hood," I said. "Over here."

He walked over to us and without any hesitation said, "He's got cancer. A fair-sized tumor that's inoperable. We can give him chemo, buy a little time. Your doctor will give you the details." He had taken the time to give my father the same information, even though, coming out of anesthesia, it had seemed like a nightmare to him.

When someone died in our family, my father pulled out his extra-large bottle of Jack Daniels. It had gotten us through the death of my cousin's young husband, my own brother's accidental death in 1982, and the recent deaths of two of my forty-something cousins. That late September afternoon, back at home, my father pulled out the bottle for his own grim prognosis. As the day wore on we got more news: Only an aggressive course of chemotherapy and radiation could help, and even then the help would be short-lived, if it came at all. "Taxol," the pulmonary specialist told us, "has given some people up to eighteen months."

But the way he bowed his head after he said it made me realize that eighteen months was not only the best we could hope for, but a long shot. My sister-in-law, a doctor too, was harsher. "Six months after diagnosis is the norm," she'd said.

Later, we would have our hopes raised and dashed again and again. At the Dana Farber Cancer Institute in Boston, Gina, my father, and I sat through a day of specialists, waiting for one of them to say he could help us. My father had dressed for the occasion in his brown tweed sport jacket and corduroy pants. Almost lightheartedly, the three of us moved from lab to lab, doctor to doctor. My research had told us that a surgeon here, with the unlikely name of Sugarbaker, could work miracles.

Dr. Meyer had warned us against radical treatments or surgeries. He did not believe my father could endure a lengthy operation. "And do me one more favor," he said. "Don't go on the Internet and try all the wacky things there." His message was clear: Take Taxol and keep your fingers crossed. But that wasn't good enough for us.

When Dr. Sugarbaker bounded in, all southern accent and good humor, he said many things. But the only one we cared about was this: "If we can shrink it, I can take that sucker out." The other doctors reconvened, studying the X rays as Dr. Sugarbaker pointed and talked. I felt elated for the first time in weeks. Every night, as I fed and rocked my baby, Grace, I sobbed in her moonlit nursery. Now there was something concrete, something to aim for.

I had gone to Barnes and Noble with the type and level of cancer my father had scribbled on a piece of paper. When I found it finally in a medical book, I sat on the floor and read that lung cancer that has metastasized to the lymph nodes is usually fatal. The only hope was surgery. Tumors that could be removed gave better chances for survival. Dr. Sugarbaker became that chance for my father. The doctors all gave us their office numbers, beeper numbers, service numbers. They were our team now, they said. And they created a team in Rhode Island to administer the chemo and radiation for my father. The oncologist's name made me shiver.

"That's Indian, isn't it?" I asked.

"Yes," they said. "Hard to pronounce. But everyone calls him Dr. Sam."

Dr. Sam's nurse, whom we needed to call, was named Grace. Sam and Grace, just like my kids. My father took it as a good sign. I tried not to let my mind go back to my dream. This was all good news. I refused to take it as anything else. Besides, in a few weeks I was going to find another kind of miracle, to supplement the medical one that possibly lay ahead.

That day of the diagnosis, sitting in the kitchen that had once held my mother and her ten siblings, their parents and grandparents every day for supper, I did some quick math. Was it possible that the man sitting across from me sipping Jack Daniels would not be alive at Easter? At six feet two and over two hundred pounds, cracking jokes about the surgeon, he did not look like someone about to die. He was not someone I was going to let die. If medical science could only give him a year and a half tops, then there was only one real hope for a cure. "There's a place in New Mexico with miracle dirt," I announced. "I'm going to go and get you some."

"Well," my father said with typical understatement, "I guess I can use all the help I can get."

my father

MY FATHER WAS THE love of my life.

I suppose most little girls have the same adoration of their dads as I did for mine. I see it with my own young daughter, the way she gazes up at the seemingly endless length and breadth of her father, the way she fits perfectly into his arms, how eagerly she climbs into his lap, accepts his kisses, delights when he calls her Sweetie Pie. He is the elusive one, away at the office all day, appearing at six o'clock, handsome in his suit and tie. After nursery school, baby-sitters, accompanying me to the grocery store and bank and other dull errands, after painting and storybooks and batches of Rice Krispie squares, he appears and she runs, happily, to him.

The only difference I've seen between this everyday father-daughter love and the one I had with my father is that mine never ended. He remained the man I happily ran to, the tall, handsome blond who, long after I was too big to get picked up by him, managed figuratively to never stop doing it. Even as an adult, I waited eagerly by my apartment window until I saw his red pickup truck arrive. Then I watched him walk to my door, carrying a box of Dunkin' Donuts and two coffees, whistling the whole way.

He liked to whistle, off-key and frequently. When I was growing up, my mother left for her job as a tax payer assistant for the IRS before he did, so my father was the one who woke me for school. The routine was always the same. First he stood whistling in the doorway. Then he came in, opened the curtains, pulled up the blinds, and sang: "I'm a-whistlin' . . . Are you listenin' . . . To my happy little washday song . . ."

Breakfast was always the same too, a jumbo hot chocolate that he made with real milk and cocoa—except on April Fool's Day when he used water and cocoa mix and saw me off with a reminder to trick someone.

My first memories of my father are of a tall, lanky man in a white sailor suit, standing at the railing of a ship that is pulling away. Black-and-white pictures of him shirtless by the sea on tropical islands were scattered everywhere around our house. My mother made my brother and me wear sailor hats, a tribute to our father while he was away. I remember picking him up at that same ship, and the way he lifted me into his arms. He smelled of Old Spice, Vitalis, and salt water, always.

I was eight when he came home to stay. That year, my brother began attending Wednesday evening coed dances in the junior high gym. They slow danced to "Blue Velvet" and tried out the Monkey and the Swim. My mother was a chaperone, driving a car full of thirteen-year-olds to the school and making sure they kept a respectable distance between one another when they waltzed.

As soon as they left, my mother in a red dress, my brother in a suit and tie, hair slicked back with my father's borrowed Vitalis, my father turned to me and asked, "So, Honey, what are we going to do tonight?"

My answer was always the same: bake in my Easy-Bake Oven. All week I planned what we would make on Wednesday. Miniature muffins, perfect round cakes, bite-sized cupcakes.

"Always read the directions first," my father would say. Then he would read aloud the instructions, always adding after each step, "Why, this is easy! We can do this!"

My brother and mother came home shortly after eight. In our two hours together my father and I had not only baked and eaten our good-ies, but he had also listened to me. I was a friendless, lonely child with a huge imagination. Over tiny slices of yellow cake, I would tell him my thoughts and theories about life and third grade. I would explain what the bullies Susan and Jill had done to me lately. I would read him the stories I wrote that week.

He marvelled at my writing, even then.

"How did you come up with that?" he'd ask me. "Why, that's just as good as anything I've ever read."

He considered my theories on things carefully, prodding for further explanation or clarity. He nodded thoughtfully. Sometimes he disagreed, and told me so. But more often he conceded that he had never thought of that in quite that way. I was special, he told me, and he convinced me he was right.

My father's wisdom came from being in the world and having experiences. After my brother outgrew the Wednesday night dances, my father and I moved our time together to Friday nights. Every Friday my mother played poker with eleven other women until well after midnight. My father and I went out to dinner or to the movies. And just like on our Wednesdays, we spent most of that time talking.

He told me stories about Morocco and China and Spain. He described typhoons, bar fights in Japan, how San Francisco's cable cars worked. In Africa he saw it rain on one side of the street and remain sunny on the other. He saw a tribe who washed with olive oil and grew rancid in the sun. He was on a South Seas island where the people did not wear clothes. In China, people fell dead from starvation right at his feet. He once ate dog stuffed with rice. He ate hundred-year-old eggs. He saw dancers: hula, flamenco, strippers in Times Square.

Those Friday nights with my father whet my appetite for travel. I would go to all those places and see all those things. He was not only wise, he was worldly. And he had a sophistication that was not immediately evident. A high school dropout, his grammar was often poor and his southern accent made him pronounce words differently: *roof* sounded like *ruff*, *Hawaii* was *Ha-wah-ya*. But he taught me how to properly set a table, to always order call liquor in my drinks. Better, he thought, to not eat steak if you have to have a poor cut of meat. Better to have fewer shoes than ones that were not made of real leather. "Remember," he used to say, "it only costs a little more to go first class."

By the time I was in high school, he was working in Providence for the IRS. During school vacations I met him for lunch at fancy restaurants. I would dress up for the occasion, and I can still see him in his expensive suit, sipping a Tanqueray martini while he waited for me. Our admiration for each other was mutual: His face lit up when he saw the hostess leading me to his table.

It was during one of these lunches that I asked his permission to take a trip alone with a girlfriend. I was sixteen, and I had worked for two years as a model, earning a lot of money. I saved that money for one thing: travel. Now I was ready.

He listened to how much I had saved and looked at all the travel brochures I'd gathered.

"I think you should go wherever you want," he said. "You've worked hard and it's about time for you to see the world."

My friend and I booked a week in Bermuda at the Princess, a first-class hotel that required men to wear ties in the dining room. My father's advice before I left was simple: "As long as you can communicate you can't get lost. If you don't know how to do something, just ask."

Our trip went without a hitch. It was my first flight, and I wore a new outfit for the occasion. I remember landing in Hamilton and easily navigating the airport and finding our way to the hotel. My father's advice and years of his stories about moving through the world guided me through the entire trip. On the flight back to Boston, I looked out the window, satisfied. I was on my way.

WHEN I LEFT FOR college the next year, my father began our custom of calling me every morning to wish me a good day, a custom that lasted until he got sick. He told me never to drink and drive, that he would drive the thirty miles to get me rather than have me on the roads. More than once he did that too.

Friends always remarked on my relationship with my father. Long ago for most of them, that special bond between father and daughter had been broken, by either distance or boyfriends or adult alienation. But as years passed, my father and I grew closer. If I had a question about boys or friends or life in general, I called him at work. He always took my call, and it was easy to forget that he was a busy man with an important job; he had the ability to make me think I was the most important thing to him.

While I was in college, my father started to work in Boston. He had an office high in Government Center, looking down on the city. Our lunches took place at Boston restaurants now, and he taught me how to navigate the city and its subway system. After I graduated and went to work as a flight attendant for TWA, I was first based in Boston. My father and I were delighted. My apartment was a few blocks from his office, and now when I met him for lunch I brought him stories of my own travels.

DURING MY ADULTHOOD, MY father grew more special to me. I moved often, from city to city, from apartment to apartment within a city. My father always came to help. He came too when I found myself confused about a decision I had to make, driving the three and a half hours to New York and sleeping on my sofa for a few nights so we could sort out the problem.

"It's not as bad as it seems," he'd always say.

At first, I would roll my eyes. He had no idea how bad it was this time. But by the time he left, he had managed to show me otherwise. Whether it was romance or finances or a career move, he showed me the way out of the problem. He did little things too, like showing up at my new apartment with a dozen juice glasses, saying, "I noticed you only have water glasses."

His honesty never flagged. The time I decided to move from my beloved Manhattan to pursue a relationship in Washington, D.C., he told me it was a bad idea. "Never give up everything for a guy," he said. Still, he was beside me in the U-Haul truck, driving south on the New Jersey Turnpike. And when that relationship proved unsatisfying, he simply listened, without reminding me how I had not taken his advice in the first place.

In 1992 I became pregnant with Sam. My father came to most of my midwife appointments, delighting in hearing Sam's heartbeat and watching him swim wildly on a sonogram. On the day Sam would be born, my father and I went to lunch and talked about the baby. "I can't remember the last time I was this excited," he said. He had big plans for this baby. Retired now, he intended to help me take care of him. Already he and my mother had attended a new-grandparents class at the hospital. He had carefully washed all of the tiny newborn clothes we'd bought, folding them neatly and helping me put them away in the nursery.

That afternoon I had a sonogram appointment. We didn't know as we sat over our turkey sandwiches that the sonogram would indicate Sam was underweight and that I would be induced to hurry his birth along. The next time I talked to him after that lunch was from my hospital bed. I made frequent calls to my parents over the next twenty-four hours. I had urged my mother to go to work, so it was my father who I spoke to with the news: "He's coming soon!" And then, a half hour later he was the first one I told: "Sam's here!"

I HAVE A PICTURE of my father holding Sam as a newborn, sitting in the rocking chair in my apartment, gazing down at him. The date on the picture is April 20, 1993. But it could have been taken any day that spring or summer because my father sat talking to Sam in that chair for hours every day. While I did the simple things new mothers can't seem to accomplish, like taking a shower or a nap, they sat together. Later, when I was writing in the next room, they sat together. They fell, immediately, in love.

By the time my father's diagnosis came, Sam was three and a half. In those years they created a bond that, even for that extraordinary realm of grandfathers and grandsons, was special. The fall my father fell ill, he had just seen me through my second pregnancy and the birth of Grace. That Friday night when he sat with the three of us, he wasn't the only one counting his blessings. I was too. Hanging over the joy of my baby daughter's arrival was the threat of my father's illness, the idea that he could be taken from me.

For my entire life my father was there for me, with constant love and honesty and common sense. He taught me simple basic morals. Never lie, he'd say. Rise above the negative people and things around you. Be whatever you want to be, but be the best at it. He taught me that love would always prevail. In many ways, he saved me. Lying there that night, I realized that this time he might be the one who needed saving. And I would do anything to save him.

A month later, I vowed to do just that.

healing sites

I DO NOT KNOW why I chose Chimayo to get my father a miracle. There were closer places, places with a bigger cultural significance, more well-known places. But without considering any of them, I knew I would go to Chimayo. Perhaps for some people the notion of seeking a miracle cure is tomfoolery, futile, or even a sign of pathetic desperation. The truth is, I believed that I would get a miracle for my father. I believed that my pilgrimage would work and that my father would be cured.

To believe in miracles, and certainly to go and look for one, you must put aside science and rely only on faith. For me, that leap was not difficult. In his 1969 essay "Prelates and Peasants," Rudolph Vecoli wrote, "Italian Catholics are only nominally Catholic." Theirs is a folk religion, he said, "a fusion of animism, polytheism and sorcery, with the sacraments of the church thrown in." Certainly the household I grew up in fits that description.

My great-grandmother, who died when I was six, healed people with a variety of ailments using prayer and household items, such as silver dollars and Mazola oil. The source of a headache was always believed to be the evil eye and my great-grandmother treated it by pouring water into a soup bowl, adding a few drops of oil, and making circles on the afflicted person's palm while muttering in Italian. Curing nosebleeds involved making the sign of the cross on the person's forehead. Around West Warwick, my great-grandmother was famous for her ability to cure sciatica. To do this, she would go to the person's house on the morning after a full moon. For a time she had a waiting list for her services.

I ONLY HAVE FUZZY memories of my great-grandmother, walking in the fields near our house, searching for certain roots and herbs. I remember people coming to our back door, speaking in hushed voices, often in Italian, and Nonna listening, weighing their situation.

Of course, most of the people she healed are long dead. But Julia Muratore, an old neighbor of ours, was alive in 1997, and Nonna had cured her husband's sciatica. She had moved from the old neighborhood, but my aunt knew where to find her.

One morning my telephone rang.

"Ann Hood?" a voice asked. "It's Julia Muratore."

I thanked her for calling me and started to explain how I'd tried to reach her. But Julia Muratore didn't want to make small talk. She had called to tell me about Nonna. It was no secret I was writing about miracles.

"You want to know about your great-grandmother?" she said.

I told her I did.

"If anyone doesn't believe you, have them call me," she said. "What I'm talking about happened way back. The early fifties. I'd heard she could do things. There were rumors about her."

"What kinds of things?"

"She could take pain away. In Italy we believe in that, you know. We believe that people can do things. And my husband Joe had sciatica so bad he couldn't stand it anymore. He'd been to every doctor and no one could help him. So we went to your great-grandmother. She came three days in a row to our house. Early early in the morning."

As Julia talked, I pictured my Nonna, her head covered in a scarf, dressed in black, making her way through our neighborhood streets at sunrise.

"We wanted to pay her but she said she couldn't accept money. I asked her what she needed and she said she could use linens, for the bed. So I gave her some new linens."

"Like sheets?" I asked, to be sure I understood correctly.

"Sheets. Pillowcases. Linens."

It seemed an odd thing to need, since Nonna lived with my grand-mother, who certainly provided her with sheets for her bed. But Julia continued.

"It had to be done behind closed doors, you know. So I didn't see anything. And she made Joe keep his eyes shut. He could hear her mut-tering in Italian. And he felt her making the sign of the cross on his back. But he wasn't allowed to look or ask questions. After three days, it was gone. He was completely cured. And it never came back. Till the day he died his back was fine. Anybody who wants to know about this can ask me and I'll tell them. It's true. Your great-grandmother could do things."

After I spoke to Julia Muratore I called my mother and told her what she said.

My mother was matter-of-fact. "I know. She healed a lot of people."

Then I told her about the linens.

"Those were for us, for my sisters and me. She used to embroider on them, our initials, little designs. She made them for our marriage beds."

"Do you still have them?" I asked.

"Who knows?" my mother told me.

Slowly, I was reaching out to this woman I hardly knew. She used to frighten me, with her Italian and her strange ways. She refused to use indoor plumbing and instead kept an outhouse in the backyard. She raised chickens, grew vegetables, pruned fruit trees. She healed people. I knew all there was to know about her, and it was not enough. These threads of information made me long to know more. I felt more con-nected to this stranger than I ever did to her daughter, my grandmother. I wanted to touch the carefully embroidered linens she earned by curing people of sciatica. I wanted to know her prayers and healing powers.

I have this one strong memory of her. It is cold. She takes my hand and leads me out our back door into the yard. Her chickens peck at my feet, frightening me. Our yard, I know now, looks like the yards of every house in southern Italy: grapevines, fig trees, wooden stakes in vegetable patches. There are small wooden buildings: her outhouse, a shed, a two-room building we call the shack where we eat in warm weather. She takes me into one of these buildings.

She is tall, taller than my own mother, and her eyes are pale blue. Her face is wrinkled, her hair snow white. She is missing many teeth. She wears a long, old-fashioned dress, a black cardigan buttoned carelessly. The sweater has holes in it. Her gloves, black, wool, are beginning to unravel. She smiles at me and speaks in Italian, but the foreignness of her words, of her, makes me want to cry.

Then she hands me a pottery bowl. She holds it in her two hands, extending it to me. I remember that bowl so clearly. It is not like anything we have in the Big House, which is what we call our house. In the Big House we drink from jelly jars decorated with cartoon characters. We have dishes that my grandmother gets free in her detergent. This bowl that Nonna gives me is pale yellow, ridged, like the clay we use in art class in school.

She calls me *fille mia*. My daughter. When I don't take the bowl, she places it in my own two hands and tells me to drink. A cat wraps itself around her legs, purring. I put the bowl to my lips. There is steam and sugar. Coffee with hot milk, sweetened. Like Nonna herself, it is strange and exotic. I stand with my great-grandmother, close, the cat purring at our feet, and I drink.

MOST MIRACLES OCCUR THROUGH the intercession of a saint. If one wants a favor, he would pray to a particular saint to act on his behalf. My great-grandmother's were no different. She had prayers to various saints to help find lost objects, answer questions, heal. Her prayer to Saint Anthony could answer important questions such as: Will I have a baby? Does he love me? Will my mother be all right? The prayer was in Italian. She would go into a room, alone, and ask the question. If she was able to repeat the prayer three times quickly and without hesitation or errors, the answer was a favorable one. But if the prayer "came slow" or she couldn't remember the words, the outlook was dire.

Legend has it that my great-grandmother learned all of these things as a young girl in Italy. She was a shepherdess for the convent on the hills of her town. The nuns took a liking to her and passed on their knowledge. Her faith was sealed years later when Mama Rose, her only daughter, was three. On a vacation in Italy from the United States, where they had immigrated, Mama Rose came down with scarlet fever. The doctors said she would not live through the night. Nonna bundled up her daughter and walked all the miles to the convent. There, the nuns prayed in earnest to the Virgin Mary to spare this child. By morning, she was completely well except for one thing: her long dark curls had fallen off at the height of her fever. My great-grandmother took her daughter's hair and gave it as an offering of thanks to the Virgin Mary. When my grandmother's hair grew back, it was red, and it remained red until the day she died seventy-five years later.

I grew up with this story, and others like it. I never questioned it. Like the story of the day I was born or the day my parents met, I accepted it as fact. But when I shared the story with a friend, he said at its conclusion, "But of course that's not true." Startled, I asked him what he meant. "Why, that never happened," he said, laughing. "It couldn't happen. Maybe her fever simply broke or maybe the doctors thought she was sicker than she was. But she wasn't cured by the Virgin Mary, and her hair probably just turned more red as she got older." Therein lies an important distinction between one who believes in miracles and one who doesn't. A believer accepts the miracle as truth, no questions asked. Although I didn't accept my friend's explanations of our family miracles, I also knew I could not dissuade him from them.

THAT WAS HOW I came to take my ten-week-old daughter an hour north of Santa Fe, New Mexico, up into the Sangre de Cristo Mountains, to the little town of Chimayo and its chapel, El Santuario. The area had been a holy ground for the Tewa Indians, a place where they believed fire and water had belched forth and subsided into a sacred pool. Eventually, the water evaporated, leaving only a puddle of mud. The Tewa went there to eat the mud when they wanted to be cured.

Sometime around the year 1814, during Holy Week, Don Bernardo Abeyta is said to have been performing the stations of the cross in the hills of Chimayo. Suddenly, he saw light springing up from the ground itself. He began to dig with his hands and there he found a crucifix. He ran to the Santa Cruz Church in a nearby town and the priest and parishioners went with him and took the crucifix back to their own church. The next morning, the crucifix was missing. Somehow it had returned to its original location. The same thing happened two more times until they decided to build a chapel—El Santuario—on the spot. This chapel contains the hole, called *el pocito* (the well) with the healing dirt.

Like many sites that claim miracles, Chimayo is difficult to reach. Grace and I flew from Boston to Albuquerque, changing planes en route. There, we met my friend Matt, rented a car, and drove over an hour to Santa Fe. The next morning we rode into the mountains on what is called the High Road to Taos, along curving roads covered with snow. Signs are few, and even getting to El Santuario requires a certain amount of faith. We had to stop more than once along the way so I could breastfeed the baby. Still, despite all this, I never grew discouraged. Before I left, my father had hugged me and said, "Go get that dirt, sweetheart." No matter what, I would get it for him and bring it safely home.

Chimayo is called the Lourdes of the Southwest because of all the healings that have been associated with it. When one thinks of miracle healing sites, Lourdes is probably the place that first comes to mind. If I hadn't had a serendipitous trip there fifteen years earlier, it is probably where I would have gone. But in 1982, when I was working as a flight attendant, I was called to work a trip one day while I was on standby. It wasn't until after I hung up that I realized the only destination I had been given was "Europe." This was unusual. As an international flight attendant on reserve, part of the fun was finding out which exotic location I would be headed for in the next hour or two.

I was twenty-five years old and at a point in my life where I had abandoned many of my childhood ways. I had moved from my small hometown in Rhode Island. I was working as a flight attendant, a job that was not usually associated with someone who had graduated sixth in her high school class and with high honors from college. Instead of the young lawyers I had been steadily dating, I was now madly in love with an unemployed actor. And, perhaps most important, I had given up not just on the Catholicism with which I was raised, but on religion altogether. Like many people I knew at that time, I liked to say that I believed in God, but not in organized religion. The truth is I didn't really think much about God back then, except in sporadic, furtive prayers for my immediate needs: don't let me be late, please have him call, help me decide what to do.

When I arrived at Kennedy Airport and looked at my flight schedule, I was delighted to see that the first part of the trip involved deadheading—flying as a passenger—to Paris that evening and staying overnight. The next morning I had to take an Air France flight to—but here I was puzzled. Of all the hundreds of three-letter airport codes I'd had to memorize over the years, this was a new one. When I asked the crew scheduler what the letters stood for, she told me the name of a city that didn't sound familiar. I saw that I would spend a day and a night there before working a flight back to New York the next morning. With images of Provence or the French Riviera in my mind, I got on the flight to Paris.

The next day, at Charles de Gaulle Airport, I spotted several other flight attendants waiting for the same Air France flight. They all looked glum. Maybe, I thought, Provence wasn't my destination after all. After introductions, I asked if any of them knew where we were headed. "Didn't they tell you?" one of them moaned. "We're going to Lourdes!" As distant as I had grown from my religion, Lourdes still conjured something large and special for me. Throughout my entire childhood, my grandmother had taken me to shrines all around New England, telling me the stories of the saints they represented and urging me to pray to one. She believed that patron saints, like guardian angels, would get you through tough times in life, even though the Virgin Mary, her own patron who had saved her life when she was three, had forsaken her.

In 1952, when her twenty-three-year-old daughter (my Aunt Ann, for whom I was named) had routine dental surgery, Mama Rose grew alarmed when the doctor had not called after several hours. She asked my great-grandmother to do the prayer to Saint Anthony to see if Ann was out of surgery and resting. The prayer went quickly and without any mistakes. But still the doctor didn't call. My grandmother then went into her room and prayed to the statue of the Virgin Mary that she had received from her mother as a wedding gift. After her prayer, my uncle appeared at the door with the news that my aunt was dead from an allergic reaction to the anesthesia. In response, my grandmother picked up the statue and threw it across the room. Still, she kept the cracked, chipped, and glued-together Virgin beside her bed, adorned with rosary beads and, sometimes, a red votive candle lit at its feet.

Perhaps this story made it difficult for me to find a saint I could trust. Or perhaps it was the plethora of saints available to me that made it so hard to choose, each of them with a glorious and tragic story—Lucy who plucked out her eyes so as to be less beautiful, Agnes who miraculously grew long golden hair to cover her naked body when she was forced down the streets without clothes, Clare who got to marry Saint Francis of Assisi and to be the patron saint of television, and, of course, Saint Bernadette. More than one Sunday I had sat transfixed in front of the television as *The Song of Bernadette* was shown on *Sunday Afternoon at the Movies*. She had briefly inspired me to want to become a nun, and I spent afternoons cleaning the wax from votive candles off the alters at church as a way to begin that journey.

Now, suddenly, I was about to see Lourdes and Saint Bernadette's grotto where the Virgin had appeared to her in 1858. I'm not sure what I would have said about miracles if someone had asked me that day; most likely I would have had a wisecrack response. But going to Lourdes was akin to visiting an idol's birthplace or tomb, like venturing to Amherst to see Emily Dickinson's house or to Rome to visit Keats's grave. I was willing to believe in something that day, to accept that there was something special and sacred about this place in the foothills of the Pyrenes, where fourteen-year-old Bernadette Soubirous repeatedly saw and spoke to a woman in a white dress with a blue waistband and rosary beads whom she called *aquero*, "that one." The Virgin directed Bernadette to dig there, and to drink the water. Only two weeks after the first apparition, people were taking away the water from the grotto, claiming it could cure illnesses. The Virgin also told Bernadette that a church should be built in that spot, and that people should come to it in procession.

Despite more than a passing familiarity with the story of Bernadette, nothing had prepared me for what I found in Lourdes. Every afternoon there is a procession of the Blessed Sacrament. Priests lead the procession, followed by the canopy with the Blessed Sacrament held high. Once that is over, the priests walk through the crowd among the sick. Each time a blessing is said, the Blessed Sacrament is held high.

Although some miracles happen weeks or even months after a visit to Lourdes, it is at this point of the day when spontaneous miracles are said to happen.

More pilgrims visit Lourdes than Rome or Jerusalem, over four and a half million a year. My visit came during Easter week, when upward of a hundred thousand people go to Lourdes, and the streets were clogged with people in varying degrees of illness and deformity, with nurses and nuns in starched white uniforms, with tourists toting cameras and snapping pictures of the dying lying prone on stretchers, the crippled atrophied in their wheelchairs, the blind with their white canes. They needn't have bothered with the photographs; the kiosks that lined the streets hawked postcards of the sick and dying, tiny vials of holy water, overpriced copies of the book *The Song of Bernadette*. The atmosphere was more like Disney World than a holy place, except instead of Mickey Mouse emblazoned on a T-shirt there was the cathedral.

I convinced myself that if I only got to the grotto, I might find a kind of peace there. In the grotto stands a tall white statue of the Virgin Mary. When Bernadette was shown this likeness, she is said to have gasped: "My God, how you deface her." Still, that is what one finds in the grotto at Lourdes. Like many people who need solace in their soul, I wasn't even aware then that I yearned for some. I wasn't to find it in the grotto, or anywhere in Lourdes. Even the sight of a sick teenager washing his legs in the water didn't move me. The carnival-like setting eradicated any communion with a higher power. When the procession began, and thousands of invalids and near-death people were wheeled, pushed, or led through the cathedral, the tourists taking pictures, the oxygen tanks bumping past, I felt further from God or a higher being than I had before I came. Disgusted, I went back to my hotel.

The writer Flannery O'Connor, a devout Catholic who suffered from lupus, visited Lourdes in the spring of 1958. She did not go there for a cure: "About this Lourdes business," she wrote, "I am going as a pilgrim, not a patient. I will not be taking any bath. I am one of those people who could die for his religion easier than take a bath for it." However, once there, her elderly cousin Sally convinced her to bathe in the holy water. O'Connor explained her reasons for doing it as a selection of bad motives: "I went early in the morning. Only about 40 ahead of me so the water looked pretty clean. They pass around the water for 'les malades,' to drink & everybody drinks out of the same cup. As somebody said, the miracle is that the place don't bring on epidemics." She concluded that "nobody I am sure prays in that water."

On the flight home, I sought out the priest who had led a group of one hundred people from Philadelphia to Lourdes. It had taken us almost four hours to board because of all the wheelchairs, stretchers, and medical equipment. Already the doctor on board had administered emergency care to a dying man. A mother had told me that her daughter, seventeen years old and blind, had a rare disease in which her brain was destroying itself. "There's nothing to be done," she'd whispered. "This is our last chance." The girl sat beside her, staring blankly from eyes the light blue of faded denim. When I placed a meal tray in front of a sixty-year-old man suffering from multiple sclerosis, he'd grunted, gathered all his strength, and thrown it back at me, his eyes ablaze with anger. "It's not you," his wife apologized, her head bent to hide the constant tears that streamed down her cheeks. "He's angry at everyone."

"Do you believe that any of these people will be cured by a miracle?" I demanded from the priest. I was young and jaded and arrogant, a stranger to death or illness.

"A miracle," he said, "is usually instantaneous. But some of these people have things that it will take X rays and tests to see if they are cured."

I looked at the young girl with the brain disorder. Certainly then she had not had a miracle.

"The church has physicians," he explained, "who study alleged miracles." He told me about the process, how a miracle case must have a medical history of the person and the records and notes of everyone who has treated him. Scientific evidence such as X rays and biopsies are examined. "And," he added, with what I interpreted as skepticism, "the cure must be a total cure. No relapses or recurrences."

"How many of these instantaneous cures have happened at Lourdes?" He averted my eyes. "I think three," he said. "But you're missing the point. This is all they have left to do. Miracles come in unexpected ways."

It seemed to me a sad journey, especially when out of the forty cases a year that pass through the Consulta Medica's extensive investigation, only about fifteen are deemed miracles. Hearing such a statistic in 1982 would have made me even angrier, angry that these people had gone so far, with such hope, only to be disappointed. But by the time I went to Chimayo, I was a different person, and that statistic actually bolstered my belief that the dirt there might cure my father. I was no longer the skeptical, arrogant young woman who had left Lourdes in a self-righteous huff. Just three months after my trip there, my brother died unexpectedly.

skip

SIX WEEKS BEFORE HE died my brother had his eyesight corrected to 20/20. Like the rest of our family, Skip was nearsighted. In photographs from our childhood, we are usually holding our glasses and myopically peering at the camera. If we forgot to take them off, the picture was considered ruined. Our mother started wearing glasses when she was in third grade and it was a stigma she regretted passing on to my brother and me, her only two children. As a result, our glasses embarrassed us. With eyesight much worse than my brother's, I had no choice but to wear my glasses all the time. But Skip could get by without his, and chose to move through the world in a nearsighted haze.

When I think of my brother now, eighteen years after his death, it is not with his eyes improved and wide open as they were the last time I saw him alive. Instead, I picture him squinting at the world, his glasses tucked in a pocket or drawer somewhere. I picture him in his orange windbreaker, the one he wore from age sixteen on, and his cutoff jeans. He was a big man—six feet three—with soft brown curls that held a hint of gold in them and a smile that never failed to make waitresses and flight attendants and saleswomen swoon. It was not just his size that was big but also his personality, the way his laughter and his grin grabbed people and held on tight. I do not let myself think of my brother often, but when I do this is what I see: the two of us walking together on the beach, Skip beside me, tanned and unshaven, gesturing and talking and smiling. He had a habit of gazing at some distant point. In retrospect it seems as if he wanted to see what lay ahead of him. But none of us had any idea what his future held, least of all him.

MY BROTHER BELIEVED HE was born blessed. He took risks throughout his life because, he told me, he was certain that our grandmother, Mama Rose, was watching over him and protecting him. He had been her favorite grandchild and the other twenty of us knew it. In life she had pampered him, cared for him, coddled him, and Skip saw no reason for her death to stop this special treatment. So he drove fast, took chances whenever he could, tried anything at least once.

All of it made me nervous. After all, I was the kid who was afraid of the dark, who preferred reading a book to anything remotely resembling an adventure. While my brother took up surfing and skiing and mountain climbing with abandon, I worried for his safety. Even his job as an environmental engineer, travelling around the country cleaning up toxic waste, was dangerous. If any of us had to guess how my brother would die we would never have chosen the pedestrian manner in which it actually happened.

"If anything ever happens to you," I used to tell him, "Mom will die."

"Nothing will happen," he'd say as he set out on his next risky venture. "Mama Rose is taking care of me."

I wasn't so sure. It was a discussion we had often, but the last time we had it he pointed to hard evidence: In the space of a few months he'd been held up at gunpoint in New Orleans and totalled a car in Alabama, and he'd walked away from both events unharmed.

At twenty-five, I had not yet decided that there was a heaven where our dead relatives gazed down at us. In fact, I thought it more likely there was not. That last week of June 1982, many things were going wrong. My brother was seeking a divorce from his wife and there were arguments over custody of their daughter. The woman he was planning to marry had, after an argument, left him alone in Pittsburgh and gone home to New Orleans to think. His soon-to-be ex-mother-in-law died, as did his soon-to-be ex-wife's best friend, who had been the maid of honor at their wedding. If my grandmother was looking after things, she was doing a pretty bad job.

On June 30 I developed a headache that no amount of aspirin would relieve. I was a flight attendant then, and reluctantly I worked my trip from JFK to Los Angeles. From my hotel room I called home, not something I usually did on layovers. "Are you all right?" I asked my mother. "I feel like something's wrong." My head pounded. She assured me everyone was fine. When I hung up I called my brother and left the same message on his answering machine. Then I went out for Mexican food with the rest of the crew.

On the cab ride back to the hotel, everyone was talking about nicknames. I thought about my brother's. He was really a Junior, and he had acquired the nickname Skip because my father was a career navy man: Skipper. But when I opened my mouth to tell the story, no words came out. Instead, my head hurt more and I grew mute. As I walked down the hotel hall toward my room, I heard my telephone ringing and I knew without a doubt that something terrible had happened. The voice on the other end was that of an old boyfriend who also worked for the airline. "I have some very bad news," he said. "Who died?" I asked him. But before he could tell me I hung up. We repeated this three times, him calling back and saying, "I have some very bad news," and me hanging up before he could give it to me. If I didn't hear the news, then everyone was still safe and alive. Once I found out what had happened, nothing would ever be the same again. What I imagined before I heard what he had to tell me was my family, the four of us, driving off in the green Chevy station wagon of my childhood. I tried to eliminate one of them, but it was impossible. We were a unit. We were a foursome that no one could separate. "Don't hang up!" the voice on the other end of the phone ordered. "Your brother Skip is dead."

IF THERE WERE A chart somewhere that listed grief in order of importance, losing a sibling would not rank high. It is worse to lose your child, your spouse, your parent. That is what you are told when you lose a sibling. But if you have lost one you know how bad, how tangled, that loss is. When my brother died, I lost my parents too. I watched them fall apart in such a way that I understood I would never get them back again. And I never did.

When my brother died, I lost my history. He had been there since the day I was born. Five years older, he'd taught me how to read, how to win at Monopoly, how to drive and do algebra and break up with a boy. He was the one in the twin bed across from me at home, in the motel bed shaking with a quarter's worth of Magic Fingers on family trips, in the backseat of the station wagon.

A sibling is the lens through which you see your childhood. Although we did not have much of an adult life together, those few years we did have before he died were often spent over a beer and saying, "Remember the time when . . ." Siblings share the experience of their first kiss, their lost virginity, their broken hearts, with each other, not with their parents. Only I know what we whispered about when our parents thought we were asleep. Only I know the secrets of my brother's heart and only he knew mine. It is true that he had a wife and many friends and more than one lover. But our shared childhood was ours alone, and without him I hold both his history and mine like a buried treasure. Without my brother to help put that history into focus, I carry it alone.

"HOW MANY BROTHERS AND sisters do you have?" people casually ask each other all the time. But for me the question is anything but casual. If I lie and say none, I get more questions about what it was like to be an only child. Even if those questions aren't asked, I leave feeling guilty that I denied my brother his life and its impact on my own life. If I tell the truth and say that I had a brother who died, I send someone else into a state of sympathy or awkwardness or embarrassment.

It is easier for people to respond to news of a parent's death. After all, parents are older than us. They get sick and they die. By the time a person is a certain age, chances are they've lost a parent. But a brother is something else. I have grown accustomed to the wide-eyed expression my news produces in people and the mumbled condolences. No one wants to be in that conversation, least of all me.

For a time I divided people into two camps: the innocent, lucky ones who had not lost a sibling, and the ones like me who had. I formed friendships with people on the basis of this unimaginable loss, despite the differences between us. Even now when I find someone else who has lost a sibling, we form a fast bond. The discovery makes us settle in to a place where we are not often allowed to go. Almost immediately we share the story of our loss: leukemia, AIDS, breast cancer, or my own story of my brother falling down in the bathtub, bumping his head, and drowning while our grandmother in heaven watched someone else. On the night my husband and I fell in love over pasta at Carmella's in Greenwich Village, we discovered that we had each lost a brother. It is odd to find love and friendship in a corner of your heart that is usually sealed off. But with this particular loss, that is how it happens.

THAT LONG HOT SUMMER after my brother died my family sat around the kitchen table stunned. When the heat finally broke and autumn arrived, I packed my bags and fled to New York City where I knew almost no one. There I did not have to be the one whose brother had died so suddenly and tragically. I could be anonymous if I liked. I could keep my loss a secret.

I coped with the death of my brother by pretending he was on a business trip and unreachable. How I coped with the loss of my parents was harder. I called them obsessively, from layovers in foreign cities, from pay phones on street corners, sometimes throughout the night; none of us slept very much anymore anyway. I called them and called them but I never figured out what to say. We, of course, never recovered. Instead, we became a different family, with three broken spokes.

OUR FIRST CHRISTMAS WITHOUT Skip, we went through the motions of gift giving and tree trimming with our relatives. Then we convened in my parents' bedroom, closed the door, and cried for hours. Usually at Christmas Skip burst through the front door in a blast of cold air, toting elaborately wrapped presents and enough holiday cheer for all of us. He would plug in the blender and make tropical drinks while Jimmy Buffet blasted from my parents' outdated stereo. He called everyone he knew to tell them he was in town and in no time our house was full—relatives, childhood friends, people Skip hardly knew, all flocking to my brother's side.

As our second Christmas without him approached I decided to do what had become a pattern for me since he died: flee. Since I was a child and saw *Hans Brinker and the Silver Skates* on *The Wonderful World of Disney*, Holland had seemed like a magical place. I called my parents and told them we were spending Christmas in Amsterdam. I imagined a vacation spent gliding along the ice of a distant canal, surrounded by strangers who would not know of our enormous loss. I imagined a fairy tale, where happy endings were still possible. But our despair was too severe for us to escape it. Still I kept trying, booking day trips to the Zeider Zee and a visit to the Heinekin brewery. In one attempt at fun at a wooden shoe factory, I forced my parents to stand beside me in pairs of over-sized clogs while another tourist snapped our picture. When it came back two things struck me: none of us had remembered to take off our glasses. And, oddly, there is an empty pair of wooden shoes beside us.

ALMOST TWENTY YEARS LATER, I realize that I can never escape. I am a sister without a brother. My brother died before I published anything. He died before I had children. To think of him now, to really conjure him, is still the most painful thing I can do. Even in dreams it is too painful to re-create him. Instead, he takes the form of James Dean. The last time I saw my brother alive I spent Memorial Day weekend with him and his girlfriend. They were planning a wedding. He was one of the first people in this country to have corrective surgery on his eyes and he could see me perfectly without glasses. To entertain him I drew before-and-after pictures of him. In the before he is squinting despite the oversized glasses perched on his nose. In the after he is wide-eyed, free of glasses. In both he is grinning. That weekend he taught me how to barbecue chicken and doctor canned beans. He promised me a kitten from his pregnant cat. When we said good-bye, he wrapped me in a bear hug; no one could hug like my brother.

Here is what I tell my children about their uncle: My brother was a big man: six feet three. But it wasn't just his height; it was also his personality that made him seem so big. He was a man who wanted to clean up the environment, who believed that love conquered all, who jogged every day with his Irish setter, who created a party wherever he was. My brother was a visionary. He was the first person I knew to have a VW bug, an answering machine, a VCR. His favorite book was *The World*

According to Garp. His favorite television show was *The Love Boat.* When he described to me what a VCR could do, I laughed at him. "This is what you see in the future?" I said. "A time when people will tape *The Love Boat* so they can watch it later in the week?" He shook his head. "You just don't get it," he said. "Someday everyone will own one of these."

After Skip died, I thought often about how he was a visionary. How angry he would be if he knew all that he had missed: CD players that shuffle music like a disc jockey, cable television, CNN and the Weather Channel, the exploration of Mars, John Glenn's return to space. But, I used to think, if he could see so well into the future, why didn't he see his own death coming? If our family believed in omens, how did we miss the ones that might have warned us or saved him?

Of course I had no answers to those questions, questions that kept me awake at night. Yet losing Skip brought me closer to the background from which I had been hiding. Turning myself over to the beliefs that I had grown up with comforted me. I did not know why a miracle did not happen for my family, but instead of doubting miracles I began to believe in them again. All of those people I had seen at Lourdes had something that I had discarded: faith. They had travelled in their various states of illness and desperation, believing they might get a miracle. Rather than feeling disdain for them, I now admired their bravery, their tenacity, their hope.

Whenever I saw a religious shop in New York, I stopped in, seeking comfort in the ex-votos, the plaster saints, the retablos and crucifixes. It was not that I returned to Catholicism; rather I returned to the hybrid Italian faith of my grandmother and great-grandmother. I believed in prayer again. I believed that if I opened my heart, I would find miracles. In the hole that my brother left, my faith returned. To have it meant that he was still out there somewhere. It meant that the childhood we had shared still lived on, with its Italian culture and beliefs, its Old World and New World traditions.

Slowly, I stepped into churches and cathedrals again. On layovers in Lisbon and Barcelona, Paris and Rome, when I passed a church I always went inside. I relished the reverence there, the sound of footsteps across stone floors, the flickering fire in glass chimneys casting shadows, the faces of others who sat in silence too. Before I returned to the bustling

the miracle

WHEN I ARRIVED AT El Santuario, I had the fear of my father's death to motivate me, as well as an open heart, a willingness to believe a cure—a miracle—was possible. My longtime friend Matt came with me to bring back dirt for his friend who was dying from Hodgkin's disease. Even the signs posted everywhere—NOT RESPONSIBLE FOR THEFT—could not detract from what we saw there. A small adobe church with a dirt parking lot, a religious gift store, and a burrito stand called Leona's, which was written up as the best burrito place in New Mexico in all of my guidebooks.

We proceeded under an archway, into a courtyard with a wooden crucifix, and into the church where the altar is a vivid display of local folk art with its brightly painted reredos by the artist known as the Chili Painter. But we hadn't come to see the local folk art. We had come for a miracle. So we quickly went into the low-ceilinged room off the church in search of the *pocito*, or well. What we found first was a testimony to all the cures attributed to this place. The walls are lined with crutches and canes, candles and flowers, statues of saints, all offerings of thanks for healings. Despite the signs asking people not to leave notes because of the fire danger around the lit candles, and not to write on anything except the guest book, the offerings have letters tucked into their corners. One statue had a sonogram picture pinned to the saint's cloak. Another had a letter in Spanish: "Thank you for the recovery of our little Luis. Our baby boy is now well. Mil gracias."

Against one wall of this room sits a shrine to Santo Nino, who is believed to walk about the country at night healing sick children and wearing out his shoes in the process. As a result, an offering of shoes is given to him whenever a child is healed. The shrine at Chimayo is full of children's shoes, handmade knit booties, delicate silk christening shoes. Roses and letters of thanks adorn the statue, which is seated and holds a basket of food and a gourd to carry water.

In this small room, I began to tremble. Unlike my trip to Lourdes, I felt I really was in the presence of a holy place, a place that held possibility. I had not felt that possibility in the hospitals and doctors' offices that had dominated my life these past few months. Even when a visit to the reknowned Dana Farber Institute resulted in that surgeon's promise to remove the tumor "if the sucker will only shrink some," I didn't get the sense of peace I had as I stood surrounded by testimonies to faith.

Not even the brochure I had bought at the tiny gift shop, which claimed that the church had never even bothered to investigate any of the claims of miracle healings, could dampen my spirits. The brochure quoted letters written after visits to Chimayo. One, from Ida P. of Chicago, stated that her husband still had six more radiation treatments to go when, on a Sunday, she brought him the dirt. On Monday the tumor was gone.

Ducking our heads, Matt and I entered the even smaller room that housed the pocito. It was just a hole in the dirt floor. The walls here are also covered with offerings, including a note that said: "Within this small room resides the stillness of souls that have disovered peace. Listen to their silence. JK, New York." Matt and I kneeled in front of the pocito and scooped the dirt with our bare hands into the Ziploc bags we had brought. I cannot say what Matt was thinking as he dug. But I had one prayer that I repeated over and over: Please let my father's tumor go away.

BUOYANT FROM OUR TIME at El Santuario, Matt and I went off to find one of the weavers that live in and around Chimayo. Carefully following the signs for Ortegas, we ended up at a small store that sold carvings and local folk art instead of rugs. "Is this Ortegas?" we asked, confused, when we entered. Each of us was certain we had not only followed the signs exactly, but turned in where another sign pointed. The ponytailed man behind the counter, Tobias, smiled at us. "You've been to get the dirt," he said. Later, Matt and I would both comment on how gentle his face was. Perhaps it was this gentleness that led me to tell him why I had come and the particulars of my father's disease. He nodded. "He'll be cured," he said. "I've seen it myself, the healings."

He told us the story of a couple who had arrived at his door—"Like you two!" The man was grumpy, angry at his wife for insisting they come all this way from Los Angeles when her doctors had told her a cure was hopeless. Sympathetic to the wife's plight, Tobias invited them to dinner. Reluctantly, the man agreed. As they sat eating on the patio of a nearby restaurant, a strange light began to emit from the woman's breast. Soft at first, it grew brighter and larger until it seemed to encompass her entire chest, like a cocoon. Then it slowly dissipated. It was the skeptical husband who spoke first. "Did anyone else see that?" Each of them had. "My tumor is gone," the wife said confidently. Although Tobias had not known what kind of cancer the woman was suffering from, he was certain then that it was breast cancer, and that she had been cured. He was right on both accounts. Back in California, baffled doctors pronounced her completely free of breast cancer.

"It works," Tobias said.

Matt asked him how, with thousands of people visiting the pocito, the dirt was never depleted.

"Oh," Tobias said, "the caretaker refills it every day. Then the priest blesses it."

This mundane refilling disappointed me. The story I had heard about the dirt was that it replenished itself in some inexplicable way.

"It's not the dirt," Tobias told us. "It's the energy of all the people who come and pray into that pocito that makes miracles happen."

Of course, there is no real explanation for what makes miracles happen. But there are plenty of explanations that attempt to disprove that they do. Just as my friend could point to many reasons why my grandmother lived through her bout of scarlet fever, skeptics can use scientific, historical, and geographical data to explain away miracles. Simply put, people either believe or they don't. In my own search for understanding miracles, I came across books and articles in support of either side.

Joe Nickell, the Senior Research Fellow for the Committee for the Scientific Investigation of Claims of the Paranormal, has written an entire book debunking everything from stigmatas to the shroud of Turin. As for miracle healings, he believes that some serious illnesses such as cancer and multiple sclerosis can undergo spontaneous remission in which they completely go away or abate for long periods of time. In addition, Nickell cites misdiagnoses, misread CAT scans, misunderstandings as explanations for miracle healings. Nickell reports that as of 1984, six thousand miracles had been attributed to the water at Lourdes, but only sixty-four of those had been authenticated as miraculous. He claims that those sixty-four cases were most likely spontaneous remissions, as in the case of a woman whose blindness was "cured," only to discover she was suffering from multiple sclerosis and the disease had temporarily abated.

In response to such skepticism, Dr. Raffaello Cortesini, a specialist in heart and liver transplants and the president of the Consulta Medica (the official board of the Catholic Church that studies miracle claims) told Kenneth L. Woodward in his book *Making Saints*, "I myself, if I did not do these consultations, would never believe what I read. You don't understand how fantastic, how incredible—and how well-documented—these cases are. They are more incredible than historical romances. Science fiction is nothing by comparison." For believers in miracles, they do not even need this substantiation.

Still, advances in medical science have made the number of accredited miracles decrease over the years. Pope John Paul II agrees that medicine has helped to understand some of these miraculous cures, but he adds: "But it remains true that numerous healings constitute a fact which has its explanation only in the order of faith." To accommodate the difficulty that proving miracle cures has become, the church has lightened its requirements on miracles for canonization. It is true that miracles were much more commonplace historically. In the thirteenth century, St. Louis of Anjou was responsible for a well-documented sixty-six miracles, including raising twelve people from the dead. Obviously, today's doctors could easily disprove not only many of Louis of Anjou's miracles, but also a good number of those that came before and after him.

But that still leaves us with the ones that no one—not even Joe Nickell—can explain since the advent of modern medicine.

Other skeptics point to geographical reasons for alleged miracles. Since many depend on the intervention of saints, and since most canonized people come from Europe, I'm not alone in my observation that a higher propensity for miracles are there. Even more specifically, certain countries, such as Italy, boast more miracles than other countries. Physicians from Italy—southern Italy in particular—believe so strongly in miracles that it can be said they are more willing to accept a cure as miraculous. Similarly, the culture of southern Italy is such that saints and miracles are a part of everyday life. As I drove through southern Italy recently I was struck by how commonplace statues of saints were. They appeared on roadsides, hanging from cliffs, in backyards, on city street corners, virtually everywhere. Almost always there were offerings at the statue's feet, flowers, bread, letters. My own ancestors came from southern Italy and I will attest to our openness in letting miracles into our lives. But other cultures share this openness, this willingness to recognize the miraculous. Rather than disproving miracles, I wonder if it doesn't support their existence. Saint Augustine claimed that all natural things were filled with miracles, and he referred to the world itself as "the miracle of miracles."

WHEN I MADE MY pilgrimage to Chimayo, I had reached a point in my life where I believed in a graced world. I believed that the births of my children were miraculous, that the love I shared with my husband was a gift, as was my ability to shape words into meaningful stories. Of course I credited hard work, talent, and character too. But I had come to believe in Augustine's view of the world as the miracle of miracles. When I arrived back in Rhode Island with the dirt from El Santuario, I felt anything could happen.

Twenty-four hours after my father used the dirt, he was rushed to the hospital by ambulance in respiratory failure. It was Christmas Eve, three months after his diagnosis. Although it would have been a perfect time to have a crisis of faith, quite the opposite happened. I simply believed that he would survive. What happened next surprised me more than his bad turn of health.

While he was in the hospital, his recovery from what turned out to be pneumonia deemed tenuous, his doctor performed a CAT scan, assuming the tumor had grown. My father had only had two treatments of chemo and he needed five before there was any hope of the tumor shrinking. Visiting him, I asked if he was prepared for a bad CAT scan.

"Oh, no," he said with great confidence. "The tumor is gone."

"Gone?" I said. Even the medical community admits there are cases of spontaneous remission in cancer, albeit rarely, and hard to document.

He nodded. "I sat here and watched as cancer left my body. It was black and evil-looking and came out of my chest like sparks, agitated and angry."

I was willing to believe the tumor might disappear, but such a physical manifestation was more than I had considered. True, Tobias had told us of a light enveloping a sick woman's chest, and it had seemed miraculous. But here was my father, a practical, no-nonsense Midwesterner, telling me a story that hinted of science fiction.

The next day my mother called me from the hospital. "Ann," she said, awed, "the CAT scan shows that the tumor has completely gone. It's disappeared."

In the background I heard my father chuckling, and then my mother made the doctor repeat what he had said when he walked into the room with the results.

"It's a miracle," he said.

his death

WHEN SOMEONE HAS A serious illness, his days, and his family's days, are taken up with doctors' appointments and tests and waiting for the results of tests. Somewhere along that medical journey, I turned forty. Unable to imagine any gift other than saving my father's life, I asked everyone not to give me any presents. When my husband had turned forty a few years earlier, he said, half-jokingly, that he wanted the two of us to spend a long weekend in Paris to celebrate. We did. And at the end of that weekend I told him that for my fortieth birthday I would like the two of us to spend a long weekend in Rome. With my father's illness and my solo trip to Chimayo, Lorne and I decided we would take that trip when—I couldn't say if—my father got better.

In January, with my father home and tumor free, we took off to Rome to celebrate my birthday. I felt such relief on that trip that everything about it seemed magnified, as if my senses had been dormant those past months and were now waking up. My father's voice on the other end of the phone when I called from Rome was strong and cheerful. Two days before we came home, he started his radiation treatments; his doctors decided he should continue with the regimen they'd mapped out for him, even though there was no tumor there to shrink. My mother and I both wondered if another trip to the team of doctors at Dana Farber was in order. But we were assured the local doctors had already talked to the ones in Boston.

"My platelets are too low to get my chemo tomorrow," my father told me.

I was standing in the small phone booth on the stairwell of our pension. Local time was 3:00 A.M. but it was only 9:00 P.M. back home. I could hear the familiar sounds of my parents' house—the television turned on low, my mother making snacks.

"Good," I told my father. "You need to get strong again."

"That's what the doctor said. I'm going to see the chemo doctor anyway. He wants to talk to me."

I frowned. My father's tumor was gone. Why didn't they just let him be for a bit?

My mother picked up the extension and the talk turned to other things. The next day I was headed home, confident and happy.

HERE IS THE PART where I would like to say that my father came home from his Christmas hospitalization and stayed tumor free, cancer free, miraculously cured. The part where I would like to tell you that, well again, he travelled with me to New Mexico, to El Santuario de Chimayo, to leave his CAT scan results in the little low-ceilinged room beside the baby shoes and notes of thanks and crutches and braces and statues and candles.

Instead, my father's oncologist decided that the radiologist was being too cautious and he gave my father one more dose of Taxol. The morning after I returned home from my birthday weekend in Rome, my mother called.

The calm in her voice belied what she was actually saying.

"Daddy's been up sick all night," she told me.

"Did you call the doctor?" I asked her. Already we were aware of how chemo could ravage a person. After his first treatment my father's beautiful pale blond hair had come out in fistfuls.

"He said it was normal. But the thing is, Daddy said he has no energy at all. He can't even walk across the kitchen."

My father had had pneumonia enough times for me to recognize the telltale sign: a lack of energy so strong that any movement seemed impossible. The fevers and cough often came after that symptom.

"Call 911," I said, "then call me back."

When she called me back to say they were on the way, I could hear my father's voice in the background.

"He's talking," I said, to comfort myself.

But it helped my mother too. "Oh, yes," she said, "he's talking. It's just that he says he can't move."

We talked nervously until finally she said, "Hear that siren? They're here."

"I'll meet you at the hospital," I told her.

My father was in respiratory failure. Pneumonia had indeed struck his weakened immune system. When I reached the hospital, he was already admitted to a room. I got off the elevator and walked down the corridor, reading room numbers as I passed. I turned a corner and saw a sight that made me taste fear, bitter in my mouth. My mother and cousin stood talking and crying to a doctor at the end of this long corridor. I thought for certain my father was dead.

Running zigzag down the hall, my own sobs made them all look up.

"Is he? Is he?" I panted.

"No," the doctor said. He was a young pulmonary specialist whom my father had met and liked during his last hospital stay. "But it doesn't look like he's going to make it."

My cries sounded like a hurt animal's.

"Here's what he has going for him. You guys. And his determination to live. Sometimes," the doctor said, "that's enough."

I ran down the corridor, away from his words and toward my father. In my panic I had run right by his room. Now I went straight to it. There was my father. The steroids had turned his complexion a healthy red, as if he'd spent a day at the beach. He was sitting up in bed, breathing through an oxygen mask. His blue eyes were lively and alert.

"Daddy," I said, but I could manage no more.

"What's the matter?" he asked me, grinning.

I tried to reconcile the information I had with the man I saw before me. For the next few months, I would find myself struggling to do that many times.

The doctor came in with Gina and my mother. He checked the blood oxygen level in my father's blood first.

"We need to get that up to eighty," my mother whispered to me.

It was somewhere in the seventies, an improvement already. Someone with healthy lungs has a level of ninety or higher, usually close to one hundred.

Like a coach before a big game, my mother instructed my father to breathe. "You can do this," she said, and he agreed wholeheartedly.

"We're moving you to ICU," the doctor said. "This is serious. And I need to know, if anything should happen, do you want extraordinary measures to save you?"

My father looked startled. "You're shitting me," he said.

My mother asked to be alone with him for a moment, and we all stepped outside the room. The doctor explained about respirators and feeding tubes. "There's a one-in-a-million chance that he will live once he goes on a respirator."

When he gave my father the same odds, my father told him, "I want that chance."

He spent almost two weeks in intensive care, diagnosed with double pneumonia. My cousin and I slept in the small waiting room outside ICU, on short plastic couches meant for watching television and waiting for news. Other families came and went. A woman whose ninety-year-old mother had just had surgery left when her mother was moved to a regular room. Another family waited for their elderly mother to recover from a stroke. She died. A fifty-year-old man was brought in on life support, a victim of an aneurism. Eventually he was removed from life support and died.

Between visits to see loved ones in the ICU and the endless hours sitting and waiting for news or sight of the doctor, people shared their stories. Telling what had happened somehow brought the person back for a moment. Every night for two weeks, my cousin and I took hourly checks on my dad. We analyzed the nurses' expressions and comments. We reported his blood oxygen level. Slowly, he recovered.

From there he was moved into a rehab floor in the hospital. Weakened by his near-death illness, he walked with a walker and had no memory of his days in ICU. My family remembered it all too well, however. The all-night vigils by his side, sleeping on chairs, waiting for doctors and tests and change. Once he was in rehab, his doctor repeated the CAT scan, suspecting a recurrence of the tumor. But there was none, and a date for his release was set.

I was scheduled to go to Vermont to be a writer in residence at the Vermont Studio Center for two weeks. Despite my initial trepidation over leaving, now that my father was actually scheduled to come home, I relaxed somewhat.

Sam and I visited my father every day in the rehab center. He was everyone's favorite patient. This attribute always impressed me above many others. He befriended everyone, from bank tellers to the teenagers who pumped his gas at the local gas station. Everyone who met him loved him, and they remembered his southern drawl and deep laugh. The hospital was no different. Lab technicians who daily took his blood joked with him and patted his hand affectionately. Nurses threatened to run off with him. Even his doctor, still baffled by the tumor's disappearance and a remarkable recovery from double pneumonia, admitted that my father's good nature and love of life had won his heart.

A few days before I left for Vermont, my father took Sam and me to the occupational therapy room where he had baked bread that morning.

"Hey, handsome!" the therapist said when we walked in. She winked at me. "You're lucky you have this guy," she said. "We don't want to let him go home, we love him so much."

I always filled with pride when my father and I moved through the world together, and this world of the hospital that we had been in for too many weeks was no different. I squeezed his arm.

My father went to the refrigerator and pilfered some Popsicles for Sam; then we sat down together in the solarium. He called hello to an especially weak elderly woman. Unable to speak, she grunted a greeting. But her eyes sparkled at my father's attention.

"Poor old thing," he said. "A stroke."

I had never hesitated to ask or tell my father anything. When I wanted to call off my first wedding, I went straight to him for advice. When I was pregnant, he was the first person I told. But now I had something on my mind that I didn't know how to approach with him.

"You're not going to die on me when I'm in Vermont, are you?" I asked, as if it were a joke.

"Hell, no," he said, patting my knee. "I'm not going to die at all.

Don't you worry. You go up there and get some time to write." He levelled his blue eyes at me and said what he had told me frequently before. "You work too hard, you know. You need time to yourself, for your writing and your thinking. I've never seen anyone work as hard as you, and do everything so well. You need this trip."

I nodded. But I was still working at the question that was really on my mind.

It was no surprise to me that when my father was first sick, before we knew his prognosis, I found myself at a particular store on Houston Street in Manhattan. In the past, I had visited their resident psychic and found him both accurate and soothing. The store sold crystals, herbs, candles, and books. Part magic, part New Age, I found it a place that reminded me oddly of my own cultural background. Here, people believed that building a shrine could generate energy in your home, that visualizing results could bring about those results. That day in late September, I told the owner about my father. He made him a special healing candle. But when he handed it to me, he said, "There are some things that can't be cured, you know."

Despite my faith in miracles, his words had stayed with me. Even that day in the solarium with my father alive before me, two miracles already achieved, the combination of my grandmother's 410 and the words of the store owner in New York, along with the pure fear of losing my father, haunted me.

"They told us you were going to die," I finally said softly.

Sam was on his second Popsicle and had curled up on the floor in front of the television.

"They said you wouldn't recover from that pneumonia. And I was so scared." I started to cry.

"They said it, but here I am," my father said, wiping away my tears. "I've got too much to live for. I'm not going anywhere."

"But when you were in ICU all that time," I said, "did you think you were dying? Did you see a bright light or any of the things they say happen?"

I was trying to gauge the doctor's accuracy in predicting the course of my father's life. If he had been close to death, wouldn't he have experienced something—a vision? a floating out of his body? a tunnel with a light at the end? I had read about such experiences and heard people interviewed enough times to find a consistency.

My father's reaction chilled me. He did not answer. He just stared at me, hard.

"Cut it out now," he said.

I opened my mouth to push further, but stopped myself. Something had happened. But what?

The day I left for Vermont, I stopped at the hospital to say good-bye. His date to go home was just a few days away, and he was excited, full of plans. As I stood listening to those plans, he coughed. Then he coughed again and spit into a small cup, the kind we used to call soufflé cups when I worked in restaurants. A nurse appeared and took the cup away.

"What's that about?" I asked. The chill of fear that came with these seemingly small events was becoming commonplace by now.

My father waved his hand casually. "They examine it," he said.

"But why?"

"Honey, I don't know."

I could tell by his tone that I was close to upsetting him, so I nodded too, trying to imitate his casual attitude.

I was in Vermont when things grew still worse.

WRITERS' CONFERENCES AND RETREATS all have one thing in common. There is only one or two phones for many people. The Vermont Studio Center had one pay phone at the top of the stairs in its main building. In February in northern Vermont, the weather is stormy, and in my first few days I enjoyed an almost constant snowfall. I stayed in my own apartment overlooking an icy river—an idyllic setting if your father was not in the hospital, if your last image of him was not coughing into a soufflé cup and a nurse whisking it away for testing.

I called too often, running through the snow, up the stairs to the pay phone, nervously punching in all of the numbers—Sprint access code, phone number, card number—thirty-two numbers in all. Sometimes, from the cold or my nerves, I hit one number wrong and had to start all over again. I called the hospital and my mother at home and my cousin on her car phone.

The day before my father's scheduled release, I called his hospital room and my mother answered, clearly upset.

"He spiked a fever," she said, almost in disbelief.

They were doing tests. So I waited a few hours and called again. This time Gina answered. Call me on my cell phone, she said. More waiting, until finally, thirty-two numbers and some minutes later, she spoke to me. Her voice too was filled with disbelief.

"He has a fungal pneumonia now," she said. "It's always fatal."

"But not always," I said, because I was thinking of miracles. I was thinking that if we were going to lose him at all, it was going to be 410 days after my dream.

"They're saying that what happens is he grows weaker and weaker, and he'll just start to sleep more and more until—"

"I'm coming home," I said.

"They said if you want to spend some good quality time with him, you probably should come home."

I hung up and pressed my face against the wall of the phone booth. Everything here smelled good, wood and snow and freshly baked bread. Right outside the phone booth were shelves of books, written by other writers in residence, writers I admired. Coming here had been an honor, one of those wonderful experiences that sometimes come in a writing life.

Soon, I was racing through the night, snow dancing almost happily across my windshield, heading south toward my father. The voices of two women with a local NPR show competed with the voice of my mother when I had called her before leaving.

"The doctors say he'll never come home again," she told me.

"That's ridiculous," I said, shivering with fear and Vermont winter. "He'll make it."

FOR THE NEXT SIX weeks, I watched my father die. Just as Gina had explained, he grew weaker and slept more. At first, the physical therapist came twice a day.

"Here's my girlfriend," my father said to her.

I saw the sadness in her eyes when she helped him to sit up, even though she gave him a grin. Soon, as my father's condition worsened, she stopped coming. We were left with nurses and doctors, grim-faced, calling us into the hall outside his room and giving us updates of bad news.

My niece, arriving from Houston, talked privately with the doctor, then met me in the lounge where we sat and did jigsaw puzzles when they came to bathe or do tests on my father.

"The doctor said he's going to die," she told me.

"Don't you read *Reader's Digest?*" I said. "People survive bear attacks, train crashes, earthquakes. You don't just give up hope."

She shook her head.

One night the phone rang, rousing me from an already restless sleep. It was late March, still wintery, and I could hear the wind howling as the nurse on the other end of the phone told me to get to the hospital.

"He probably won't be here when you arrive," she said.

I drove through a blinding icy rain, much faster than the speed limit. Running through the parking lot, I heard myself praying out loud. The automatic doors were locked, and somehow I pulled them apart with the strength of my fear. A hospital at night has an eerie silence. In every room there is someone being born or dying or mending, but the dimmed lights and stillness mask all of that.

The sound of my footsteps were deafening as I ran off the elevator to the wing of the hospital where my father lay, perhaps dead already. He was on the cancer ward, a place filled with crying families, gray-faced patients, solemn chaplins, death. But as I turned the corner I heard one of my favorite sounds: my father, laughing. I froze, unable to believe what I was hearing.

A nurse looked up and recognized what she saw in my face. "He pulled through," she said.

I started to laugh and cry at the same time.

But when I reached the nurses' station where she sat, she said, "The time is going to come soon when he won't," she said. "You have to prepare yourself."

I had one thought when she said it: Fuck you. Fuck all of you.

Then I ran to my father, calling out to him in the dark silent hall. "Daddy!" I called. "Daddy!"

THAT NIGHT MY MOTHER, Gina, and I slept in a semicircle around my father's bed.

"We're like a fortress," we told him, "keeping out bad things."

We dragged cardiac chairs from the hallway into his room. I always stayed by the lamp so I could read after everyone had gone to sleep. When we asked him if we should stay every night, he said yes.

It became our nightly ritual for the next month.

Even as I watched him grow weak, I could not accept that he was going to die. At first, the nurses seemed to be on our side. One taped up a picture of a snazzy sports car on his bulletin board, right beside the large tear-off calendar with the black numbers that marked off the passing days.

"That's what you'll drive out of here in," she used to say.

"You bet," my father said.

But there was no improvement. His bed digitally recorded his weight and soon, when he stopped eating, those numbers began to drop. The nutritionist made him a high-fat concoction of Ensure and ice cream. Even though he thanked her profusely and said it was great, he never ate it.

Every day I dressed Grace in a pretty outfit, often with a matching hat, and brought her with me to the hospital. My father would hold her and play with her, the way he had with Sam. Except instead of the green rocking chair in my cozy living room, he was in a hospital bed, immobile, on a cancer ward.

"She's going to be a beauty," he always said before he handed her back to me.

We all tried to engage my father in the everyday acts he performed before he grew so ill. Gina and I still asked him for advice, told him jokes, complained about our worlds outside the hospital. Almost jauntily we'd walk in and announce, "There's no place to park out there!" as if to show him that everything was still normal. The world was waiting for him to rejoin it. My mother turned on *Wheel of Fortune* and *Jeopardy* each evening at seven.

"What's your guess for the final *Jeopardy* question?" she'd ask, mulling over her own choices.

She read to him from the newspaper. "Come on," she'd say. "How are you going to get better if you don't keep up with things?"

I started to show up with his favorite danish from Zaccagnini's bakery. "Look," I'd say, opening the box for him, "cherry, blueberry, cheese."

In retrospect I suppose we were demonstrating control over our lives, trying to triumph over the loss we were about to suffer, rather than helping my father fight his inevitable death. But we could not know that then. So we brought him the latest Tony Hillerman mystery and lottery tickets and doughnuts.

While he slept—which was more and more often, just as the doctor had predicted—I went into the lounge and worked the jigsaw puzzle that was always on the table. Other hands, strangers' hands, had added to it while I was in my father's room, or asleep myself. I began to notice the different stages of illness people were in. There were the ones who were like we had been once: frightened but still hopeful, in a fighting mode. There were the ones who were confused that all of that fighting had somehow led them back here.

And there were the blank-faced ones, already in the throes of grief, on a deathbed vigil. They stumbled through the corridors, unaware of night or day, often clutching someone's hand—a priest or loved one. Even amid the daylight hospital sounds of intercoms calling to people and messengers delivering bouquets of balloons and food carts and nurses and doctors hurrying about, stethoscopes swaying, I would still hear the high-pitched wail of death, someone's loved one slipping away despite medicine and prayers and love.

One day I saw a man I took to be a doctor. He was tall and paunchy, probably in his midfifties, and dressed in jeans and a sweatshirt. Round-faced and balding, when he passed me, rolling an IV pole, he smiled warmly. That night, unable to find three cardiac chairs, which allowed us to stretch out almost flat to sleep, I went into the family room where I knew there was a couch. Unlike the lounge, where a television ran all day and people ate Dunkin' Donuts and played cards, the family room was used when doctors wanted to talk to families. It had a somber air, as if it had absorbed all the tears that had been shed there.

I was surprised to see the man from earlier that day sitting there in a hospital johnny, the IV pole by his side. Was he a doctor or a patient? I wondered. Again, we traded smiles. Gina and my mother had developed relationships with other families. They knew who had what kind of cancer and who was treating it. But I avoided these conversations. As long as I stayed out of what was going on around me, I thought, I'd be less a part of it.

The next day my mother told me someone's story. She'd met a woman in the restroom who had also spent the night. That woman's husband had just been diagnosed with leukemia and was given only a few months to live. They had agreed on an aggressive chemotherapy treatment that had to be administered in the hospital. It was a desperate attempt to save him, a last resort.

"I wonder if that's the man I keep seeing," I told her, explaining how I'd seen him in street clothes during the day and a johnny at night.

It turned out to be him, and my mother and his wife derived some strength from each other over the next few weeks, both holding out hope of a reversal.

ON APRIL 1, A SPRING nor'easter attacked the state. Snowbound, I worked desperately to shovel out my car. Even when I had, the roads were impassable. I spent my first night in weeks at home. But I couldn't sleep. Awake and edgy, I called my cousin, who was in Boston that night. She had taken to calling the hospital several times during the night whenever she could not sleep. Lately, the nurses had told her to stop. But here we were, both awake at 3:00 A.M. She called, patching me in so I could hear the news and we could both sleep.

"We were just about to call you," the nurse said. "We're losing him. Come as fast as you can. Your mother's already on the way."

Again I dressed hurriedly and left my house, driving as fast as I could down the freshly plowed Route 95, calling to God or someone to help my father, to help me. Again I raced through the dim empty halls to his room. And again I found him sitting up, breathing, looking around at all of us gathered there. This time my aunt had come too, and she shook her head when I walked in. "Scared the hell out of us," she said.

I had come to think of these weeks since I left Vermont as a bubble of hospital and illness. The only way I saw for the bubble to break was for my father to die. I wanted this hell to end, but not at that cost. Collapsing into a chair, I wondered if we would ever resume our lives again. They had long since stopped trying to wean my father off oxygen. He wore two tubes in his nose and a mask over his face, and still he couldn't get enough to keep him alive. The 410 days I thought Mama Rose had warned me about now seemed like just another cruel trick at my expense.

An uncle and another aunt arrived, and Gina came bursting in from Boston. Dawn cut the dark sky, allowing light to filter in. Usually I greeted everyone and tried to maintain some semblance of normalcy. But this time I was too spent. I said hello, numbly. Across from me, the calendar hung on the wall, beside the picture of the car that I could not imagine my father ever driving. It was still too early for the nurse to have changed the date; it said 4/1 in its big black numbers.

I gasped, loud enough for people to hear.

My aunt rushed over to me. "What?" she said. "What?"

By now, everyone had heard about my dream that fall. So she knew exactly what I meant when I said, "It's not 410 days. It's 4/10. April 10."

AFTER THAT NIGHT, THE hospital—doctors, nurses, social workers—began a campaign to get rid of my father. They gave up on him, and they wanted us to give up on him too. Just a few weeks earlier, my mother and I had toured nursing homes when a hospital representative informed us that he'd had pneumonia for too long. He couldn't stay anymore. Fungal pneumonia killed people faster than my father was dying. We found a nursing home nearby and were ready to have him transferred until we learned that in an emergency, they were not equipped to treat him. If one of his respiratory failures happened, they'd have to call an ambulance and have him taken to a hospital. He would surely die en route. We began a campaign to take him home.

"He'll be housebound," his doctor said.

To this we replied, "We don't care."

Sometime during the long hospital stay, I watched a *Frontline* episode on infertility. One of the women interviewed adamantly said she would never try in vitro fertilization or other invasive techniques. In the next show, she was at an in vitro clinic. When the interviewer reminded her of her earlier, strong statements, the woman explained: "You keep moving the line. First you say if nothing happens, you will simply adopt. Then you say you'll try the simplest things. Then you say you'll try more invasive things, moving the line each time something fails."

I began to see my father's illness in the same terms. At first, we wanted him better. Then we were happy to have him come home, even with a walker. Then we accepted that he'd be on oxygen all the time, then that he would be housebound. As long as we moved the line, he was alive.

His health failing, he instructed us on how to prepare the Easter breakfast specialties he had been in charge of for the last twenty-five years—how to turn a frittata so it doesn't break, the secret to making light pizzeles.

The day before Easter he began to die. His oxygen supply was so low that his legs grew blue and mottled. It was our turn to be called into the family room, where his doctor urged us to let him die.

"Even if he pulls through, and antibiotics could allow that to happen," the doctor explained, "he'll just get another infection tomorrow or next week. He's not going to get better."

I thought of all the stories I'd heard over my lifetime, stories about people letting their loved ones go, or loved ones asking their families to let them go. My father had asked us to do everything, even if the chance was one in a million.

"Give him the antibiotics," I said. *Save him*, I begged, hoping the doctor could see into my heart.

But the doctor and the nurses were fed up with us. "Don't stay one night," one of the nurses whispered to me outside my father's room. "That way he'll die. They won't go with their loved ones right there all the time. It always happens that you stay and stay, and finally go home and in the time it took to drive there, the person dies, like they've been waiting for you to leave them alone."

One afternoon the doctor called me at the hospital.

"Ann," he said, "you're logical. You're smart." What he didn't say was that I was the stronghold, not relenting to his unarticulated pleas to let him let my father die.

"And?" I asked him.

"Let me tell you a story," he said. "My father's a doctor too. And he had this dog who was old and sick and couldn't be cured. I kept telling him that he should put the dog to sleep, and he refused, saying he wanted to spend as much time as he could with the dog while he could. The dog's not suffering, he said. And I said, But he can't get better. What's the use?"

"Let me tell you about our dog Maggie," I said. "Same scenario. Sick but not in pain. Do you know what my father did?"

The doctor didn't answer.

"He let her live as long as he could. He pet her and played with her and had those last few weeks with her."

"Ann . . ." he began.

"The thing is," I said, "we're not talking about dogs. You cannot take whatever minutes or hours I can have with my father. You can't. I won't let you."

That Easter weekend, the man with leukemia had also taken a turn for the worse and the nurses pointed out to us how his wife was learning to let him go. Why do we have to learn that? I wondered. There was only one person who could answer that: my father. And I was determined to fight for his life until he told me to do otherwise.

A priest was called and administered the last rites, now known as the sacrament of the sick. But when the priest walked away, I grabbed my father's hand and sought a miracle yet again: "Daddy," I said, "please come back. For me and Sam and Grace."

At the sound of my children's names, my father struggled not only to open his eyes, but to breathe, a deep, life-sustaining breath.

By that evening, he was sitting up. "I thought I was a goner there," he joked.

Easter morning he told my mother that her frittata was too dry. I stayed with him all day. That night, we watched the movie *A Few Good Men*. He always enjoyed movies about the military. I sat on his bed and held his hand.

"Daddy," I said, "they didn't want to give you antibiotics today. But I told them you wanted to do everything to make you better."

"Hell," he said, wide-eyed. "If I didn't get antibiotics, wasn't I going to *die*?"

I nodded.

He looked into my eyes. "Honey, you make sure they do whatever they have to. You understand?"

Knowing how close I was to tears, I nodded again.

I sat like that, holding his hand, until he went to sleep.

Later, I told the doctor that if I had listened to him, I would not have had that final day with my father. He would have taken it from us.

THE DOCTOR SUSPECTED THE cancer was back and had spread to my father's brain. He did CAT scans on his bones, lungs, and head. But my father remained tumor free and cancer free. Despite that, on April 10—4/10—he slipped into a coma. That day, my father's oncologist, a man from India, took us into the hallway outside my father's room.

"He's a fighter," he told us, and I knew exactly what his words would be because Mama Rose had already brought me to this moment. "But there's nothing we can do."

The next day, my uncle's birthday, my father opened his eyes for the last time.

"Hey, buddy," he said. "Happy birthday."

He pointed to the calendar.

"It is today, right?" he said, taking my uncle's surprise for something else.

In that moment, we both thought we'd gotten another miracle. My father and my uncle shook hands. Then my father slipped back into his coma and died early in the morning, three days later.

More than once since then I have found myself wondering not *if* I got a miracle or not, but whether I prayed for the wrong thing. Should I have bent over the pocito and asked for my father to live rather than for the tumor to go away? What I am certain of is this: I got exactly what I prayed for on that December afternoon at El Santuario de Chimayo.

hope

DESPITE EVERYTHING, I STILL believed.

A few weeks before my father died, I dreamed that it was a Friday night and we were out together, the way we had been for so many Friday nights in my life. We were at a local rib joint in Providence, Sticky Fingers. Since I'd moved back, it had become one of our favorite spots. We had a favorite waitress, who flirted with both my father and Sam. Sometimes her own young daughter was there, and Sam would eat with her. Mostly, I suspected that this waitress was struck by the same thing most people noticed when they saw my father and me together: the strength of our relationship.

In this dream, my father and I sat in the center of this busy restaurant, drinking beer. He was laughing and happy, but I felt nervous.

"Where are you, Daddy?" I asked him.

He laughed and sipped his beer. "I have no idea," he said.

"But you must know."

He laughed again, shrugging this time. "I don't know. But wherever I am, I'm okay."

I remember waking from that dream and believing that my father had somehow transcended the state he was in to assure me he was happy. At that point, he had started to confabulate. One day his doctor came into the lounge to tell me that my father had stopped recognizing him.

"That's impossible," I told him. "I was just talking to him and he made perfect sense."

I went back into my father's room. He was in bed, the television on.

"Was anybody in here while I was gone?" I asked, settling into the chair beside him.

"Dr. Osmanski," my father answered with great clarity.

Relieved, I told him that the doctor thought he hadn't recognized him.

"He said that?" my father said, surprised. "What's wrong with that guy? I was riding my bike down Main Street and he rode his bike right by me and I waved right at him."

Although he always recognized me, more and more he stayed in a world all his own. But that dream brought me some comfort. Apparently that world was a good one.

Later, as he lay in a coma, I used to hold his hand and talk to him. As hard as it was for me to imagine my world without him, one of the worst parts of that world was that we would not have the tradition of that morning phone call. In the emotional roller coaster of his illness, one high point that I especially remember is the morning he called me after he left the ICU.

"Hey," he said, as naturally as if the calls had not ceased those awful weeks. "Now there's something I wanted to tell you."

That was how he always started our telephone calls. But this time his words made me cry.

"What's wrong?" he asked me.

"Nothing at all," I explained. "You just have no idea how good it is to hear your voice. To have you call me like this. I've missed our morning talks so much."

When they stopped again, I convinced myself it was possible they would once again resume. Those last days of his life, understanding they had ceased forever, I begged him to find a way to call me.

"Daddy, you have to try," I said, squeezing his hand. I could see the faded colors of his once-vibrant tattoo, the blond hairs on his arm. "Find a way to call me. Please."

My father was never good at memorizing phone numbers—he always had to look up my mother's number at work even though it had remained unchanged for years—so I wasn't surprised to find a folded piece of paper with my phone number written on it among his personal effects after he died. Even in the hospital he had kept it close by him.

The day after his funeral, I sat alone in my bedroom. I wasn't crying. Rather, I was numb and empty. It was the first day in months that I did not have to race to the hospital. I was free to cook in my own kitchen, to wander the rooms where I'd hung pictures and arranged furniture. I was home, and it felt strange. My mother had taken both Sam and Grace for the day, with the hope that they would keep her busy. As a result, except for our nanny on the third floor, I was alone with my grief.

The phone rang. I didn't want to talk to anyone, yet I answered it instinctively.

But after I said hello, there was silence.

"Hello, hello," I called. Still no response. "Daddy? Is it you?" I said, then immediately felt foolish and hung up.

I sat down again, and the phone rang right away.

"Hello?" I said.

This time I heard perfectly my mother and Sam making dough boys. My mother was instructing Sam on how to stretch the dough.

"Like this?" he asked her.

"That's it!" she said. "Now we fry it and when it's all done we sprinkle it with sugar."

"Mom?" I called. "Sam?"

Instead of answering me, they kept talking to each other, about making dough boys and what they would do when Grace woke up.

"Mom!" I said again. "Pick up the phone!"

I could picture the two of them in the pantry, standing at the stove. Sam would be on his little stool, at my mother's side. And the phone would be two rooms away, in the living room. Even if my mother had brought the portable phone down from her bedroom, where was it placed so that I could hear them so well but they couldn't hear me, shouting for them now? And if they had called me, why weren't they talking to me?

I hung up the phone and considered all of this. Then I dialled my mother's number.

It took her several rings before she answered. So the phone *was* in the living room, I surmised.

"Mom—" I began.

"What do you want?" she said. "I'm busy."

"I know," I told her. "You're making dough boys."

"How do you know that?"

I repeated everything I heard. "You're crazy," she said. "We didn't call you and the portable phone is upstairs."

"I may be crazy," I said, "but am I right?"

She paused. "Yes," she said finally. "That's exactly what we said."

We were quiet for a moment, then she said, "I'm burning the dough," and she hung up.

Slowly I made my way to the third floor and knocked on the nanny's door.

"Did you hear the phone ring?" I asked her.

She nodded. "Twice."

In that moment I felt certain that my father had reached me. In her 1980 book *Walking on Water: Reflections on Faith and Art*, Madeleine L'Engle wrote: "If it can be verified, we don't need faith. . . . Faith is for that which lies on the *other* side of reason. Faith is what makes life bearable, with all its tragedies and ambiguities and sudden, startling joys." That defines the type of faith that I had been raised to believe, the faith that I still held at my core. Because of God, things happened that could not be explained. I believed Mama Rose had come to me on that September night to foretell my father's death. And I believed that my father, wherever he was, had found a way to call me. There is no logical explanation for these events; they seemed demonstrations of faith.

What I'd heard that day on the telephone made me feel good about Sam and my mother. They would forge a relationship that would be different from the one Sam had with my father, but that would fill the void my father's death had left. I believed too that my father had figured out a way to reach me, and that he had done it in the very way I asked him to. It was ten o'clock in the morning, close to our usual time to talk. I would keep open to all possibilities. He would find me again.

I GREW UP WITH ghosts.

They roamed our house while we slept, kissed us, pinched us, brought warnings and advice. Sometimes they came in the form of animals or presented themselves as shadows, though mostly they looked very much as they had when they were alive. Even though they were all related to me, I did not want to see them. "They won't hurt you," Mama Rose used to tell me. But I wasn't convinced. Everyone else in my family was delighted to have visits from long-dead people. At breakfast they exchanged stories about who had come the night before and then tried to interpret the meaning of the visit while I blocked my ears and concentrated on my Cocoa Puffs instead.

Along with our ghosts came their stories. My great-grandfather died in our basement when he fell down the stairs carrying bottles of his homemade wine. My Aunt Ann died when she was twenty-three having her wisdom teeth removed at the hospital down the road. My Uncle Brownie died in the arms of his young wife as they danced a waltz one Valentine's Day. My great-grandmother, Nonna, died at the age of ninety right upstairs in what later became my parents' bedroom. All of them returned to check in on us and, although I never actually saw them myself, they terrified me.

"Oh," my mother would say, sighing happily over her morning coffee, "Nonna came to see me last night. She sat right on the side of my bed and stroked my hair." Then she'd add, "She looked good." Or my grandmother would tell us that her daughter, my Aunt Ann, had visited in the form of a bluebird. "She comes every year like that on her birthday," she'd say, as if it were the most normal thing in the world for a long-dead woman to appear annually as a bluebird. My newly dead Uncle Brownie liked to sit on the sofa and smile as we passed. A great-aunt was sometimes seen peeking out of our cuckoo clock. There was a never-ending stream of sightings and visitations.

Even my father, a Midwesterner who could trace his roots back to the Virginia settlement, claimed to see ghosts walking around upstairs in the middle of the night. They often appeared to him as three puffs of white smoke, and they always liked to catch up on family news when they visited. Some mornings he would wake up with an arm or leg covered in bruises, which my grandmother attributed to angry ghosts. Even when a routine blood test revealed that my father had a low platelet count, the appearances of bruises still led to a discussion of which dead relative was boxing with him as he slept.

The ghosts were part of a larger string of the idiosyncratic beliefs of my family. We believed in strange forms of healing, in dreams as portents, and that Saint Anthony could—through prayer—predict the outcome of any situation. The story went that my great-grandmother passed down to my grandmother the healing and special prayers she had learned tending sheep for nuns in southern Italy. When we woke up in the morning, we were not allowed to talk until Mama Rose fed us a piece of toast. To tell the dream on an empty stomach, she said, would make it come true. After we ate she'd demand: "What did you dream last night?" No matter what the dream, Mama Rose had an interpretation for it. Clear water meant bad luck. A wedding meant bad news. Losing a tooth was an omen of death: Front teeth foretold a death in the immediate family; back teeth indicated the death of someone less intimate. A happy dream in which I spent an afternoon on a boat in a lake became a nightmare because the water was so clear I could see the bottom. "Oh, no!" Mama Rose moaned, rocking back and forth and covering her face in her hands. "This is terrible."

Every headache we had was attributed to *mal occhio*, the evil eye. My joy at getting to ride in my Uncle Eddie's red Cadillac convertible through the streets during a parade, all white-gloved and waving, was ruined when my grandmother decided I'd gotten mal occhio from jealous onlookers. "But I don't have a headache," I insisted as she poured Mazola oil into a bowl of water. "Ha!" she said, closing her eyes. "You will!" She pointed to the bowl and began to chant in Italian. When I peered in I saw beads of oil floating in water. But to Mama Rose, those beads were proof positive of mal occhio. Whenever my brother or I had a nosebleed—something we experienced frequently because of allergies—Mama Rose pinched our nose shut, tossed our head back, and made the sign of the cross on our forehead over and over until the bleeding stopped. Years later in a first aid class, I was taught the same procedure to stop a nosebleed, minus the sign of the cross, of course. But as a child, my grandmother's abilities seemed miraculous.

Mama Rose and Nonna frequently consulted Saint Anthony. When one of us had a question we would ask them to do "the prayer": Will I get that job? Will I marry this guy? Will our trip be a safe one? Alone in the bathroom with the door closed and our question in their mind, they prayed to Saint Anthony, learning their answer by how easily they were able to recite the prayer. They always returned from the bathroom solemn, sat at the kitchen table, and explained the results for us all to help interpret.

Similarly, Nonna kept a dried bunch of twigs bent into the shape of a rose in her top drawer. This "rose" had supposedly come from Jerusalem and had somehow been touched by Jesus. Placed in a glass of water—the same kind of glass from which Mama Rose and Nonna drank their anisette—and prayed to in some systematic way, the rose either opened to indicate "yes" or stayed shut to indicate "no." Unlike the prayer to Saint Anthony, the rose was only used for monumental questions.

Despite all of this superstition and eccentric behavior, it was the ghosts that bothered me the most. Stopping a nosebleed was, after all, a good thing, even if the manner in which it was stopped was conventional. Waiting for a twig in a shot glass to open up was more like a game to me than anything scary. But ghosts were ghosts, and even as a child I thought that dead people should stay away, even from the ones they loved. It was easy for me to link the healings and the prayers to religion or culture or custom. But a ghost walking around a house made that house haunted, and I did not want to live in a haunted house.

My family lived with my great-grandmother and grandmother in the house they bought when they immigrated to Rhode Island. It was old, a jumble of rooms constantly filled with relatives who spoke in broken English, dressed in old-fashioned black clothes, and emanated the smells of garlic and mothballs. In their pockets they kept rosary beads with large wooden crucifixes hanging from the ends. They would finger the beads almost nonstop, praying every time there was a lapse in conversation. Each room was dominated by a large-as-life statue of a saint—Saint Anthony, Saint Christopher, the Virgin Mary—draped with rosary beads, votive candles burning at its feet.

There was always food cooking, but it was the peasant food of Conca della Campania, the small town outside Naples from which we had come. I would wrinkle my nose at the strange smells. "What is that?" I used to demand. Often the answer was something that sent me running outside for air: lungs, intestines, hearts, livers. But what I found in our yard was not necessarily more comforting. Roosters and chickens pecked at my feet. In winter the fruit trees were wrapped like mummies. My great-grandmother, muttering in Italian, might emerge from her outhouse. Although my mother and all nine of her sisters and brothers could speak Italian, none of them wanted their children to learn. In school, it had marked them as different and they wanted to protect us from the teasing they'd endured. So when my great-grandmother called to me in Italian, I could not understand her. The more she shouted to me, the more she frightened me. "Speak right!" I used to shout back before running into the house.

At night in our house, Mama Rose and her daughters often sat up late talking. These conversations always ended up delving into the supernatural goings-on in our neighborhood: children spontaneously combusting; a woman up the street who, with one glance at a pregnant woman, could turn the baby into an unsightly monster; another woman who used candles to predict a husband's faithfulness, measuring the height and brightness of the flames. Most nights I would lie awake trembling, listening to the frightening stories being told downstairs, afraid of what would happen in our creaky old house once I fell asleep.

When I was very young, I accepted all of these things as the realities of my life. But once I started school and entered my first split-level ranch, I realized that my family was different from everybody else's. I became infatuated with a little girl named Michelle, who seemed to embody America in the 1960s. Cute and blond and pigtailed, her ancestors hailed from Kansas, a big square state colored pink on the map at school and situated smack in the middle of our very own country. Her grandmother drove a spiffy car—a Chevy Impala!—and baked M&M cookies and snickerdoodles while Mama Rose stood in my kitchen skinning rabbits.

Eager to visit Michelle every day, I became a pest, staring wide-eyed at the neat boxes of macaroni and cheese that lined their cupboards, the glasses of Hi-C her mother poured for us, the gurgling dishwasher and garbage disposal they used with such ease. While grapevines and fig trees and rows of tomatoes took up all of our backyard, Michelle 's was dominated by a fully equipped swing set. Usually talkative and personable, I became mute in the face of all these modern American trappings. Unlike our house with its old furniture and old people coming in and out, entering the Kincaids' house was like stepping into the pages of the Sears and Roebuck catalogue. Everything there was new and shiny. I longed for a canopy bed like Michelle's instead of the iron one I shared with Mama Rose. I wanted a vanity, a silver hairbrush, an ivory bureau with antique gold trim. I wanted a bathroom in sea foam green with a sliding opaque door on the shower. I wanted to be 100 percent American, 100 percent ghost-free.

I begged my parents to move to Brookfield Plat, the development where Michelle lived. Each street there was lined with identical houses, all of them filled with modern life. "But our family has lived here forever," my mother explained. "We don't leave." Apparently that was true even after death. For the other thing I was certain did not exist in Brookfield Plat was ghosts. The houses and families there were too young, too modern, to be haunted. Afraid to invite any of the girls from the Plat to our house for sleepovers, I longed for their slumber parties. Dressed in baby-doll pajamas, I could do the Swim and the Jerk to the latest Beatles 45, eat slightly scorched Jiffy Pop, do everything just like all the other girls. Then I could sleep easily, tucked into a trundle bed or a lower bunk, the smell of new paint still faintly evident. Unlike at home where I insisted on sleeping with a light shining right in my face, at slumber parties I treasured the darkness and the sound of real live girls breathing beside me.

As it always does, change came. Nonna died and my grandmother reluctantly allowed renovations in our house. The outhouse was demolished, the fruit trees were dug up, and a fancy two-car garage was erected in the spot where they had stood. I finally got a coveted room of my own and chose an antique white bedroom set trimmed in gold. We got new furniture, put panelling on the walls. But this modernity did not scare away our ghosts. While the Mr. Coffee dripped and my mother prepared menus from *The Galloping Gourmet*, the ghost stories were still shared. "My father came last night," my grandmother might say. "He looked so handsome," she'd add. And she would smile so happily that I would shout at her: "You're giving me the creeps. I don't want to hear about it!" Long into high school I lay awake in horrified anticipation of some dead relative stroking my hair or commenting on my choice of boyfriends.

My first apartments were always new. I liked the shiny appliances, the stark white walls. I slept peacefully then, the lights turned off, no threat of these places being haunted. Then one day, searching for a place to rent, I looked at an old Victorian. The floors tilted familiarly. Touching the glass doorknobs brought flashes of childhood memories into sharp focus. I saw the face of my grandmother, now dead. Remembering her red curly hair and the way she tilted her head as she listened made me oddly content. I rented that apartment, and this began a life-long attachment to old homes.

I did not expect to encounter ghosts in any of these rented places. After all, the ghosts I'd grown up with were loved ones roaming the very house they had lived in. I was certain someone else's ghosts would not bother with me. Oddly, the idea of ghosts no longer frightened or embarrassed me. As time passed, the traditions I'd grown up with vanished. Nonna's "rose" was lost, the prayer went unlearned by my generation of cousins; even the food we cooked became sanitized versions of the kind we used to eat. And the people I loved began to die. The family I had known for forty years was shrunken, disappearing altogether. Just as my mother lost siblings, I lost Skip. The uncles and aunts who kept my childhood home so full began to die too. Then my father died. The notion that any one of them might come to me and give me advice or comfort was actually appealing. But they stayed away. Perhaps, I sometimes think, with my frequent relocations and rented homes, I am difficult to find.

My mother still lives in the same house. Whenever I ask her if she sees ghosts, she smiles sadly and shakes her head. It is the old stories she likes to tell, the sightings and visitations of forty years ago. When pushed, she admits unexplainable occurrences. "Once," she says, "before Daddy died, I was sitting at the kitchen table looking out the window and Skip's face appeared on the wall across the street. All day it was there, looking at me. Finally, I asked Daddy if he saw anything and he was relieved. He'd been seeing Skip all day too." She talks of seeing two white doves fly off together one morning after she wondered if my father and brother were together now. She says she sometimes smells the particular cigar smoke of an uncle, feels an arm around her shoulders when she sleeps. These stories would have frightened me once. But now I find myself hopeful that there will be more of them.

Alone now, my mother talks frequently of selling the house. She imagines a small condo with fresh paint, no stairs, and a new kitchen. The idea alarms me. Where will our family go if she abandons them? In June, when her sister appears as a bluebird, who will greet her? When Nonna stops in to check on things, what will she find? I don't say this to my mother. Instead, I tell her I will help her pack up when it's time for her to move. "It's only a house," I say, struggling to sound lighthearted even as my stomach lurches at the thought.

With my own husband and young children, there is no reason for me to sleep at my mother's house. But its proximity to the airport and my departure on an early morning flight kept me there overnight recently. My room looks different than it did when it really was mine. A crib for overnight visits from grandchildren takes up one corner; my mother's winter clothes take up another. Still, when I climbed into my antique white bed with the gold trim and turned off the light, I could easily imagine myself as a young girl again, in this room. I could imagine my brother working at his desk in the next room, doing problems on a slide ruler. I could hear my father snoring, my mother's breathing making harmony with it. I could remember my aching to leave this place, my desire for everything new.

But unlike my younger self, who used to fear sleep and the ghosts it might bring, I closed my eyes and willed them to come to me. I finally understood my grandmother's elation at seeing her dead father again, even if it was during sleep. The thought—the hope, really—that my own father might kiss my cheek one more time, or that I might see my brother after almost twenty years, filled me with peace. For the first time, I slept happily in this haunted house.

In the morning my mother told me she didn't really want to sell the house. Relieved, I asked her what had changed her mind. "Our family has been here forever," she said. "We don't leave."

AUTUMN 1997.

Six months after my father's death, I found myself plunging into despair. As time passed without those morning phone calls or one of his bad jokes, I became immobilized by my sadness. My heart seemed to take on extra weight. Friday nights were the hardest, all of our past ones spent together stretched into a blur of memory; all of my future ones looked lonely. Foolishly, I had expected him to find me. I was willing to accept anything. One night I heard a psychic on *Larry King Live* describe the scent of cherry blossoms as a communication between a mother and daughter. If I were to catch a hint of Old Spice, I decided, it would satisfy me. I waited for a bird to pause on my windowsill, or a bottle of beer to fall out of my refrigerator. Anything, even that small, would bring me some comfort. But none came.

For me, this despair was like staring over a cliff into a vast spiritual abyss. I did not want to take the step that would send me dropping into that abyss. I believed in God, and that belief kept me from falling over the edge; still, I teetered there, unsteady. I had always found solace in church. As a child, I spent every Sunday morning at Sacred Heart, the Catholic church where my parents were married and my brother and I were baptized. I found comfort in the rituals there, in the prayers recited by rote in unison. The smells of incense and candle wax provided comfort to me even as an adult.

Over the years I had attended many different places of worship— Unitarian, Episcopal, even Quaker meetinghouses and Buddhist temples. Often location determined my choice. When I lived in Greenwich Village I worshipped at the Episcopal church around the corner from my apartment. The winter I spent in the Berkshires in Massachusetts I attended Quaker meetings. During my years working as a flight attendant, I visited the churches and cathedrals of the cities where I stayed. It wasn't so much a denomination that felt right to me. Rather, I needed a place for prayer and reflection, a holy place where I could feel closer to God.

Prayer had always been a big part of my life. Mama Rose prayed the rosary every night. Sitting in her oversized pale pink chair, she mouthed the words silently as the beads moved, one by one, prayer by prayer, through her fingers. If I interrupted her, she kept her eyes closed and continued praying, as if she hadn't even heard me. Her collection of rosary beads was large—pale blue crystal, rough wood, clear plastic, black, collected at various churches she visited around New England

and Canada. The rosary beads hung draped around the statues of saints' necks or sat tucked in Mama Rose's apron pockets or nestled in drawers with our kitchen spoons.

But it wasn't just Mama Rose who believed in the power of prayer. We all did. My mother said her prayers faithfully every night and made sure my brother and I did too. No matter where I slept or how old I was, the last thing I did was say one Hail Mary, one Our Father, and an Act of Contrition as well as a thank-you to God for whatever that day had brought. Prayer and church mingled with the other less traditional beliefs of my family to shape and strengthen my faith.

My husband and I attend a Congregational chuch in Providence. The minister there often gives sermons that leave me thinking about faith and spirituality long after I hear them. During the months of my father's illness, the church provided me with a source of comfort, as did the chapel in the hospital that I visited every day to pray. But after my father died, church and prayer did not keep my despair at bay. In fact, I found that going to church made me feel worse. I found myself questioning the theories of faith that I had always held as true. Still, I kept going and kept praying, hoping that God would show me a way back.

When comfort did arrive, it was in a surprising package. Unexpectedly, I found myself pregnant late that fall. I did some calculations and realized the due date was July 21. But both of my babies had been born early—Sam exactly two weeks, and Grace exactly one week. If this baby were two weeks early, it would be born on the Fourth of July, my father's birthday.

Once again, my steadfast hold on my faith, even when it felt shaky, had delivered me. Somehow my father and God were sending me a baby born on his birthday. So precious and comforting was this idea that I kept the pregnancy to myself for a bit, as if it were a private communication with my father. This baby, I realized, was a true gift, another sign of faith when I was about to lose mine.

THAT DECEMBER, EAGER TO keep the optimism this pregnancy had infused in me and struggling to find examples of faith at work, I visited Mexico City during the Feast of the Virgin of Guadalupe. It was there, in

1531, that Juan Diego, while walking outside, heard birds singing, saw a bright light from atop a hill, and heard someone calling his name. He climbed the hill and saw a young girl, radiant in a golden mist, who claimed to be the Virgin. She told him she wanted a church built on that spot. When Juan Diego told the bishop what he had seen, the bishop asked him to go back and demand a sign as proof that this was really the Virgin. When he returned, the apparition made roses miraculously bloom, even though it was December. Convinced, the bishop had a cathedral built there. More than ten million people visit the shrine in Mexico City, making it the most popular place next to the Vatican in the Catholic world.

While my then four-year-old son Sam and I walked toward the basilica in the crowd, people whose eyes had been fixed on the cathedral ahead of us suddenly turned around and gazed up into the sky instead. A murmur passed through the crowd. Some people dropped to their knees and began to pray. I turned too. In the sky, the sun had passed behind the clouds in such a way that it appeared to make a cross of light above us. I blinked and looked away, then once again turned toward the sky. The cross of sunlight was still evident. The crowd pointed and made the sign of the cross.

"Sam," I said, tugging on his hand, "do you see anything in the sky?"

It was hard for Sam to take his eyes off the dancers in feathered headdress up ahead of us. But he did for a moment.

"You mean that X in the clouds over there?" he said, pointing.

"You see that?" I asked him.

"I see something," he said, and then he turned his attention back to the dancers.

But I could not turn back so easily. Just a few weeks earlier I had felt a despair that seemed to be powerful enough to take me away from all the things that had kept me going in the past. Now my faith was renewed. At night in our hotel room in the Roman district of the city, Sam and I lay in bed eating quesadillas from room service and watching *Rugrats* in Spanish. My exhaustion from this still-young pregnancy pleased me. Everything felt possible again, including miracles and unexplainable phenomena in the sky above Mexico City. Even as the crowd pushed me along toward the basilica, I craned my neck to better see this sign from God.

My cousin Gina saw the same phenomenon of light in the late 1980s when she visited Medjugorje, which was then part of Yugoslavia. Since June 1981, six young people claim to have seen the Virgin Mary there daily. Gospa, as they call her, gives them messages for humankind. Gina took a side trip from a vacation to make the steep climb up Mount Krizevac, where many pilgrims have claimed to see the sun "dance" or other mysterious light effects. Medjugorje is now part of the war-torn country of Bosnia, and although many people go there for miracle healing, the miracle that had occurred since the war is perhaps even more astounding: Rockets and bombs aimed at the church have failed to explode. Medjugorje remains untouched by the war around it.

Gina remembers looking into the sky and seeing a blinding light. Yet she could look directly at it without blinking or getting the usual spots in front of her eyes that such a bright light would cause. She nudged her companion and told him to look at what the light was doing in the sky.

"I don't see anything," he said.

"How can you not see that?" she said, continuing to stare, mesmerized by the vision.

He shrugged. "You're crazy," he said. "There's nothing unusual up there."

Gina continued to keep her eyes fixed on the bright light she saw as she climbed. Her companion never saw it at all. Years later she can recall the bells ringing that day, announcing the presence of the six young children in the church. She remembers too the unusual song of dozens of birds. She left Medjugorje with what is known as "the Medjugorje effect," a state of euphoria that follows an initial feeling of hostility or doubt about the events at the shrine. Her companion did not experience this feeling, but recalling her trip there, Gina always gets a far-off look in her eyes and struggles to describe what happened to her that day, both externally and internally.

ALTHOUGH IT WAS AN impressive sight to behold the December 12 that I made the walk to the basilica along with people who had come from all over Mexico, many on their knees, that national pilgrimage and the spectacle of light were not what struck me about Mexico and its relationship to the miraculous. Rather, it was the way the culture as a whole viewed miracles that impressed me. Street vendors everywhere sold milagros, the small silver charms that mean, literally, "little miracles." The charms take the shape of body parts—arms, legs, hearts—and are pinned to saints in churches, to the inside of people's own jackets, everywhere. When I told a vendor that my mother had recently broken her hand, he gave me a milagro in the shape of a hand, at no charge.

These milagros are not unlike the silver ex-votos sold in a small shop in Palermo, Sicily, that are made into the shape of body parts that have been cured by saintly intervention. Most common of these are the silver ovals with a pair of eyes to honor Saint Lucy. But one can also find noses, hands, breasts, lungs, intestines, kidneys, even entire bodies of men, women, and children or farm animals.

Throughout Mexico one can also view *retablos,* paintings made on wood or tin that request favors for everything from curing someone of pneumonia to asking that children do not fall out of windows, that a woman have a safe childbirth, or that a house not catch on fire. Although many churches have glorious collections of retablos, they also adorn the walls of shops and homes, humble requests for miracles large and small. "Oh yes," a friend of mine who lives in San Miguel de Allende told me, "here in Mexico it is a miracle if someone's ox does a good job or if it doesn't rain on a special day. Miracles happen everyday here."

As if to prove her point, the night before I left Mexico City several of us climbed into a cab to go to a restaurant. The driver was unfamiliar with the address. Everyone studied a map and planned a route, but still we couldn't find the street. Several times we stopped and asked directions. Still we couldn't find it. After forty minutes and yet another set of directions by a pedestrian, the cab came to a screeching halt. "We're here!" our driver exclaimed happily. "It's a miracle!"

despair

THREE DAYS BEFORE CHRISTMAS, when we would give our news of the new baby to my grief-stricken family, I began to throw up violently. This was a good sign. Ten years earlier, during my first marriage, I'd suffered a miscarriage after several weeks of feeling great except for fatigue. I'd later heard an old wives' tale that babies who stick make you sick. My next two pregnancies certainly did that, and they went without a hitch. I was now almost eleven weeks pregnant, and the dizziness and nausea I'd been experiencing had turned into morning sickness. This baby was fine.

The next morning I was shocked to find a smear of bright red blood when I went to the bathroom. The midwife scheduled a sonogram for that afternoon. All day I lay in bed, worried. In my first trimester with Sam, I had bled quite a bit, and everything turned out all right. But I also remembered how my miscarriage had begun just this way—a smear of bright red blood when I went to the ladies' room in a Middle Eastern restaurant in Brooklyn. What worried me most was what a miscarriage would do to my faith. This pregnancy had lifted me from my sorrow in inexplicable ways. That July baby meant something larger than just a new baby to me. If it didn't happen, then what was I to make of this pregnancy? And of my father's death?

That afternoon, my belly full of water and smeared with gel, the technician moved the monitor carefully over my stomach while my husband and I watched the monitor. Twice before we had delighted at the early movements of our children. But this time we were quiet, holding our breath. The technician paused. There on the monitor was our third child. But the sonogram showed no heartbeat.

"If your dates are off," the technician explained, "then there wouldn't be a heartbeat."

Since this pregnancy, unlike Sam and Grace, was unplanned, I had no idea when I'd actually conceived. I was still willing to hold out for the hope that I would have this baby after all. But that hope was erased that night when I began to bleed profusely and suffered debilitating cramps. There was no doubt now; I was losing my seed of faith.

On Christmas Day 1997, a year after my father's tumor disappeared and I had believed in a miracle, I sat among my family and believed in absolutely nothing at all. My despair began in earnest that day. And so did my search to conquer it.

"FAITH IS NOT A series of gilt-edged propositions that you sit down to figure out, and if you follow all the logic and accept all the conclusions, then you have it," Mary Jean Irion wrote in *Yes, World*. "It is crumpling and throwing away everything, proposition by proposition, until nothing is left, and then writing a new proposition, your very own, to throw in the teeth of despair." That was what I had done when the doctors gave us my father's prognosis. I went to New Mexico full of faith and hope, throwing that faith into the teeth of despair, believing in a miracle.

So when despair once again took over, I turned to my very own proposition. I would search for miracles, and in that search I would try to find one to save my spiritual self. I began to read everything I could find about faith and miracles. The more I read, the bleaker I felt. Pictures of pilgrims praying at different sites around the world filled me with pity for them, and for me. My faith, so recently renewed, was once again disappearing. I tried praying, alone and in church, but what had once comforted me now left me emptier than when I began.

On Sunday mornings, while my husband and children went to church, I stayed in bed poring over more books about miracles and faith, highlighting passages in brightly colored marker, leaving hot pink and fluorescent orange streaks across the page. I started compiling lists of places where I had been and received spiritual solace and other lists of places where I might go.

A part of me was drawn to Italy where I'd always felt at home, as if I really did belong there. My husband liked to tease me about the way, when we visited Rome together, he saw expressions and gestures that he also saw in me. But, for a small country, Italy had more than its share of miracle sites. When I studied maps, carefully marking off Siena, Assisi, Padua, Palermo, the trip looked as disconnected as I felt.

Whenever my husband and I plan a family vacation, we always make sure that his eight-year-old daughter Ariane can join us. Ariane lives in Michigan with her mother and stepfather and their two children. Despite the geographical distance, my husband makes sure Ariane visits us every month and for a good part of summer and holidays. With her school vacation ahead of her, we agreed that we should go back to Italy with all three children.

The story of Padre Pio, a Capuchin monk who is said to have performed miracles even after his death in 1968, sparked my interest. Almost a cult figure, Padre Pio was being considered for sainthood. It is said that people flocked to the remote Italian town of San Giovanni Rotondo on the Monte Gargano, the "spur" of the Italian boot that divides the plains of Apulia from the Adriatic Sea, in search of miracles. Perhaps there I would find a miracle too.

No ordinary man, Padre Pio had the stigmata, the gift of transverberation (a wound in his side like Jesus had), and the ability to bilocate—to be in two places at one time. In many ways, I was bilocating too. Struggling to move through my grief and maintain a strong marriage and good parenting, I moved between these two emotional worlds daily. Memories of my father alive coincided with my life without him. I tried to be optimistic and hopeful while inside I was back overlooking that spiritual abyss, closer than ever to falling into it.

Another bilocation of sorts was also at work. Over the sixteen years since my brother's death, I had managed through faith and sometimes sheer willpower to avoid the despair of grief. But my father's death catapulted me into a double loss. The realization that my once-strong family of four was now cut in half added to my emotional pain. My family history and memories became more fragile and more precious as I lost people with whom I shared them.

From 1952 until 1955, my parents and my young brother had lived in the Vamero section of Naples. When I studied my maps, I always lingered there in southern Italy. Not only had Nonna come from somewhere outside Naples, but my parents and Skip had been a young family there together. Miracles come in all different ways. Perhaps there was a miracle for me around Naples, a bond that could be forged, a loss that could be recovered. For me, this loss was literal with the deaths of my father and Skip, but also symbolic. My faith in God and the unknown that allowed for miracles had been shaken, perhaps for good—unless somewhere in Italy I could find what I needed to resurrect it.

PACKED TIGHTLY INTO A small Fiat, the five of us—Lorne, Ariane, Sam, Grace, and me—drove the winding roads toward Naples. Only a few hours off the airplane in Rome, we were already heading south, where a small suite of rooms in a hotel on a promontory in Sorrento awaited us. But I had convinced my husband that a stop in Naples, in Vamero, would help me. Fortified with fresh buffalo mozzarella and cafe lattes, we arrived in Naples late that sunny March afternoon. Vesuvius towered above the sparkling Bay of Naples, its peak long ago blown off during an eruption, leaving it almost heart shaped. Capri jutted from the water and, in the distance, Ischia.

While my husband explained Pompeii to the two older ones and Grace slept in her car seat, I fought back tears. I had grown up with stories of my parents' years here with Skip, and this was the first time I had seen any of what they had described. There was Vesuvius, and below it Pompeii, where for free they would wander on Sunday afternoons and watch archaeologists uncovering bits of the city. And there was Capri, where my mother bought a new red hat. Her stories of the terrifying boat ride into the Blue Grotto used to keep me mesmerized as a child. The large destroyers and aircraft carriers in the waters now reminded me of our family slides, my father atop a ship just like one of these, in his navy uniform, young and handsome, a cigarette dangling almost cockily from his lips.

On the map in my lap, I searched for the town where Nonna had lived. Its name was vague, its location vaguer. I read all the names of small towns outside of Naples, then gave up.

"I come from somewhere around here," I said, looking at the Bay of Naples sparkling beside us, Vesuvius looming above us.

Sam laughed. "No you don't. You come from Rhode Island."

"You're right," I said. Inside, I felt untethered and lonely.

We ventured into Naples, a city of great chaos and an almost sad beauty. The traffic was heavy, the signs confusing, our jet lag mounting. Although we easily found Vamero on the map, no matter how hard we tried we could not get there.

"It's at the top of the funicular," I said, remembering the tales of my mother and brother riding it home. There were palm trees there, and large stone houses with marble foyers. A shop sold the best cameos in the world.

But after trying for over an hour, we agreed to give up. What had I expected to find there anyway? I chastised myself as we continued to Sorrento. The little girl with the red-and-white-checkered underpants that used to chase my brother? The old women who used to wash the marble steps of houses on their hands and knees each morning? My parents, young and alive, a round-faced three-year-old boy in their arms? No, I decided, turning my back on Naples. There was no miracle for me here. And a small nagging thought crept into my brain: Perhaps there were no miracles anywhere, after all.

ON OUR WAY FROM Sorrento to San Giovanni Rotondo, an all-day car ride through mountains and rugged terrain, I read the story of Padre Pio aloud. My husband kept rolling his eyes. More than once he whispered to me, "The guy was a kook." But when I'd finished, I asked Sam and Ariane if they believed that Padre Pio was capable of everything the book said. Did they believe he could heal people too? "Oh, yes!" they both said without hesitation. Their eagerness to believe struck me. Not long ago, I had believed too, and for the rest of the day a sadness stayed with me.

It was a brutally cold March afternoon when we arrived at the cathedral there. The wind blew at over fifty miles an hour. But still the church was packed. I made my way downstairs to Padre Pio's tomb, where the kneelers around it were full of pilgrims offering roses. A father stood beside his young son, who sat hunched and twisted in a wheelchair. As they prayed, the father lovingly stroked the boy's cheek. Watching them, I was convinced that the boy would not walk out of here, leaving his wheelchair behind. I did not believe the boy would ever walk.

True, Padre Pio has been given credit for many miracles. In one, a young girl was born without pupils in her eyes. Her grandmother prayed to Padre Pio without any results. A nun urged her to make a pilgrimage from her small town to San Giovanni Rotondo. There, the monk touched the girl's eyes and she could see. On their way home, they stopped to visit a doctor who, upon examining the child, was puzzled. The girl could see, but still she had no pupils. Like all places where miracles are said to happen, the legends of the healings are whispered among those who go. They are described in the small brochures one can buy for a few dollars at the church. But it is only the hopeful, the desperate, who crowd around the water, the dirt, the heart, the tomb.

As I stood to leave Padre Pio's tomb, a middle-aged man and his mother hurried into the room. The woman held a statue of the Virgin Mary, an offering. But what I saw on their faces was a look that I recognized too well, a look I wished was not so familiar. They wore the shocked and grief-stricken expressions of those who know they are about to lose someone they love. Perhaps they had just received the bad news. Or perhaps the person had taken a turn for the worse. They had come here because the doctors had told them there was nothing else that could be done. It was a matter of days or weeks or months. The only thing left to do was ask for a miracle. And with a coldness that was unfamiliar to me, I did not think they would get one.

MY FATHER DIED TWO days before Sam's fourth birthday. Once, before my father was even sick, Sam came to me upset because he'd seen his favorite baby-sitter crying. "She was sad," Sam told me. "I've never been sad before." Then he added, "Not ever."

It was true. Sam's young life was a happy one. And just as my father had enchanted me, a good part of Sam's happiness came from him too.

As Sam liked to tell anyone who would listen, he and Pa were best buddies. My father agreed. Ever since Sam arrived, all four pounds, twelve ounces of him, my father became his best friend. He washed all of Sam's new clothes with a gentle detergent to rid them of chemicals that might irritate a baby's skin. While I wrote in my tiny study, Pa rocked Sam in the next room, singing and humming to him, getting up to point out everything outside the window.

As Sam grew, Pa took him places in his red pickup truck, carefully buckling him into the car seat. They frequented restaurants around town, the two of them charming waitresses and customers. On walks around the block, they had special places to stop and rest; Sam imitated my father's cough as they sat side by side on stone walls or grassy corners. They even dressed alike in pocket T-shirts, baseball caps, and jeans. Whenever Pa arrived to pick him up, Sam would first run into his arms, then check to be sure they were dressed the same before throwing me a kiss and shouting: "Bye bye, Mommy! I'm going with Pa!"

When my father became ill, I worried about the effect it would have on Sam. He ridded me of one concern when I took him to visit my father in the hospital. "Pa might scare you," I told him, explaining about the tubes in his nose and the mask over those, all pumping oxygen into him. I warned him about the IVs and the bruises they left behind on Pa's arms. But Sam only met my careful descriptions with surprise. "Pa could never scare me," he said. And he was right. Adults who visited showed much more trepidation than Sam, who raised and lowered my father's hospital bed, played with the television remote, and sang him "Grand Old Flag."

"Are you coming home soon?" Sam always asked Pa before his visit ended.

"I'm trying," Pa said.

Sam and I have always had a good relationship. Both of us are verbal, and like to talk about everything in great detail. But trying to explain what eventually became inevitable was difficult for me, and understanding it was almost impossible for Sam, who had imagined he and Pa together for a long time to come. Then came the day when I had to tell Sam that he would never see Pa again.

As I struggled to cope with not just my father's death and the once again shifting dynamics of my shrinking family, but also the larger questions of faith and miracles, I became unable to articulate the thoughts that plagued me now. But Sam remained as open as ever. "So," he'd say as he settled into his car seat, "Pa is in space, right?" Or, pointing at a stained glass window in church, he'd ask, "Is one of those angels Pa?" Without me to guide him in his search for answers, he came to his own conclusions. Heaven, he said, was located somewhere near Cambodia. When you faint, Sam speculated, you disappear a little. But when you die you disappear completely.

I thought his solutions were as good as any I could come up with. The part I had trouble with was what he did right after he posed them: He'd look me right in the eye with more hope than I could stand and wait for me to agree with him, or give him the right answer. But in this matter my fear and ignorance were so large that I grew dumb in the face of his innocence.

At night, Sam pressed his face against his bedroom window and cried, calling out into the darkness, "Pa, I love you! Sweet dreams!" Then, after his tears stopped, he'd climbed back into bed, somehow satisfied, and sleep. I, on the other hand, wandered the house all night, haunted by the past few months and the turns they had taken. Sometimes I sat on the couch and simply tried to conjure my father's face before he got sick. But as soon as my eyes closed, that other image came to me—my father in the hospital and me unable to save him.

Other times I replayed the events, as if I could find and then change some crucial one. Should we all have moved up to Boston so that he could have been in the hands of the Dana Farber Institute? Should we have insisted that he not get any chemotherapy or radiation, put our faith in the belief that our miracle of the tumor vanishing would last forever? I remembered how certain the oncologist had been when he explained that even one tiny stray cell of cancer would find his brain or liver and kill him. We had opted for every piece of insurance we could have to save him, medical and spiritual, and ended up losing him anyway.

Like Sam, I cried too. But when I looked out at the spring night those few weeks after he died, with crocuses and daffodils sprouting, the snow melted away, the hint of warmth in the air, I did not find comfort.

I found instead emptiness, a world without my father. Just the spring before he had called to tell me of my cousin's unexpected death; now he too was dead. He had waited at my house while I went for an amniocentesis exactly a year earlier. Then he brought me a turkey dinner, videos, Tylenol for my cramping. He sat by my bed and held my hand, assuring me that this baby was fine. "Honey," he'd said, "we deserve another baby and I can't wait to love her and dress her up. I do love your babies," he added, sighing. But he had mostly held Grace in his hospital bed; he would never love her or dress her up. My thoughts sent me into fresh tears and more doubts about the miracle I thought I'd had.

One day in the supermarket parking lot, I saw a red pickup truck like my father's and for an instant I forgot he had died. My heart leapt as I thought, Dad's here! It wasn't an unfamiliar feeling. In my darkest hours he had always shown up to comfort me. But this time I realized immediately that the truck belonged to someone else; my father was dead. I began to cry hard. Sam climbed onto my lap and jammed himself between me and the steering wheel.

"You miss Pa, don't you?"

I managed to nod.

"You have to believe he's with us, Mommy. You have to believe that."

I wanted to believe that more than anything. But I was losing my grip on what I believed. Too young to attach to a particular ideology, Sam was finding his own ways to deal with losing Pa. I couldn't show him heaven on a map or explain the course a soul might travel, so he found his own way to cope.

That night, as I cooked dinner and Sam sat at the kitchen table coloring in his new Spider-Man coloring book, he said, "I love you too."

I laughed. "You only say 'I love you too' after someone says 'I love you,'" I explained.

"I know," Sam said. "Pa just said, 'I love you, Sam,' and I said, 'I love you too.'" He kept coloring.

"Pa just talked to you?" I asked him.

"Oh, Mommy," Sam said, "he tells me he loves me every day. He tells you too. You're just not listening."

I watched my little boy's bent head as he colored Spider Man all the wrong colors. I had grown up learning how to listen to what no one else can hear, to find answers in what is around me, to believe in the unbelievable. But now I found myself unable to do what Sam had figured out on his own.

That night, when I paced my house crying, the image that came to me was of Chimayo, how I'd been so full of hope that day I'd bent beside the pocito and scooped the healing dirt into a Ziploc bag to bring to my father, how I'd kept that bag in my pocket like a talisman, touching it from time to time as the plane brought me home.

When I saw him, I broke into a run, until I reached the safety of his arms. There, with the faint aroma of Old Spice and cold December air, I told him I had the dirt. "That's good, Poopers," he'd said. "Because it's going to work."

What I needed to do, I decided, was go back to Chimayo. That very night I wrote a letter to the priest there, Father Roca. "Dear Father Roca," I began, "last year I travelled to El Santuario de Chimayo to pray for a miracle for my father. . . ."

TWO WEEKS AFTER I returned from Italy, I took another trip. It was almost a year to the day that my father died, and I went back to El Santuario de Chimayo. Father Roca, who has been the parish priest there for forty years, talked to me in his tiny office inside the church. He is a man who dispenses smiles and stories as easily as holy water; several people came in while I was there and, without missing a beat, he blessed their medals and crucifixes, sprinkling holy water, murmuring prayers.

"I have reread your letter many times," he told me. "I am so happy for your family."

Thinking he was confused, I said, "But my father died."

Father Roca shrugged. "It was God's will. The tumor went away, yes?" I nodded.

"Do you know who came here one month before he died? Cardinal Bernadin. From Chicago. He came here and asked me to take him to where the dirt was. I led him to the pocito and then left. Fifteen minutes later he emerged, smiling, at peace. 'I got what I came for,' he said."

"He wasn't cured," I said.

Father Roca smiled. "I know."

I spent about twenty minutes with Father Roca. He told me about the crucifix that was found there. He told me about the miracles he had personally witnessed: the woman who was so sick that her son had to carry her to the pocito but who walked out on her own; the young man who came to pray en route to throwing himself off the mountain in despair but, after praying at the pocito, decided to return to his wife and baby. To Father Roca, the miracles of El Santuario de Chimayo are not just physical. Rather, they are miracles of inner transformation. "There is," he told me, "something very special about this place."

Later, I returned to the small room with the offerings, and the smaller room with the pocito that the caretaker refilled every day. I prayed there, a prayer of thanks for good health, the love of my children and my husband, the closeness of my family, and, finally, I asked for the courage to accept what had come my way. If someone at the shrine on my first visit had told me the miracle I would receive was peace of mind, I would have been angry. Miracles come in many forms, both physical and spiritual. Was it possible I would get that other kind of miracle? One that would restore my faith and lead me out of my despair?

Before I left El Santuario, I again removed a Ziploc bag from my pocket and filled it with dirt. Back at home, my aunt had recently been diagnosed with lung cancer. My mother, whose faith had not flagged, asked me to bring home some dirt for her sister. She needed a miracle too.

WHEN I RETURNED FROM this second trip to Chimayo, I did not have a miracle. On the plane home, I stared out the window, remembering something my mother had said. Whenever we lose something, we pray to Saint Anthony to help us find it. "Saint Anthony, help us look around . . . There's something lost that must be found." The stories of the successes after appeals to Saint Anthony are numerous: eyeglasses, wallets, keys, all returned by Saint Anthony.

But one day my mother told me she had lost her paycheck. "Can you believe it?" she said. "In one week I've lost a new set of curtains still in the bag, my driver's license, my car keys, and now my paycheck." The other items had all been found after praying to Saint Anthony. But not this one. "I said the prayer," my mother told me, "and I could almost hear his answer: 'Enough! You lose everything!'"

That was how I felt. How could I keep asking for miracles from God? How could I expect answers? I thought of the day I dug into that dirt for my father and how strong my faith had been. Now, that faith was weak, almost extinguished. I knew better than to only believe in God when we get what we want, but for me the miracle of my father's tumor disappearing had been a sign that all I believed was true—God and prayer and the power of things larger than the world we know. If I believed that, then his death, the loss of that baby, the emptiness in my spiritual self could only mean that I had been wrong.

My despair held fast, even deepened as I marked my first year without my father. I feared that everything was random, that God was not out there, that no matter what we did or believed we could not have an impact on any of it. Back at home, I kept researching miracles, trying to find the one place where I might find one for my soul. But slowly I began to realize that no matter how many miles I travelled, there was another, more difficult journey to take, the one that led me backward and inward.

After all, had I been born into a different family, I would never have gone to find my dying father a miracle, or believed I would get a sign from him. It was time to look at that family, I realized. In them lay the foundations for a faith that had endured for a century or longer. Despite the cultural props of Italy—the superstitions and curses and traditions—my family had a strong faith in God and miracles. Church and prayer played as significant a role in that faith as did the other, less traditional things. In my dictionary, one definition of faith is: "Belief that does not rest on logical proof or material evidence, as in *faith in miracles*." That is the kind of faith that helped me through losing my brother, through a devastating breakup, that led me to Chimayo. Without it, I could not find God or the comfort of church or prayer. That *faith*, part familial and part religious and part cultural, was my "very own proposition." Without it, I had nothing left to throw into the teeth of despair.

"Faith is what makes life bearable," I remembered again from L'Engle. The miracle I needed now was for my spiritual Odyssey. It was the most important miracle of all. Although I would make several trips on my search, the most important one was when I looked back over a hundred years to a people and a place where, in many ways, I began.

the simones

MY FAMILY BROUGHT THEIR belief of miracles with them from the Old Country. That is where, near the end of the nineteenth century, my great-grandmother, Angelina Simone, a poor village girl from Conca della Campania in southern Italy, was a shepherdess for the local church. A tall, blue-eyed beauty, she caught the eye of a local boy, Giuseppe Urgolo, who had made good. Giuseppe, who was to become my great-grandfather, came from a family that had acquired some wealth and moved to Sorrento. He had a highly respected job as a tax collector in the southern provinces for the king. His family did not like that their son fell in love with a peasant girl. They gave them enough money to immigrate to America.

No one knows exactly when my great-grandparents came to America, but it was around the year 1900. Some family stories place their first attempt to move here in 1901, when my grandmother, their only daughter, was two years old. What is certain is that they were part of the large-scale Italian immigration of the late-nineteenth century. The turning point for Italian immigration to the United States was 1880, when a plant lice ruined many of the vineyards in southern Italy. Around the same time, the United States began getting most of their citrus fruit from Florida and California rather than southern Italy, as they had for decades.

Those two important factors, combined with poor health conditions, overpopulation (the population of Italy doubled around that time), heavy taxes, weakened soil, primitive agricultural methods, and poor health conditions, forced a major immigration. In just forty years, four million Italians—most of them from the south—moved to the United States, where industry was booming. Italy's farmland was owned by wealthy landowners, and the peasant farmers who worked the land for them were widely exploited. The promise of jobs lured men away from their families, often with the hope of saving money to return to Italy and buy their own land. More than any other group, the Italian immigration and return migration was frequent. Of the 3.8 million who came during the boom, 2.1 returned.

The first to leave the small villages of southern Italy attracted others from their village to the same area where they had moved and found work. This chain phenomenon produced Italian communities where Old World villages were simply transplanted to the New World. As they had in Italy, families all lived together, even after marriage. Grocery stores and churches where only Italian was spoken were common. Marriages to non-Italians were discouraged. And, like back home, the family was ruled by the women.

Italian women know that they hold up the entire structure of the family; without them it would collapse. As Luigi Barzini describes them: "They devote the same zeal, enthusiasm, and spirit of sacrifice to their families which heroes dedicate to King, Leader, Flag, Fatherland, Constitution, Revolution, and 7 Year Plan . . ."

Rhode Island, a state that had twenty-five Italian immigrants in 1850, had over nine thousand when my great-grandparents arrived. They followed their own relatives to the small village of Natick in western Warwick. Twenty years after they arrived, Italians made up the largest immigrant population in the state, peaking at over fifty-one thousand in 1932. All of them came from the south. The people of southern Italy, who tended fruit trees and vineyards, came to America and worked in the mills as unskilled labor, earning about ten dollars a week, a third less than the Italian and French immigrants who arrived before them.

The name *Natick* is Native American for "a place of hills." Natick straddles the Pawtuxet River, and it was one of the dozen or so factory villages that sprung up along it around 1803. By 1815, the area was the most outstanding place in all of New England. Within a thirty-mile radius of Providence, 140 cotton factories operated 130,000 spindles, producing almost 28 million yards of yarn a year.

At first, cheap labor came from the local women and children. But as the industry expanded, want ads were placed in *The Providence Journal* and through the Providence Emigration Office for people from England, Ireland, Scotland, and Wales to come to America and work in the mills. The Irish were the first to come, settling along Providence Street. Then came the French Canadians, beginning in the 1850s. They settled in the village called Arctic. Other ethnic groups, like the Polish and the Portuguese, arrived to work in the mills too, settling in their own close-knit communities. The unwritten rule was that everyone worked together but stayed apart. You married your own, living in the same village if not the same house as your family.

The Italians were the last to immigrate. They settled in Natick on Prospect Hill, which overlooked the pride of the area: the Natick Mill. In 1850, two brothers—Robert and Benjamin Knight—combined several of their textile mills to form the largest cotton manufacturing firm in the world. The name they gave this company was Fruit of the Loom, inspired by a beautiful painting of an apple that caught their eye. After the Civil War, immigration went crazy, especially in the industrial northeast. In 1884, the Knight brothers got the idea to combine four mills into one. The result of that combination was the Natick Mill. Seventy feet wide, over thirteen hundred feet long, and six stories high, the Natick Mill had ten thousand spindles and three thousand looms and employed two thousand people. The village in which it sat was home to five thousand French Canadian immigrants. In fact, more French than English was spoken in Natick.

Then the Italians arrived. Among them were Angelina and Giuseppe Urgolo. With this great Italian immigration Natick changed. And who my family was, and who we would become, changed too.

MY GREAT-GRANDMOTHER NEVER LIKED America. Italians, it is said, always feel exiled and unhappy in alien lands. This was certainly true of Nonna. She was homesick and alienated much of the time, even though the hilly village of Natick looks very much like the hilly region from which they had come, and the neighborhood in which they settled was 100 percent Italian. Italian was spoken with as much if not more frequency than English. Gardens were laid out exactly as they had been back home. Every family had grapevines and made homemade wine that they stored in dirt cellars.

Still, despite all the familiarities and similarities, it was America, not Italy, and my great-grandmother did not like it. She never learned English, and she never gave up the ways of the Old Country. Back home, life had been hard and poor; but there was a certain comfort in it, a life she never quite relinquished. Like many other Italian immigrants, the plan was to save enough money to go home. Often, she talked about going back for good. Finally she and Giuseppe decided to go home and stay home. My grandmother, Rose, their only child, was two when they packed up and, relieved, moved back to Italy.

When Rose got sick and almost died, her parents blamed it on the Old Country. It was dirty there. The doctors were ignorant. In the few years they had lived in America, they had learned enough and seen enough to feel dislocated in Italy. Trapped between two worlds, they reluctantly moved back to Rhode Island for good. This sense of being caught between the Old Country and the New, of being Italian and American, defined not only Angelina and Giuseppe, but also their daughter and grandchildren, and me, their great-granddaughter.

MY GRANDMOTHER, ROSE URGOLO, had an arranged marriage to a man she'd never met when she was sixteen years old. She was beautiful. Just under five feet tall, slender, with curly red hair and green eyes, she was an anomaly in many ways: the fair skin and red hair and light eyes, an only child, with some money sent from her rich grandparents back in Sorrento.

The man her parents chose for her to marry was an only child too. Born in Providence—an American!—Anthony Masciarotte's father had died when he was young and his mother had inherited a good deal of money. Tony had a trade. He was a barber with barber shops in Wickford and on Block Island. But Tony was not attractive. A small man with a hook nose and glasses, my grandmother told me that the first time she saw him she cried and promised to run away rather than marry him. When I asked her what was wrong with him, she shook her head. "He was homely," she told me. And he was twenty-three, seven years older than his beautiful bride.

My grandmother told me that the morning after the wedding, her new mother-in-law marched into the bedroom and tore the sheets from the bed. Concetta Rossi was famous for two things: She was mean and she was stingy. Everyone was afraid of her. The sixteen-year-old bride rose from her marriage bed, blushing, scared, while her new mother-in-law gathered the sheets. She inspected them for blood, a sign that Rose was indeed the virgin her parents had promised. When she found what she was looking for, she threw open the windows and hung the bloody sheet outside for the neighborhood to see.

I have the marriage certificate for Antonio C. Masciarotte and Rose Urgolo. It has long ago been taped together; even the tape is discolored. The ink is faded, the paper itself spotted brown like age spots on an old hand. According to the certificate, the marriage took place at Parrocchia di S. Giuseppe—Saint Joseph's Church, in Natick, Rhode Island. Saint Joseph's Church still stands on the corner of Providence Street and Wakefield Street, high on a hill with a dramatic set of stairs leading up to it.

Built in 1872 to serve the large French Canadian population in Natick, Saint Joseph's was called the French church even when I was a child. The Italian church, Sacred Heart, is half a block away. Made of stucco and wood, Sacred Heart would not be built for another fifteen years, when Father Tirocchi arrived in Natick from Rome to create a church for the Italian population of Natick. So beloved was he for giving them this church that a riot broke out when news came that he would be transferred. He stayed, perhaps longer than anyone would have imagined: His crypt sits in the wall at the front of the church.

The ethnic villages that had developed around the mills were so strong that my grandparents' marriage certificate states the location of Saint Joseph's Church as Natick, Rhode Island. In fact, they now lived in the newly incorporated town of West Warwick, which in 1913 gathered all the different villages together to form one town. No one seemed to notice. Well into the 1970s, my grandmother still received mail addressed to her in Natick, Rhode Island. Although the villages existed because of the mills, their center became the church. If I told my grandmother which church someone went to, she could immediately and accurately tell me their ethnicity and which neighborhood they lived in. She only liked Italians. And even though she had biases against most other nationalities, it was the French she liked the least. The French, she always insisted, could not be trusted.

Coming to America as a minority, surrounded by French Canadians who owned the land and earned more than Italians for the same work, her prejudice was based in her own bad experiences. And it never faded. Not even a little. Seventy years after she came to America, when I introduced Mama Rose to my first boyfriend, she asked him what church he went to. He told her. "Oh," she said, "you're French."

I waited for her to say more, to insult him or embarrass me. But she remained polite and distant.

As soon as he walked out the door she grabbed me by my waist-length hair and gave me a good hard tug.

"What's wrong with you?" she said. "All the boys who come around here and you pick a Frenchman."

"Mama Rose," I told her. "He's *American. I'm* American," I reminded her. She began to swear in Italian. Then to pray in Italian.

"You're Italian," she said, pulling my hair again. "Don't you ever forget it. And don't you ever trust a Frenchman. You hear me?"

When Rose Urgolo married Antonio Masciarotte on September 6, 1914, these lines were strongly drawn. For the most part, like the immigrants around them, they were more firmly rooted in the Old Country than in the new one they called home. Even though automobiles were introduced in 1907, Natick in 1914 preferred horse and carriages, or the streetcars that ran through town. The Natick Mill had put in the streetlights and they had built a stone water tower on Prospect Hill, so that there was running water in every house. Rose and Tony moved into the house at 40 Fiume Street (*fiume* is "river" in Italian) with Rose's parents. Fourteen months later, their first child—Giuseppe—was born in the bedroom off the kitchen. Over the next nineteen years, nine more children were born in the same room.

By the time my mother, number nine, came along—seventeen years almost to the day after her parents were married—my grandmother had run out of names. She had honored her father and mother (my Uncle Joe and Aunt Angie), her husband (Uncle Tony, whom we called Brownie), her mother-in-law (Aunt Connie), the Virgin Mary and her mother, Saint Ann (Aunt Ann-Marie), and even herself (Aunt Rosie). September 5, 1931, was a hot day. My mother made her entrance early that morning and my grandmother, exhausted and perhaps not prepared for nine children, glanced out the window to see the morning glories in bloom. That is how my mother came by her name. Gloria.

I imagine my grandmother in her bed, in the very room that many years later I shared with her, tired and spent from childbirth and the constant pregnancies and births that had taken up her life for twenty years. I imagine her porcelain skin and red curls against the white hand-embroidered linens. She turns toward the window where morning is arriving. And she sees the bright blue of newly opened morning glories. She has no energy, no creativity, no more names. Yet she kept having children. Almost three years later when her tenth and final child was born, my grandmother simply named her after the month in which she came into the world: June.

Despite the amount of people who lived at 40 Fiume Street, the house is small. Three bedrooms upstairs, one so tiny it is more like a walk-in closet. In that tiny room the three boys slept, each in their own single bed. In the center room were the six oldest girls, pressed into two double feather beds. In one was Connie, then Gloria, then Rosie. In the other, Emma, then Anna, then Angie. Each one of them had their own nail to hang their clothes on; there were no closets. The largest room was for Angelina and Giuseppe, the children's grandparents. Giuseppe went off to work every day at a textile factory in Apponaug, a nearby village, where he worked as a bleacher. Downstairs, Rose and Tony slept in the bedroom where all the children were made and born. The youngest, June, slept on the green vinyl sofa that sat against one wall in the kitchen.

Three rooms of the house were blocked off and given a separate entrance for Rose's unmarried cousins: Rum, Carmine, and Annie, who we called Nuneen. Their lives too were touched by tragedy. Their parents both died young, as did another sibling and a set of twins. Nuneen was born with a displaced hip, which was incorrectable at that time, and so she was deemed unmarriageable. Rum and Carmine suffered broken hearts.

The three of them helped with all of the children, the cooking, tending the garden, running errands. Carmine was a rag man, a junk picker. He showed up with gifts from the local dump: cracked china platters, discarded toys, appliances and clocks that no longer worked. He fancied himself a ladies' man and was always doused in too much cologne that someone had thrown away.

They had a sister, Etta, who married and had two sons of her own. She lived in East Greenwich, a pretty nearby town that sits on Narragansett Bay. She was Rose's best friend. The two of them spent weekend afternoons together at the brown-and-green enamel table in Rose's kitchen. They drank strong black coffee and chewed Black Jack gum, fast. Etta's father and Rose's father were brothers. These two women were as close as sisters, with Etta baking delicate butter cookies decorated with small silver balls, or the special Italian cookies that are rolled in honey and topped with colorful sprinkles. She brought these to 40 Fiume Street when she visited. Her husband, also named Joe, had tuberculosis and was sent to recover at a sanitarium in New York. After he returned, he refused to eat or drink in anyone's house for fear of spreading the dreaded disease. He believed this even though he was cured.

In this loud, big, busy, Italian-speaking family, there was my mother. Quiet, slightly overweight, with thick, long dark hair and glasses bought only after a long argument with her father who did not believe she really needed them. It wasn't until a teacher called to insist that they buy her glasses that she finally got some. The world she was born into began and ended in this small village that straddles the Pawtuxet River, in this house on top of Prospect Hill.

Natick was beginning its decline when she was born. A mill strike in 1922 lasted for thirty-three weeks and began a southerly migration in manufacturing. In 1935, when my mother was four years old, Knight closed twenty-two plants and Rhode Island lost more than a million spindles to the south. Only three mills were left in West Warwick, the town that was once considered the most outstanding place in all of New England.

But the thirties were the last decade that Natick thrived as it had, when it was the best of both the Old and New Worlds. The Italian baseball teams were the champions of all the village teams of the 1920s and 1930s, and there were games on hot summer nights. One year, my mother was chosen to be the Virgin Mary in the parade for the feast of Our Lady of Carmel. Every July the men of Natick made a wooden platform to carry the statue of Our Lady of Carmel. It took five men on each side to hoist the statue and carry it up Prospect Hill and through its streets. Three hundred people lined up to watch, pinning money on the statue just as they did back in the Old Country. Then everyone went to Sacred Heart Church and the feast began. My mother dressed in a pale blue long cotton dress, and she wore a veil on her head. She walked behind the statue, proud that she was chosen.

Then, on the night of July 3, 1941, sandwiched between her older sisters Connie and Rosie, my mother was awakened by the sound of screams. The whole neighborhood, it seemed, had gone crazy. All of the sisters got out of bed and rushed to the window where they watched flames leaping into the night sky. The smell of smoke was so strong that when they breathed in, they could taste it. The fire department wetted down all the houses, shouting instructions. The older girls dressed and ran outside to see what was happening. But Gloria and her sister Ann ran to their grandmother. She held them close and together they huddled with her in a corner of her bedroom, where she prayed in Italian to the Blessed Virgin to keep them safe. The girls prayed too, in the Italian she taught them.

Hours later they learned what happened. The big Natick Mill was destroyed by vandals, burning completely to the ground before the fire was finally put out on July 4. All six stories, all thirteen hundred feet of it, gone. Only the stone foundation was left. And for the rest of that hot summer of 1941, the air in Natick smelled acrid. It burned the back of their throats. Cotton manufacturing in the Pawtuxet Valley disappeared for good. World War II was about to begin. Natick, and my mother, had to figure out who they were. Despite what they had lost, they still held certain things close to them: family, tradition, and a belief that miracles can and do happen.

the hoods

THE HOODS ARE PRACTICAL Midwestern Baptists, as far removed from the southern Italian beliefs as possible. Among the mostly dark-haired, dark-eyed, animated, and loud population of Natick, my father stood out. For one thing, he looked different. Tall, blond, blue-eyed. For another, he sounded different. Greensburg, Indiana, where he grew up, is close enough to Kentucky to leave the imprint of a southern drawl on its inhabitants. In a town where everyone had come from somewhere else, my father's cavalier attitude about ethnic backgrounds could be disarming.

The Hoods had been in America long enough to consider themselves simply American. The only immigration in their history was in 1857—as the French Canadians flooded into the small village of Natick along the Pawtuxet River—when my great-great grandfather James Ralph Hood moved his wife and children two hundred miles north from Flemingsburg, Kentucky, to Richland, Indiana. His father, also James Ralph Hood, had been born in Virginia in the 1780s and was still alive when his son was run out of town because he freed his slaves. That man became my grandfather's grandfather.

If you travel around the cemeteries in Flemingsburg, Kentucky, or Richland, Indiana, you will learn the story of my family, because the Hoods do not travel far. They are all buried in these small towns surrounded by rich farmland. James's son, James Napoleon, was a farmer there when he returned from fighting in the Civil War. A monument erected on the battlefield at Chickamauga has his name on it.

At the age of twenty he was discharged from the army and went home to Richland, Indiana. There he married Nancy Noland, who had been orphaned as a young girl and sent to live with an aunt and uncle in Cincinnati. How they met remains a mystery, but her young parents' graves are in Fairmount, famous as the hometown of James Dean. On September 21, 1885, an early frost hit Richland. So remarkable was this frost that James Napoleon and Nancy gave their son, born on that day, the name Charles Frost. That's how my grandfather got his name.

Charlie Hood moved to Greensburg with the train company he worked for and probably stayed because of my grandmother, Bessie Robbins. Her people had lived in this small farming community for as long as they can remember. The Robbins family, it is said, was a notorious clan. It is accepted as common knowledge that they are kin to the Hanks family, and that if anyone bothered to look hard enough they would find that Nancy Hanks, Abraham Lincoln's mother, is a cousin; but anyone who has investigated this cannot substantiate that link. There are Runyans and Irelands and Mileses, but no Hankses. If disputed to a Greensburg Robbins, however, you would just get a smile. Well, they'd tell you, we *are* related to President Lincoln on his mother's side. What everyone does remember is that Bessie's mother, Cora, was a pipe-smoking bootlegger who often put her grandchildren to work gathering and cleaning old bottles for her moonshine.

Charlie and Bessie lived in Greensburg, where he worked at a variety of jobs. He managed the local liquor store. He worked for the railroad. For a while he was even the chief of police. The Greensburg of the early 1900s was a town with only one family with any ethnicity to speak of, and they were called the German family, and they owned a bakery. There were two blacks, a brother and sister, who worked as a janitor and a cleaning lady. There was one Catholic church and the people who went there were called "fisheaters" because they did not eat meat on Fridays. Although I cannot know this for sure, I believe that if someone had told Charlie and Bessie Hood that someday their son would marry an Italian Catholic, they would not have believed it. For one thing, there were no Italians around. To them, the combination was as strange and unfamiliar as marrying a Martian.

HALFWAY ACROSS THE COUNTRY from 40 Fiume Street, in Greensburg, Indiana, Charles and Bessie Hood and their nine kids moved from house to house. Big families were the norm in this farm town, as were large square houses with wraparound front porches that had swings and rocking chairs. The Hoods lived in town because Charlie was the chief of police. The farm kids went to school barefoot and late from having to do chores. The Hoods were poor, but they had shoes and three square meals a day. Bessie served food at six, noon, and six. Beans and homemade bread and her own canned vegetables and relishes. She cooked with lard and fatback. In the summer, when she was waiting for her pies to cool and her bread to rise, she sat in the kitchen and listened to her beloved Cincinnati Reds on the radio. Bessie loved baseball and her children knew better than to interrupt her during a game.

Bessie was sick with a bad heart for a good part of the younger kids' lives, sick enough that there was talk for a time about sending them to live with other relatives. When Bessie got mad at them, the kids knew to run up the stairs because she couldn't chase them. But she liked to quilt, and the town's women would come to her house to thread the needles for her so she could make quilts, one for each of her kids.

My father, like my mother, was born next to the last, on July 4, 1929—three months before the Great Depression hit, which left little impact on the Hoods, who were already as poor as they could be. His family, unlike the Masciarottes, had roots only on this land. They were American through and through, and it is fitting that my father, the most patriotic of them all, was born on the Fourth of July. All of his brothers, except one, were tall, well over six feet. The girls were mostly tall too. And they all had blond or red hair. My father was the blondest, a towhead with pale blue eyes, the ultimate Midwestern farm boy, tall and lanky and blond in his denim overalls, chewing on a blade of grass.

He did not like school. He did not like Greensburg. He wanted only to leave and see the world that lay beyond this small town, which was famous for a tree that grew out of the courthouse roof. That was all. He dreamed of the sea, even though he had never even glimpsed it.

When he was fourteen he ran away with a carnival, only to be sent home when they discovered his age. When he was sixteen he lied to get in to the National Guard, only to be sent home again when his real age was discovered.

His parents did not know what to do with him. He was wild and reckless. He got thrown out of school. Finally, when he turned seventeen, he told his father he wanted to join the navy and go to sea. It was 1946. The war was over. My grandfather, relieved, maybe even happy, took him to enlist. When my father, Lloyd Edward Hood, joined the navy, he reinvented himself. Sent first to San Francisco, he took on the city ways, riding the cable cars up the steep hills, courting society girls at swanky hotel bars.

Everyone called him Hood. He even referred to himself that way. When he was sent to China to fight communism, his family nicknamed him Wong. He went home to Indiana when his mother died in 1949. Except for rare visits, he never went home again. Not really. Instead, he embraced the world as his home. He loved being at sea, even though he never got over his seasickness. He loved visiting foreign lands—Japan, Spain, Africa. Women loved him, loved his southern drawl, his blond hair and blue eyes, his sassiness. He was a handsome wise guy who liked to drink beer and dance with pretty girls. He read Zane Grey, and detective books by James Cain and Dashiell Hammett.

When he was sent to Rhode Island he expected to do his time there and get out. He had never even heard of Rhode Island, wasn't sure exactly where it was on the map. But on his first weekend pass, he went with some buddies to Newport to go drinking. They were all new to the state and did not know where to find some good cold beer. Walking, they turned down an old cobblestone street.

My father stopped, overcome by a feeling of such strong familiarity that he had to remind himself that indeed he had never been to Newport before. He had lived in China. He knew San Francisco as well as he knew Greensburg, Indiana. But he had never been this far east before.

Still, he heard himself say, "Follow me. I know a great little place."

The men followed him for several blocks, at which point he turned, walked a little way, then opened a door and led them down some steep stairs to a basement tavern that dated back to the late 1700s.

"Order me a beer," he said. "I've got to go to the head."

Without asking for directions, he made his way to the bathroom, which was located down a complicated, mazelike series of corridors.

Back at the bar, beer in his hand, that same feeling washed over him. He was certain of two things: he had been here before, in a time he could not recall clearly; and he was meant to be here again. The young man who loved to travel, who wanted nothing more than to be carefree and at sea, was certain he was meant to stay in Rhode Island.

A week later, at a dance hall in the village of Crompton in the town of West Warwick, a dark-haired girl with sad eyes and an hourglass figure caught his attention. He did not know that days before the boy she thought she would marry had left her for someone else. That boy, Pinky, was dancing with his new girlfriend that very night. And my mother's two best girlfriends were keeping her company, reminding her that Pinky wasn't good enough for her anyway, that someone else, someone handsome and funny, would come into her life soon.

Then a tall, handsome blond in a white sailor's uniform stood in front of her and, sassy as ever, said, "Who's your tent maker, kid?"

At six feet two and only one hundred thirty pounds, my mother found this guy a joke. She laughed at him and kidded him right back. They started to dance. That night he proposed to her. It was September of 1949. Earlier that summer, her father was bit by a mosquito that carried equine encephalitis. He grew delerious, and he was rushed to Mass General in Boston, diagnosed, and sent home to die. For days he lay in his bed in the room off the kitchen, ranting. Frightened, my mother moved silently through the house, or snuck cigarettes with her friends.

She had dropped out of school when her best friend's father died the year before, the two of them finding work in various mills. They worked in the bleachery, then making artificial flowers. She was her class social committee chairman, smart and funny; these jobs left her dissatisfied, but she didn't know why. They gave her enough money to buy cigarettes and smart clothes in the women's stores in Arctic, the downtown section of West Warwick. She had no desire that she could name, just a gnawing yearning for something more.

Her father died on August 31, 1949. His funeral was on my mother's eighteenth birthday. In Italian tradition, the family was in mourning for a year. My grandmother wore black. They were forbidden to listen to the radio. Most of the older ones were married by now; June, the youngest, was only fourteen. It was my mother who, at eighteen and single, could not play records or go dancing.

The last thing her family expected was for her to come home with a sailor from Indiana, a Protestant, only weeks after her father died, and ask permission to marry him. The answer, firm, loud, and in Italian, was No.

I WAS RAISED TO believe in love at first sight.

Here are my parents, proof that it is possible. My father had a large Italian family, ready to reject him. He was *American, Protestant, a sailor*—in short, he had nothing going for him. But he and my mother were determined to triumph. This belief in the possibility of beating the odds stayed with them for their lifetime together. Even as he lay dying in the hospital forty-eight years later, they believed he could beat the odds and come home.

He could not change his ethnicity, or lack of it. He had to be a sailor; it was the only thing he wanted to do. That left his religion. He was a lapsed Protestant, at best. Why not become a nonbelieving Catholic? With my mother at his side, and her mother and grandmother watching warily, he began the conversion process. He smiled at the priest, nodded with forced enlightenment, chose my uncle as his godfather, and got baptized. Now all they had to do was wait the required year for the mourning period to end, and they could be married. My father believed in God, and despite his lack of conviction toward Catholicism he went to church every Sunday and his voice sang above everyone's.

As I grew older and we discussed religion together, he often said, "It's not *what* you believe but *that* you believe." Ultimately he accepted that ghosts roamed 40 Fiume Street and that Nonna could heal through prayers, ideas that would never have occurred to him back in Indiana. His faith in God and a hereafter never wavered. In the hospital he befriended all the priests who visited the patients, always saying after they left, "A nice guy, that Father."

When he and my mother got engaged, he gave her a set of luggage instead of a diamond ring. He was going to take her everywhere with him, even though she did not share his enthusiasm for travel. She preferred the comfort of her family, the house where she had been born, the familiar streets of West Warwick. She knew what had happened at each corner, the bridge where her friend's brother fell into the river and drowned, the streetlamp where another friend crashed one icy night, the church where she prayed every Sunday, the dark places where they parked the car and kissed until late at night.

Her sisters all lived within walking distance of each other and 40 Fiume Street. They built new houses with knotty pine walls and refinished basements. They made casseroles with canned soup. They drove big Chevys, gave their children American names—Debbie, Gail, Michael, David. This generation was moving away from their immigrant past. They only spoke Italian to their grandmother, or when they didn't want the kids to understand them. This new world was enough for my mother, a new world right in her own backyard. She didn't need to see foreign lands, to eat strange foods. She didn't want to leave her mother.

Still, she took the luggage instead of a diamond ring and began to plan her wedding. Set for November, she chose burgundy velvet for her attendants, her sister's satin wedding gown. My father's family was going to come from Indiana, these strangers who were about to become part of her family. And then, after the wedding, the newlyweds would take a honeymoon in Greensburg. Her sisters had gone to Florida, driving south, staying in small motels, wearing new bathing suits on white sand beaches, sipping tropical drinks. But she was driving west, to the place where they cooked with lard and called Catholics fisheaters. She was terrified, and excited.

By the time I was born six years later, she'd had my brother, Skip, her beloved sister Ann had died, and she and my father and brother had lived in Naples, Italy. My father had been away at sea when my brother was born; this time he was home for the weekend from his new station in Annapolis, Maryland. Soon enough, we would join him there.

leaving the old world

LIKE AUNTS AND UNCLES and cousins and my mother and brother before me, I spent the first weeks of my life at 40 Fiume Street, tended by three generations of women. In the Italian tradition, they placed a silver dollar on my belly button to keep it from sticking out. At night, they tightly swaddled me in a cotton cloth from waist to toes. This would keep me from becoming bowlegged. They rubbed olive oil on my scalp to prevent cradle cap. On my undershirt they pinned a little gold horn to keep away the evil eye, a gold heart, and a blessed medal from my patron saint, Saint Ann. When I cooed, they prayed in Italian to Saint Nicholas: Saint Nicholas, bring the words to her mouth. This ensured that I would talk early and well. Because I did not sleep at night, Nonna turned me upside down over the flame on the stove. This ensured that I would no longer mix up night for day.

Thus taken care of, my father drove his family, now a foursome, to our new home at 3 Fig Court in Annapolis, Maryland. It was late January 1957. Dwight D. Eisenhower had just been sworn in as our new president. This move away from Mama Rose was easier on my mother than the move to Italy. She was a ten-hour drive away, in her own country. And she had a son and daughter, exactly what she had hoped for.

Our large extended family, the generations of relatives mingling at Mama Rose's house all weekend long, the sixteen cousins, the siblings and their spouses all living nearby, Nonna and Mama Rose cooking and making decisions and giving opinions, the two of them trying to keep the Old World and the old ways alive as the hope and prosperity of the 1950s gobbled up those ways—all of these things and people intruded on our life. This first move together, driving south to Fig Court, began our immediate family's private history, the one we did not share with everyone back home.

Just as Nonna and Mama Rose had straddled two worlds, so did my mother. A part of her would always long for Natick and the house at 40 Fiume Street where Italian was still spoken and shrines with statues of saints and flickering votive candles occupied the corners of every room. But another part began to grow too. In it, we were a typical American family. We got our green Chevy station wagon. My mother made fried chicken or hamburgers for dinner instead of veal and peas or braciola. Back home, at breakfast, Nonna crumbled milk crackers into a bowl with milk and sugar; in my mother's house we had Fruit Loops, pancakes with maple syrup, bacon. Our furniture was Danish modern, all sleek light wood, an orange bucket chair, a green sofa instead of the dark wood and iron beds that filled Mama Rose's house. We took swimming lessons at the neighborhood pool, played miniature golf, put a mat covered with footprints on our living-room floor, and learned to dance the cha-cha, while the cousins in Rhode Island went to saints' feast days, ran to Nonna to stop their bloody noses, reported their dreams and sightings of dead relatives faithfully to Mama Rose for interpretations and signs.

When we came back to visit, the old relatives in black with their garlicky breath and broken English scared me. The old-fashioned house, so different from the modern apartment we lived in, suffocated me. The doorknobs were glass, the upstairs was cold, and coal burned in the stove in the kitchen. Outside of Natick, the world had converted to gas heat, electric stoves, linoleum and Formica. I would spend a good part of my life vacillating between these two worlds—the outside modern one and the one at 40 Fiume Street, which was still dictated by the traditions and superstitions Angelina Simone brought with her from Italy at the turn of the century.

Into her old age, Nonna walked rather than rode in cars. She made her pasta by hand, expertly shaping gnocchi and ravioli. If she wanted to eat chicken for dinner, she stepped into the backyard, grabbed one by the neck, killed it, plucked its feathers, and cooked it. She never stepped foot in a supermarket; she raised rabbits to eat, grew her own fruits and vegetables. Indoor plumbing frightened her.

While we awaited my father's next orders, we took up residence back at Nonna's house. For almost three years I had lived among Americans in Maryland. This world, of which I was also a part, frightened me, even as my mother struggled to keep the new ways. At night, Nuneen set my pale blond hair in rags to make fat banana curls. Mama Rose made me kiss the statues of Saint Anthony and the Virgin Mary. She showed me pictures of dead relatives. In the morning my mother dressed me in Capri pants and brand-new white Keds. I sat in the yard beside fig trees and tomato plants, under a clothesline full of clothes drying in the sun, and shelled peas with Nuneen, helped her knead bread in a big blue metal pan, then picked the clothes.

In Maryland, we did not attend church. My mother longed to send my brother to a Catholic school, but my father did not share her enthusiasm. His faith was a more personal one and he remained a reluctant Catholic. Saints and miracles were private rituals that my mother kept to herself while we lived on Fig Court. But here at Nonna's they dominated everyday life. Still, as would happen throughout my life, the old ways began to seduce me. What had once frightened me now drew me in.

Skip embraced Catholicism. In years to come he would serve as an altar boy at Sacred Heart, earn the Order of the Cross, and become an Eagle Scout at Sacred Heart's Boy Scout troop. But that was all awaiting him after one more move: My father's orders came. We were moving to Washington, DC. As word spread, aunts and uncles arrived to hear the details and give advice. My father was going there first to find us an apartment and enroll my brother in school. As my mother talked, she looked past her mother and her grandmother. Already she was rearranging our Danish modern furniture, imagining where the orange bucket chair might go.

OUR APARTMENT WAS IN a complex called the Shirley Park Apartments in Arlington, Virginia. It was our two years alone here that forged the bond that we believed could not be broken. Still, each of us feared that it would somehow. I remembered the prayers Mama Rose taught me over the summer and I said them every night, terrified that something would happen to one of us. My mother was the same. She knew how easily you could lose someone, the way she had lost her sister during a routine operation. She worried over us even more. Unlike the kids around us, we had strict rules to follow. We could not go to any playground in the complex, just our own. We could not move from apartment to apartment without telling her. Our mother was always there somehow. Her voice found us no matter where we were. Her face was always pressed against the window, watching us, keeping us safe.

None of us wanted this time together in Virginia to end. It was as if we had moved into a cocoon from which we did not want to emerge. We continued to become a wholly American family. From the long hallway in our apartment my brother and I watched our parents hosting cocktail parties. My mother served Ritz crackers topped with Cheez Whiz and half an olive; my father mixed highballs. The women all wore fancy dresses, shiny green, deep red, pale soft blue. They smoked cigarettes from long black cigarette holders. The men wore skinny ties and black suits. They had crew cuts.

Everyone was excited. John F. Kennedy was our new president and there was a hope that we could practically taste in the air. My parents took us to his inauguration on a bitter cold January morning. We sat, shivering, drinking hot cocoa, as he passed us, waving.

"Wave to the president!" my mother directed us. "He's Catholic," she added, proud.

My brother obeyed, standing up, one hand over his heart, but I wouldn't let go of my hot chocolate. Skip was chubby—husky, my mother made us say—crew cutted, brown eyed, and serious. At home in our bedroom every night he tried to learn to dance the twist. He took a towel and pretended he was drying himself, shimmying awkwardly. When I laughed he pinched me. He had a chemistry set and made me look at my spit under a microscope so I would cry. At night he told me that his armies—Roman gladiators, Civil War, Revolutionary War, doughboys, World War II GIs, all of them—would attack me while I slept. I adored him.

"She's not so pretty," my mother said of Jackie Kennedy. "I don't think she's pretty at all."

The boy next to me had a runny nose and it was so cold that the snot froze on his face. I couldn't stop looking at him.

My mother jerked my arm. "There goes President Kennedy," she said.

"Uh-huh," I said. I never knew that snot hardened like that. "I want to go home," I said.

Home was a three-bedroom apartment on the second floor of one of the Shirley Park Apartments. My brother and I shared a room with twin beds. They were supposed to be bunk beds but my mother was afraid we would fall from the top bunk so they sat side by side instead. The second bedroom was a playroom. I had a dollhouse and a pink play stove and refrigerator. I had a Barbie with a blond bubble cut and a lavender Barbie case. I was not allowed to get the wedding dress because it cost five dollars. I was also not allowed to get the black cocktail dress because only puttanas—whores—wore black cocktail dresses. I was not allowed to get Ken, because dolls should not be boys. Instead, I had Tiny Thumbelina, who squirmed spasmatically when I turned her on, and my most prized possession, Chatty Kathy. When I pulled her string, she talked.

We had a plastic kidney-shaped dish with a plastic palm tree in it and two turtles we got from the five-and-dime. My mother hated those turtles. She thought they carried diseases. We also had two goldfish in a bowl. The turtles were named Speedy Gonzalez and Slowpoke. So were the goldfish. Mine was always the one named Slowpoke. On our windowsill my father raised African violets. They were rare and exotic and difficult to keep alive. My mother worried that she would kill them.

My best friend was from Bolivia. Her grandfather had been the ruler of Bolivia and was killed during a coup. The family escaped to America. She had dark skin and curly hair and a brother named Germann. I was infatuated with Maria and her family. She called her father Poppi, so I called my father Poppi too—except I forgot the full name and used Pops. My father started to call me Poops. Then we both called each other Poopers. The name stuck forever.

I began to collect small Disney characters. Every week new ones were available at the Drug Fair and I could hardly wait for the next one to come. I had Jiminy Cricket and Pinocchio, Snow White and the Seven Dwarfs, Alice in Wonderland, Chip and Dale. I kept them in a shoebox. When I took them out I spent hours lining them up. I called them my parade.

Every Sunday night my mother made Jiffy Pop popcorn and we all watched *The Wonderful World of Disney* on television. I held my breath during the beginning, when Tinkerbell flew across the screen and fireworks exploded over Cinderella's castle. Even though our television was black and white, I saw those fireworks in Technicolor. Disneyland and I were practically the same age. I knew that park as if I had already been there. The pink teacups, the flying Dumbos, Tomorrowland.

Disneyland became our family's ultimate dream. Someday we were going to drive there, all the way to California. We were going to stay at a hotel right near the park, in Anaheim, and every day we would go to Disneyland. I made my father show me on maps, thick road maps from AAA. His finger traced the route we would take across the country. We would visit his family in Greensburg, we would go see Old Faithful. We would see America. My mother rolled her eyes. "California," she said, as if it were the moon we were talking about. "It's so far."

I looked at the miles and miles we would have to travel to get there. Nothing was better than the four of us in our Chevy station wagon. We took road trips all the time. We drove along the Blue Ridge Parkway and went deep into the Luray Caverns. We went to Mount Vernon and Monticello. We visited our friends who left the Shirley Park Apartments and moved back to West Virginia. My mother always packed a picnic, and we stopped along the road to eat fried chicken and potato salad. Then we washed our hands with Wash and Drys, wet towelettes that smelled like lemons.

It was easy for me to imagine the four of us driving together all the way to Disneyland, to California. "It will take over a month," my father explained to me. My heart raced at the thought. On very long rides I got to have Underwood deviled ham straight from the can, bags of potato chips, bottles of Coke. My brother and I sat together in the way back with the pillows from our beds. Even though my mother found the idea preposterous, she wanted to believe it too. Disneyland was our dream vacation. But we never got there.

Instead, the next time we travelled it was east, not west, back to Rhode Island and 40 Fiume Street. It was 1962, and my father was sent to Cuba, a post that did not allow families. Once again, we settled in with Nonna and Mama Rose. At first, I struggled against them and their superstitions. They shouted in Italian if we put shoes on a bed, walked out of a different door than the one we'd walked in, or didn't cross our legs when we were in the presence of someone who could be a witch.

But when first grade started, I realized I didn't fit in there either. The girls, with their pixie cuts and jump rope games learned together in kindergarten, lived in sleekly modern split ranches in neighborhoods that did not have shrines to the Virgin Mary or grapevines clogging the yards. I was more than the new kid in school; I lived like a foreigner.

The gray-haired, powder-cheeked teachers, with their soft flowered dresses and the rulers they held to rap knuckles, gave me books to read to ease the loneliness of recess. Even this school—the same one generations of my family had attended—straddled the Old and New Worlds. A mile away, my cousins went to a modern yellow brick-and-glass school, with young teachers who looked like Marlo Thomas in *That Girl*. My teachers routinely checked us for lice and asked if we had enough coal in winter; across town they were learning songs to Broadway shows. At home, my mother struggled to modernize the house. She talked of getting an electric stove and wood panelling. But Mama Rose and Nonna refused. "We've always lived this way," they argued. "We're happy."

ODDLY, MY REJECTION BY those pixie-haired girls and my growing love for my old-fashioned teachers made the Old World of our house a comfort. True, the steady flow of relatives, many of them old women dressed in black, speaking in Italian, with faces populated by a topography of moles and liver spots and wiry hair, still bothered me. But I grew to love running downstairs along the cold floor to huddle in front of the kitchen stove. I waited for the coal truck to arrive, and followed the man, his face and hands blackened from soot, as he filled our coal bin.

I took refuge from the schoolyard taunts and cheek-pinching relatives in the Shack, the outbuilding used to feed us on hot summer nights. The Shack consisted of two rooms, one small, one large. The small one held a slate sink and a butler's pantry of shelves and cupboards. The large one was mostly table, a table that could seat a dozen people comfortably. There was another sink and a beat-up sofa to curl up on and read, alone. Built to accommodate Mama Rose's ever growing family, we still used it in summer, shuttling food from the Big House to the Shack.

On those nights, the Shack was the essence of summer: Rhode Island bread and butter corn that we had husked on the bench in the yard; fresh peas shelled by a bevy of cousins; green beans from an uncle's garden, served cold with lots of crushed garlic and mint from our garden; tomatoes and cucumbers, from our own backyard, that had marinated for days in oil and vinegar and oregano; battered and fried squash blossoms—*coguzza*, we called it; stale bread, blackened on top of the stove, wet with water and olive oil, and topped with lots of salt and oregano.

The finale was Mama Rose's blueberry pies. We were sent to the boundaries of the yard with cups and buckets to pick the blueberries that grew there. Blueberry bushes lined two sides of our property, and all summer they appeared in our cereal and cold bowls set out for nibbling. An aunt had mastered what she called blueberry muffins, but they were more like cupcakes, dense and sweet and topped with a hefty shine of sugar.

Finally Mama Rose brought out the pies, three or four or five of them, gooey with blueberries. She always made a lattice top, its scalloped edges forming a perfect crisscross pattern. She had secrets for her pie crusts, and she shared them only reluctantly. A brush of cream on top for even browning. A sprinkling of sugar for taste. We never had ice cream or whipped cream with pie, just fat wedges oozing with fruit. In the morning we ate it cold for breakfast.

On summer nights, when all the food had been eaten and crickets sang in the yard, the grown-ups played cards at the long table in the shack. The table was covered with a thick oilcloth littered with small round holes from cigarette burns. They all smoked, stogies or Pall Malls, the crushed red packs growing into small heaps as the night wore on. The cousins stayed mostly outside, although the slam of the Shack's screen door could be heard, followed by a complaint or whine: Someone had taken someone else's army men, a cousin wasn't sharing, another cousin had skinned a knee or had too many mosquito bites. An adult's voice rang out: "Go outside and play!" Then another slam of the screen door and a new game began—frozen tag or Mother, May I.

But my mother wanted progress. That New Year's Eve Nonna died. And her death catapulted us into our era of modernization. For the two years that my father was in Cuba, our household shot out of its immigrant days and into the 1960s with a vengeance. At the helm of these changes stood my mother. She had tasted all that technology had to offer while we lived in Virginia, and she became determined to bring it to the old house at 40 Fiume Street. My uncle the electrician came at night after supper to inspect the wires. My uncle the oil man spent time in our cellar. My uncle the carpenter brought tape measures and notepads and walked around the house, serious and frowning. There was excitement in the air as my mother talked to them. She gestured widely with her arms, tapped on walls, pointed at glossy pictures in magazines.

Already she had moved her contemporary blond wood bedroom set from her old childhood room to the one Nonna had occupied for over half a century. She'd had my uncle the carpenter build a closet with a modern-looking, sliding straw door instead of a regular wooden one. She'd had drawers built into one wall, long sleek things that looked as if they belonged on a boat. She bought wild sheets, with bright red poppies, another covered in a field of electric yellow daisies. The old embroidered ones got packed away.

After Nonna's somber room, with its dark bureau, the iron bed that had long ago turned from silver to black, and its smell of stale urine and medicine, this newly conceived room was a shock. I always stepped into it with caution. When Nonna occupied it, I simply stayed away, especially after glimpsing her once in her old-fashioned, long white cotton underwear as she unpinned her long gray hair. Now, it was the sunniness of the room that held me frozen in the doorway.

THE NEXT WINTER, MY father sent us baby alligators from Cuba. Like all of our pets, they died quickly. My mother set them up in the big double sink behind the Shack and they froze to death on Christmas night. He also sent alligator shoes for my mother and a purse for me. The purse was made from alligator skin and snapped shut with an alligator face, its eyes shiny yellow, its grinning mouth the part that snapped. This would have been remembered as the Christmas of the alligators, but instead, it was the blue year. My mother decided to get an artificial Christmas tree. My brother and I fought this change the hardest.

"These are amazing," my mother told us as she pored over advertisements and sales in the Sunday newspaper. A discount store called Ann & Hope offered the largest selection. "No needles to vacuum, no smell, no mess. You just pop it in the stand and it's Christmas."

Of course we argued that Christmas was all about the smell of pine trees, the hard work of choosing the perfect tree, somehow getting it home and straight up in its stand, the decorating.

But she waved us away. "Nonsense. There's no need for any of that anymore."

Progress had even invaded Christmas.

One day we came home from school and our mother was waiting.

"I got the most beautiful tree in the entire store," she said proudly. "I put it up all by myself. That's how easy it was."

We followed her through the pantry and kitchen into the living room where the ugliest thing I had ever seen stood in the corner reserved for the towering trees we usually had. A squat, round silver tree met us. My mother happily explained how the tree itself was just a stick covered with holes. All she had to do was place the "branches" into the holes and she had an instant tree. The branches themselves were covered in a silvery foil, with fat pom-poms at their tips. From these tips my mother had hung blue balls.

"Blue is our theme," she explained.

She'd bought plastic candles for every window. With a flourish she opened the heavy gold drapes to reveal blue-tipped candles. She plugged them in and they glowed the same color as a blue lava lamp.

"Trees are not silver," my brother said.

"Where are all of our real ornaments?" I asked, staring at the blue balls dangling from the silver pom-poms.

But our mother was too busy setting up what she called the pièce de résistance: a multicolored pinwheel that, as it slowly spun, shone swaths of yellow, blue, or red onto the silver tree. We stared, horrified. But our progress had just begun.

Maybe it was because of the new kitchen. Or maybe my mother's introduction of TV dinners and casseroles made with Campbell's soup somehow won her over. Or maybe all these years my grandmother had been secretly dreaming of leaving the Old World behind too. Whatever the reason, Mama Rose fell in love with Graham Kerr, the Galloping Gourmet. And our meals were modernized too.

Mama Rose loved to watch television. She liked *The Virginian* and *The Big Valley*. She watched one soap opera, *As the World Turns*. She always caught *Saturday Night at the Movies*, no matter what the movie was. And she liked *The Galloping Gourmet*. *The Galloping Gourmet* came on every afternoon, just before *Dark Shadows*.

"Isn't he cute?" she'd say, pointing at the zany Englishman drinking too much wine as he cooked.

Anything English became popular. Twiggy, the Beatles, Davy Jones, Mary Quant and Yardley and Carnaby Street.

"He is cute," I agreed.

Carefully Mama Rose wrote down his recipes.

Before the Galloping Gourmet, our meals had a predictable pattern. Monday we had soup or stew. Tuesday we had a roast, pork or beef. Wednesday was macaroni. Thursday was either chicken, usually cooked in what Mama Rose called "in the oven"—oil, vinegar, garlic, oregano—or pork chops, fried, or—worst of all—veal cutlets dredged in an eggy batter and fried. Friday was meatless: eggs in purgatory (sunny-side up eggs in red sauce), creamed tuna on toast, fish and chips from the fish place, chow mein and fried rice from the Hong Kong restaurant in Arctic, or clam chowder.

On Saturdays we ate in the afternoon because there was always a card game on Saturday nights for the grown-ups. We had boiled hot dogs and beans, or fried hamburgers, or cold cut sandwiches, or pizza, or steak, also fried. Then at night Mama Rose gave us a TV dinner. My favorite was Salisbury steak, a fat hamburger with sweet brown gravy and mashed potatoes that tasted nothing like a potato. We also had our big Sunday meal in the afternoon. We never called the afternoon meal lunch, it was dinner. We ate supper at night.

Sunday dinner was cooked on the grill in the summer. My father had two specialties. One was Chicken Bountiful, chicken cooked in foil with some kind of Campbell's soup. The other was shish kebab, chunks of beef marinated in whiskey and sugar, set on a skewer with peppers and onions and cherry tomatoes. The rest of the seasons Mama Rose made three- or four-course Italian meals, macaroni and antipasto and some kind of meat, a meat loaf stuffed with hard-boiled eggs and olives, or braciola, a flank steak braised in red sauce, or sometimes sausage with peppers and potatoes.

But once Graham Kerr entered our lives, none of us knew what to expect.

Mama Rose never allowed anyone in the pantry with her when she cooked. We all sat at the table in the kitchen and waited for her to produce dinner. She appeared, sweating, with huge platters of food that her four-foot-ten-inch frame seemed unlikely to actually carry. But she always just made it to the table, sliding her heavy load of meatballs or roasted potatoes to the edge of the table, then going back for the next platter.

With her Galloping Gourmet meals, she appeared as usual, in her apron, sweating, carrying a heavy platter that seemed about to drop from her arms to the floor. But this time when she slid it onto the table, we all stared.

"What is it?" my brother asked.

"Swedish meatballs," Mama Rose said.

We kept staring. To us, meatballs were large and firm and round. Without gravy, they were a crisp brown with flecks of parsley, still wet from the oil they'd been fried in. We ate those as snacks, happily popping them into our mouths in two or three bites until Mama Rose slapped our hands. "Enough! I need them for the gravy!" she'd say. In the gravy they were covered completely in red, the sauce dripping from them onto our chins.

These meatballs were tiny, the size of marbles. And they sat in brown gravy, lots of it. They did not smell of garlic or parsley.

My mother sniffed, and frowned.

"Allspice," Mama Rose announced.

The next platter was heaped with noodles. But not the kind of noodles we knew, spaghetti, ziti, penne.

"Egg noodles," Mama Rose said.

She wiped her hands on her apron and grinned.

"*Mangia!*" she ordered.

But we didn't know what to do.

"Like this," she said, frustrated, and she began to slap egg noodles onto our plates, then top them with mounds of these tiny meatballs.

Another night she brought out a large pot instead of a platter. She placed it in the center of the table.

"There," she said.

We all leaned over to look. I'd never smelled anything like the aroma wafting from this.

"Beef bourguignon," she said.

"Ma," my mother said, "what is beef bourguignon?"

"It's fancy," Mama Rose said. "It's French."

The Galloping Gourmet was starting to get under our skin.

"Coq au vin," she said another night. "Delicious."

I found myself longing for her fried pork chops. Was nothing going to stay the same?

THERE WAS TALK OF the war. My father, home from Cuba, had been in the navy for twenty years. I did not realize how close he had come to danger while he was away. The Bay of Pigs and the Cuban Missile Crisis had both occurred while he was stationed there. Now, Vietnam was heavy on everyone's mind.

My father was a Seabee. I had a small silver fighting bee pin that I wore on my jacket. But my father had never fought any war. He had just missed World War II, and he had been stationed in Italy during the Korean War. His job was storekeeper, and he purchased and procured supplies. The rumors were that Seabees would be sent to Vietnam. With twenty years, my father could retire. But he loved the navy, loved the different duties he had, loved moving and travelling. His hope had been for us to all go somewhere new together, maybe even to Europe.

The more he checked, the more certain it became that he was destined for Vietnam. Reluctantly he signed up to retire. He was thirty-seven years old.

What surprised him was that he would now settle down. No more sea bags to pack, no more waiting for orders. Even more surprising was that he would settle down here, in Rhode Island. At first, my parents spent Sunday afternoons looking at houses. We saw a farmhouse in North Kingstown, a yellow house in a subdevelopment in Cranston. My father liked them all. He had never owned a house before, and they each had a certain appeal. But at night, when my parents talked enthusiastically about the merits of each house, Mama Rose groaned and grabbed at her chest.

"What is it, Ma?" my mother would ask.

"Nothing, nothing," she'd say, smiling weakly. "Just my heart. I'm fine." Mama Rose had a heart murmur from her bout with scarlet fever as a child.

With all of her children married and in their own houses, our departure would mark the first time she lived alone, ever. Weak heart or not, she did not want to live by herself. Discussions began in the kitchen and continued in my parents' bedroom, late into the night. My father reminisced about how happy we had all been as an autonomous family in Virginia. He pointed out that it wasn't just Mama Rose who came along with the house, but Nuneen, Uncle Rum, and Uncle Carmine. Soon they would be old. Did my mother really want to take care of so many old people?

Even this thoroughly modern version of my mother could not leave 40 Fiume Street. The old ways dictated that someone stayed with the mother, that someone took care of the relatives, that someone made sure the family house remained in the family. Despite the linoleum and Formica and amber sliding glass doors, my mother could not let go of these traditions. Reluctantly on my father's end, we stayed: 40 Fiume Street became ours.

One day a man with a clipboard appeared at the front door. They were rezoning the street, he explained. Some lots had been sold. He pointed vaguely up the hill. As of the first of the next month, our house was no longer number 40. We were now number 10. He gave us an official document and said good-bye. We watched him go from door to door, renumbering the street. As big as that change was, an even bigger one was about to come.

MY FATHER GOT A fancy job as the East Coast head of a company that shipped supplies to Vietnam. Like many jobs, it was headquartered at the Quonset Point naval base, called simply "the base." Uncle Rum worked at the base, as did Uncle Chuckie, both in civilian jobs. But after twenty years as a Seabee, my father kept all of his privileges, and much of our life still revolved around the base. My parents shopped at the commissary there, and they bought liquor and cigarettes at the navy exchange. We all had ID cards, and we even went to the navy hospital for routine checkups.

For the first time in his life, my father did not wear a uniform to work. He went to a men's store and ordered six suits, beautiful wool and tweed and pinstriped suits. We traded in our station wagon for a Chevy Caprice, a fancy green car that was followed by a two-tone Ford LTD. My father, a beer lover, started to drink martinis. He took us to a fancy restaurant near the base for lunch where we ordered club sandwiches. A few times a week we ate dinner out and had filet mignon and Caesar salads. We entertained out-of-town business associates. Suddenly, we were no longer a navy family. Our Italian roots seemed more and more distant. We had entered the middle class.

Around the time of my father's new job, my mother's youngest sister was widowed. Her daughter was only two, and they could not afford the apartment they'd been living in. To Mama Rose, there was only one solution. They would move in with us. At this, my father put his foot down. Bad enough that Mama Rose was underfoot and that the relatives in the back moved in and out of the house all day. But two more people living right with us?

Again, late-night discussions ensued. Before I knew it, the uncles were back with their wires and measuring tapes and notebooks. But this time they were taking over the yard.

Despite all the changes my mother made after Nonna died, the yard remained untouched. Right at the road we had a garage where our fat gray cat had a litter of kittens twice a year. A white fence ran from the garage to the house, and in the middle of that fence was a gate. When you walked through the gate, you could have walked into a yard in southern Italy. There were benches for sitting or husking corn. A red wheelbarrow rested beside the rakes and hoes and spades near the double sink. There was always a bag or two of manure there. And behind all of that stood the Shack. If you meandered through the fig trees and the vegetable garden, you came to the fruit trees: peach, pear, and a large cherry tree. Beyond those stood Nonna's outhouse, and then the grapevines, and finally the blueberry bushes.

Now my parents took me outside and showed me a different yard.

"The garage will be knocked down," they explained, pointing, excited, "and the fence too. We'll put in a big driveway, and at the end of it will be the new garage. We'll build an apartment for Auntie Junie and Gina above the garage."

They continued, talking about the two bedrooms, the modern bath, the kitchen that would sit on the first floor and the harvest gold carpeting that would line the stairs and living room.

I looked at the yard.

"But what about the cherry tree?" I asked, realizing it sat approximately where this carpeted living room had to go.

"We'll have it chopped down."

My eyes settled on the spot where the new driveway would be built.

"What about the Shack?" I cried.

"We don't need the Shack anymore," they said. "It's an eyesore."

In a panic I ran inside. Surely Mama Rose wouldn't let this happen.

She stood at the stove in the pantry, carefully reading a recipe to herself.

"They're going to tear up the yard!" I told her.

"Sssshhhh," she said. "I'm busy."

"But the trees." I thought of the hard pears we collected each spring, the taste of the dark cherries.

"Can't you ever be quiet?" Mama Rose said. "You made me forget what I'm doing!"

"They're going to knock down the Shack," I said.

"Jesus Crest! Go out and play!"

I watched her overlap thin slices of potatoes in a pie plate. The recipe card said: potatoes au gratin.

"Where the hell do I keep my nutmeg," she muttered to herself.

A month later, construction began.

OUR REFUGE FROM LIFE at 40 Fiume Street, with its boisterous relatives coming and going at all hours of the day and night, became our car. Early in the morning, before it was completely light, the four of us crept out of the house and drove away. On these trips, it was the way it had been briefly when we lived alone in Virginia. One Saturday we drove to New York City for the day, riding the elevator to the top of the Empire State Building, buying souvenirs. We ate hot dogs on the street. We shopped at Macy's. We drove home the long way so we could gaze at the Statue of Liberty.

"Where the hell have you been?" aunts and uncles shouted at us when we got back home. "We came to visit!"

Frequently we drove the hour to Boston, the four of us. We parked in a big parking garage and then walked to the T and rode it to Fenway Park. Before we left home, my father would gather the exact change for each of us to buy two subway tokens. We always sat in the bleachers, and rooted for Yaz and Carlton Fisk, Dewey and Fred Lynn.

"Why didn't you tell us you were going to a game?" aunts and uncles chided us. "We would have come with you."

On hot summer nights, we slipped out after dinner but before the relatives arrived for coffee, and drove to the beach for a dip. My mother set up a gray navy blanket on the sand and we all ran into the waves. None of us hesitated, or dipped just a toe. We charged those waves, running in headfirst and then riding the waves back into shore. Later, we'd go for clam cakes or ice cream. It would be dark when we got back, but there still might be a few aunts and uncles sitting at the kitchen table.

"Why didn't you wait for us?" they'd say. "We're dying for clam cakes."

Every few years we drove to Indiana to visit my father's family. That was always best. A couple of weeks with just the four of us. On the way we would stop a few days for pure vacation. In 1967 we headed for the

Montreal Expo. But my mother read that Jean Dixon had predicted that the Expo, built on an island, was going to sink and thousands of people would be killed. She let my father drive us by it, and then we headed into the city where we ate French food and stayed safe.

My mother worked hard to keep us safe. At Niagara Falls we were not allowed to ride the *Maid of the Mist* that travelled below the falls. Instead, we stood together across the street at an overlook and watched the rushing water. I glimpsed lucky rain-slickered sightseers, floating close to the falls. But not us. From this distance, we would stay out of harm's way.

Danger seemed to always be around the corner. I was aware of it. We all were. But in our car, together, singing songs off-key, we felt safe. Our large extended family could not penetrate. The outside world stayed away. Yet at any moment we understood that could change. Somewhere deep inside I knew all along that this family, trying so hard to stay together, would come apart. Like our turtles and fish and alligators, like my father's delicate African violets, like my mother's sister and brother, one of us could be taken away. I prayed at shrines and churches for God to keep us together. At least for a while, we were. We snuck away, and in our metal-and-glass cocoon, we stayed together and safe.

OF COURSE, WE WEREN'T safe. The sixties arrived in full force, splintering families and the country itself. My brother went off to college, grew a beard, had long-haired friends who reeked of the sweet smell of marijuana. Eventually, he got married, had a daughter, moved away. I write these things without details because what happened to him, to all of us, requires such care in the telling. I am building up to it, trying to encapsulate the years before we lost him, because it is losing Skip that matters. That is what happened. Our foolish family, believing in its strength and love, lost him and grew lopsided, three-legged, unsteady.

But first Mama Rose died. She chose the bicentennial year, dying unlike how she lived: quietly. Appropriately though, she died sitting at the kitchen table, where we had shared so many family dinners, where she used to stand on Easter mornings and sprinkle us with holy water as a blessing. I was already away at college, where I had redefined myself as totally American. I highlighted my dark blond hair so that it was gold, cut it into a Dorothy Hamill wedge, wore Izod shirts and khaki pants. With Mama Rose gone, most of the telltale signs of my Italian background vanished. There was no one speaking in broken English anymore at home. When friends visited they saw an American family with a big car, a father who wore a suit to work, a mother in cashmere sweaters. We ate filet mignon for Sunday dinner now. Our relatives stayed home more often.

Eventually I moved away too. I even acquired a hint of a New England accent, as if my family had been there for generations. When I went to work as a flight attendant, I adopted a new sophistication. I studied the way people dressed, what they bought in European cities, where they went. Before long, I was going to the theater in London, shopping in Paris. My Italian heritage was like a secret. To everyone I met, I was a blond New Englander with the innocuous name of Hood.

Then, in June of 1982, Skip died, and this facade of safety that had nurtured me for so long shattered.

the search

FOR FIFTEEN YEARS I cobbled together a life without Skip. Again, the details of those years are not important. What matters is that during that time I slowly began to reclaim my heritage. I liked the shock on people's faces when they learned I was Italian, a fact I no longer kept to myself. But rather than embrace my traditions, I reinvented them. My Italian cooking was out of cookbooks, and never southern. When I visited Italy, it was to its cities—Venice, Florence, Rome. Inside churches, I remembered how to light a votive candle in someone's memory, and lit them for my brother. I began to collect religious art—statues and crucifixes and candles, the things of my childhood.

But when my father died, and our once indestructible family of four was now cut in half, I felt a desperate need for comfort. Those things from my childhood took on a new importance. Still, in my search for miracles, I mostly looked for the external kind, the kind you journey to find. By the summer of 1998, with an advance on a contract for this book, I began to plan trips in search of a miracle. I doubted that anything could cure me of my despair and restore my faith again, unless my father could intervene. I longed so much for his conversations, his laugh, him, that the sight of intact families made me weep. Desperately, I made plans.

I am a modern American pilgrim.

That means many different things. For one, I am disconnected from any organized religion. How much simpler it would be to know my pilgrimage must be to Mecca or the Western Wall. How much simpler to know that, like the Hopi Indians, on Niman the kachinas go home and every July there is a dance to bid them farewell. But we American pilgrims have a mixed culture, leaving nothing clear.

I am an Italian-American woman. I could go to Italy and visit the homes of saints: Catherine, Francis, Claire. I could wait until September and visit Naples to see if San Gennaro's blood liquefies, as it has done most years since he was martyred in A.D. 305. I was raised a Catholic. I could go to Fatima or Medjugorje or any of the places where the Virgin Mary has appeared. I could go to the principal shrine of the Catholic Church, Saint Peter's Basilica in Rome.

I am a mother. Can I expect a two-year-old, a five-year-old, and a nine-year-old to climb mountains, crawl into caves, visit third-world countries, all so I can find whatever this elusive thing is I am seeking? There are school vacations to coordinate, limited time to travel, the childhood pressures of learning how to read and divide—these loom larger than my spiritual yearnings.

I am a wife. For two years my travels centered on miracles. I have gone alone or with one of the children or with our whole family to shrines and feasts. There was my original trip to Chimayo, a visit to Mexico City for the Feast of the Virgin of Guadalupe, a return to Chimayo, our family trip to Padre Pio's town in Italy. Lorne, despite his patience with my search, would like a vacation that can satisfy my journey and our family's need for relaxation and fun. We are not a family who enjoys vacations spent lying on the beach at a resort in Aruba, but the children have walked the stations of the cross a lot lately. One day I came home to find Sam lying on the kitchen floor, arms spread wide.

"What are you doing?" I asked him.

"I'm Jesus on the cross," he said.

Like most families I know, we are paying our mortgage and school tuitions and American Express bills. I have spent more than our usual funds allotted for vacations as I've travelled. Despite a little money from my publisher, a few magazine articles that paid some expenses, we have a budget to consider. I cross off Japan, India, Sri Lanka, Peru from my list.

Close to home, only an hour's drive away, a miracle is supposed to be happening. While I continue my search for a longer miracle journey, I get in my car with the kids and drive to Worcester, Massachusetts.

Worcester is an unlikely place for miracles. For the most part, places associated with miracles, visions, and shrines, and even the birthplaces of saints, are beautiful. Think of the Pyrenees in France where Lourdes is nestled, or the dramatic Himalayas, which, according to the Hindu tradition, lie in the country of the gods. Think of Tuscany and Umbria, two regions of Italy rich with miracles and saints. A volcanic rock formation shaped like a sleeping bear, Bear Butte is lush with conifers and ash trees that the Lakota Sioux and Cheyenne believe are sacred. It is said that Crazy Horse prayed there before Little Big Horn. Today, people still go to Bear Butte and leave small bundles of cloth filled with tobacco as offerings to the Spirit. These colorful "prayer ties" blow gently in the South Dakota breeze.

Mountains and rivers and springs and caves, majestic demonstrations of nature at her best, have ancient sacred traditions. So it is surprising that the industrial city of Worcester is a modern miracle healing site. Worcester, in central Massachusetts, is known for other pursuits. Its location on the Blackstone River led to its rapid industrialization in 1822. Initially producing mainly machinery and metal goods, Worcester later added chemicals and pharmaceuticals to its industry.

Worcester also has a violent history. In 1675 and 1683 it was the scene of Native American attacks. One hundred years later, Daniel Shays led an armed rebellion of economically depressed farmers demanding relief. The Shays Rebellion, as it came to be called, was dispersed by state troops.

Today, Worcester is the home of Holy Cross College and Clark University. But it is better known as the site of a large complex of shopping outlets. Glimmers of a more beautiful city can be seen in the maze of one-way streets and traffic circles that perplex visitors. Grand Victorian houses line one main boulevard. A grassy park forms the center of downtown. The Worcester Art Museum is a proud and still-lovely building.

Mostly, though, one sees strip malls with convenience stores and fast-food restaurants, small and often shabby houses. And churches. Everywhere one looks in Worcester a steeple jabs the sky.

In one neighborhood, off the ubiquitously named Pleasant Street, in an ordinary ranch house of the type that became popular in the early

1960s, lies a fifteen-year-old comatose girl named Audrey Santo. The sign outside the house asks people not to ring the bell or knock on the door. PLEASE RESPECT OUR PRIVACY, it says. Anyone who wants to can show up at the house between ten and two any Tuesday, Wednesday, or Thursday and visit. Inside, it is said, miraculous things are happening.

Fifteen years ago, at 11:03 A.M. on August 9, Audrey's mother, Linda, found the toddler floating facedown in the family's above-ground swimming pool in their small backyard. The family was told that little Audrey would not live. Linda Santo refused to believe that. When in fact Audrey did survive, they were told she would never wake up from the coma that was brought on by a combination of her accident and an overdose of hospital-administered phenobarbital. Linda refused to accept that either. Instead of putting little Audrey in a long-term nursing facility, she brought her daughter home.

Audrey requires round-the-clock care. She breathes through a tube in her trachea and eats through a tube in her stomach. Her pediatrician, Dr. John Harding, says that Audrey is not in a coma, but rather suffers from what is called akinetic mutism. People in a coma show no signs of awareness of what is going on around them. The Santos and Dr. Harding believe that Audrey is aware of her surroundings. They know when she is agitated or happy and say that she expresses herself with her eyes.

In 1988, Linda Santo took her six-year-old daughter, who had been in a coma already for three years, to Medjugorje in what is now Bosnia, the site of apparitions of the Virgin Mary where people have reportedly been miraculously cured. In an interview with Lesley Stahl, Linda Santo said that she believed that Audrey would be cured at Medjugorje. Instead, Audrey went into cardiac arrest and had to be flown home.

It was after the Santos returned to Worcester that inexplicable things began to happen in their home. Nurses hired to help with Audrey's care reported smelling roses in the room when there were no flowers. The scent of roses is believed to be a sign from God. Padre Pio was said to have an intense fragrance of roses emanating from him. His followers called it the odor of sanctity. The technical name for this phenomenon is osmogenesia.

Besides osmogenesia, the religious statues in Audrey's room began to weep what appeared to be an oily substance. *The Catholic Free Press* reports that initial analysis of this substance has determined that the oil is neither animal nor vegetable. It is of a mysterious origin.

Priests who have said mass in the Santos' garage chapel have said that spots of blood have appeared on the Communion host. At present, the Catholic Church is investigating the strange occurrences around little Audrey. The process is slow and careful. The church does not embrace situations like the one in Worcester. Even revered and famous sites such as Fatima and Lourdes are designated by the church as "private revelation." Catholics may accept or reject them. However, even in the early stages of the investigation, the church has already eliminated trickery as a cause for the weeping statues and bleeding Communion wafers.

Then, of course, there are the miracle healings.

In an article in *The Hartford Courant*, religion writer Gerald Rener reported that through Audrey's intercession, Joey Parolisa of Methuen, Massachusetts, recovered from injuries sustained in an automobile accident in 1994. Joey was told he would probably never walk again (doctors unconnected to his case claim that injuries of the type he suffered result in about a 50 percent recovery rate). His mother, Sheryle Parolisa, went to Worcester and prayed through Audrey for her son to walk again. When she returned home, Joey was on his feet.

Several years ago, Audrey developed a terrible unexplainable rash. A dermatologist biopsied it and learned that it was from a certain type of chemotherapy. Audrey had never received any chemotherapy. Rumors have circulated since then that shortly after the rash appeared, the Santos received a letter from a cancer patient who had visited Audrey and prayed for a cure. She was undergoing the type of chemotherapy that produced the rash Audrey had. And her cancer disappeared after she prayed to Audrey to intercede.

There is a term in Catholicism for someone like Audrey: a *victim's soul*. A victim's soul takes on the suffering of others. She takes on the pain and suffering of those who file past her three days a week in what is called on the instruction sheet distributed by the organization the Apostolate of a Silent Soul, Inc., "Pilgrimage Day at Little Audrey's Chapel." The Xeroxed sheet has a boxed picture of the comatose Audrey, eyes open, lips parted, seemingly gazing at a distant spot, with the words

"Little Audrey Marie Santo, Our Precious Gift." "Praise be Jesus and Mary," it begins, "the moment has arrived—the Holy Spirit inspired us to open the doors to Audrey's Chapel."

Fourteen instructions follow, including where to park, warnings that police will tow cars, and when you can arrive. Number six reads: "You may drop off anyone who cannot physically walk to Audrey's." You are told that you can bring a priest/priests and that oil from the weeping statues will not be distributed, though you can write and request some. Numbers ten and eleven read: "You will not see Audrey, but she is present in the home where the chapel is," and "Audrey will know you are here."

The end of the sheet reads—as if the authors are teenagers signing off in a letter—"Hope to see you soon!" The other side is an order form for the video of Little Audrey's life and the monthly newsletter. The two-hour video includes "moving and touching footage" of Audrey's birthday party, miracles, the four Eucharistic occurrences, and oil and blood exuding from images.

Oddly, many Worcester residents are not even aware of what is going on in the house on South Flagg Street. The news is being spread by a coterie of Catholics who believe that Jesus and Mary are calling for prayer and repentance by creating the weeping statues and bleeding Communion wafers. After Mother Angelica reported on Little Audrey for the Eternal World Television Network, four thousand people showed up at Christ the King Church in Worcester. In 1998, Holy Cross's twenty-three-thousand-seat football stadium was filled for a mass on the anniversary of Audrey's accident.

In 1999, the church made an unofficial request that people pray *for* Audrey, not *to* her, which was interesting considering that her mother, Linda, has said that each time she was pregnant she prayed God would give her a saint. After what has happened to Audrey, *The Hartford Courant* asked, would Linda still pray for God to give her a saint? "I can give them life but I can't give them eternal life. God answers your prayers," she replied, "and it may not be the answer you want but it is much better to give him the issue. It works for me." Still, in that interview and others in newspapers and television, Linda Santo has said that she too is praying for a miracle: that her daughter Audrey will wake up.

Fearing that Little Audrey is becoming a spectacle, the church asked that the Holy Cross debacle, in which she was rolled on a stretcher into the stadium, not be repeated. Weeping statues and bleeding wafers are not part of the Catholic pedagogy, and the church does not support such events.

Still, especially on the August 9 anniversary of the accident, people will flock to Worcester. Last year, the Santos, in an effort to respect the church and Little Audrey's followers, arranged for a prayer vigil at Christ the King Church. From 1:00 to 5:00 P.M., the crowd could file into the church two by two and view Little Audrey behind a glass partition. Remembering the twenty-three thousand at Holy Cross a year earlier, I arrived at the church in Worcester at 10:00 A.M. with my cousin, Sam and Grace, and a bag full of snacks and crayons.

A bus from Pennsylvania had already deposited a large group, who stood saying the Hail Mary in front of the modern yellow brick church. The parking lot was not yet full, though it would be jammed by the time we left that afternoon. Cars with New York, New Jersey, and Pennsylvania license plates were parked there when we pulled in. Leaflets had been tacked up to posts. There was the same black-and-white photograph of Audrey at the top, and in big letters was written NO MASS OR BENEDICTION. ATTENTION: READ CAREFULLY, followed by seven items. Number one read, "Little Audrey will be in the church—you will see her."

We joined the line of people. Many had brought coolers and sat comfortably on lawn chairs on the grass. Poking from shopping bags were large crucifixes and statues. People fingered rosary beads as they waited. A Mexican family posed for pictures, snapping happily away. In front of us, an Indian man cradled an infant wrapped in a bright Barney blanket. His wife looked solemn and sad despite the cheerful pale green flowered dress she wore. Her eyes were ringed with dark circles, as if she had not slept well in a long time. Their five-year-old daughter chattered happily and skipped in circles around them.

The large group's bus driver came to tell them he had parked in a shady spot down the street. Now he was off to McDonald's for some breakfast. Many of them tried to convince him to stay.

"No," he said loudly, addressing all of us, it seemed. "It's a political decision."

The priest in the group pleaded with him. "But you're so close."

The bus driver smiled. "I'm closer than you know," he said. He explained to the growing crowd that he had never missed church once until 1968. "I didn't fall away from the church," he said. "I walked away."

Behind us, an elderly couple commented on Grace's glasses.

"Isn't she cute?" the woman said. Her denim hat had a large artificial daisy pinned to it and the daisy bobbed as if it were nodding agreement.

"Where did you come from?" I asked her. Everyone in the crowd was eager to talk.

"New Mexico," she said.

Her husband, a gaunt man with skin tinted yellow, grinned. "Yup," he said. "She wanted to come."

I assumed he was ill and she had come hoping for a miracle.

"Did you come to get a miracle?" I asked her softly.

"I came for strength to accept what comes my way," she said.

I nodded, admiring her knowledge that perhaps that was all she could get here, or anywhere.

"Yup," her husband said. "She's got cancer."

Startled, I looked at the robust woman standing beside me. "You?" I blurted.

"I've had three operations and almost died twice," she said. "Ahh," she added almost dismissively, "I've had hard times my whole life."

The Indian family had rearranged itself. Now the mother held the baby while the father quizzed the little girl from Brain Quest cards for ages seven to eight: "1,000 Questions and Answers to Challenge the Mind," the box boasted.

"How do you spell baby?" the father asked.

"B-A-B-Y," the girl said slowly.

That was the first time I saw her baby brother convulse. He had several more convulsions as the morning passed.

I turned from the mother and her sick baby to see a family setting up lawn chairs in the shade beneath a tree. It was easy to see who was who in the family: parents in their late sixties and their two daughters. Both appeared to be around my age, somewhere in their forties. One was tanned and blond and apparently healthy except for a cast on her foot. The other, I knew, was dying. She was thin with a sallow complexion.

Her body seemed to sink into itself, and she moved as if she were in pain. Her eyes were glazed, her mouth set hard. Her husband buzzed around her, arranging the chair and making sure she was comfortable. His gentleness broke my heart.

Behind them a Benedictine monk dressed in a long black robe appeared to hear confessions in folding chairs. He was from Latrobe, Pennsylvania, the home of the oldest monastery in the country.

I went to talk to him, sitting in the wobbly chair across from his.

I meant to ask him what he thought of all this—Little Audrey, the weeping statues, everything. But instead I blurted the story of my father's illness and how I'd gone to Chimayo to find him a miracle. I started to cry, but I continued to talk to him. He had a long gray beard and dark eyes. In his robes he looked like a visitor from another era, and somehow that appealed to me. If he was surprised to hear my story instead of a confession, he didn't show it.

When I finished, I felt drained.

"Why did God do this?" he said. "He didn't do it. He allowed it and we choose to either grow from it or let it ruin us. God allowed your father to die. Now you must choose what you will do. Through God's grace you have a talent, the ability to write. With this you can comfort others in grief."

Then he leaned toward me the slightest bit. "This is real, you know," he said. "Something is really happening here."

I looked back at the crowd. Two more busses had pulled up, along with two TV news teams. A woman stepped out of the crowd and posed for one of the news cameras with her statue of the Virgin Mary. Another bus arrived. It was bright green with a picture of a leprechaun on its side and the words CATCH THE MAGIC. Something was happening here. But what?

I moved back to my place in line, where the Indian father was removing a tube from the baby in the mother's arms.

"Wouldn't it be weird if Little Audrey woke up today?" Sam asked me.

I wondered how many people here were hoping for that very thing.

The mother with the sick baby was talking to a man from Wisconsin. Although he was dressed with a priest's collar, he was standing with his wife, both of them draped with large wooden rosary beads. The Indian woman explained how her husband didn't want to come. But she prayed that he would change his mind and he did.

"What can you give me?" she asked the man. Her eyes darted from his face to his wife's.

"When you have a baby who will never be normal—" he began.

"I'm not ready to say he will never be normal," she interrupted passionately.

"Fine," the man said. "But children like this are little saints. He is a little saint."

Disgusted, the father walked away.

Seeing such pain and desperation made me want to walk away too. I proposed a trip to the bathroom with the kids. The bathrooms are in the basement of the church, a cool, plain place where it is easy to imagine bingo games and Girl Scout meetings and Christmas bazaars. But today it was filled with smiling women wearing pink ribbons beneath that black-and-white photograph of Little Audrey. They answered questions and pointed the way to the bathrooms.

As we waited for a stall to open up, a woman from a bus group whose name tag read HELLO MY NAME IS VERA said to another woman, "Someday she will just get out of that bed."

"That's right," the other woman said. "You're right."

It was noon. In one hour we would be allowed inside the church. As we made our way back to our place in line, more busses arrived.

The Indian woman still talked to the man and his wife.

"Life is valuable at any level," the man told her.

The woman grew frustrated. She told a story she had clearly told many times and believed no one understood. Her eyes grew feverish as she talked.

"I am telling you," she said forcefully, "that there are mysterious things with him. The similarities with my son and Audrey are unbelievable. Even with the things the nurses did. I read about what they did to Audrey. The same thing with my son. The things she can move, he can move. The very same things!"

She held out a sheet of paper that she received in the mail when she wrote to the Apostolate of a Silent Soul for some of the oil from the weeping statues that the family collects in plastic cups.

"I don't have all the dates and things like they do. But I am telling you the similarities are incredible."

I listened carefully as she talked. Did she think her baby was also a victim's soul? I was not certain. The only thing that was clear was how desperate she was. She wandered back to her place in front of me in the line. I smiled, hoping to emit the compassion I felt.

"Did you drive far to be here?" I asked her.

"We came from New Jersey," she said. "My husband didn't want to come. We are Hindu. We don't believe . . ." Her voice trailed off. She obviously believed.

She grabbed my arm conspiratorially. "Everything about my baby is mysterious. The seed came from nowhere. Do you understand? We had taken care of it so we would have only the one child." She pointed toward her daughter who was playing a game of tag with Sam and Grace. "An astrologer told me I would have two children and I laughed. 'It's impossible,' I explained to her. Then one week later I am pregnant." She shook her head as if she still could not understand the course her life had taken. "At first, when you have a baby like this, you can't believe it."

"Well," said the woman from New Mexico with the nodding daisy on her hat, "what's wrong with him anyway?"

"It's mysterious," the woman said, now turning her full attention to her new listener. She hoped, I supposed, that someone would hear what she was trying so desperately to say. "He is fifteen months old but he is like a three-month-old."

"I noticed how he just lies there," the woman said, clucking her tongue sympathetically.

"Yes! But the doctors cannot figure out why. Whenever they do tests, the results disappear. There is mystery here, I tell you!"

At 12:50 an ambulance pulled up. A murmur spread through the crowd: Little Audrey was here. The church group at the front of the line resumed their long-since-abandoned Hail Marys.

I chatted briefly with a reporter from *The Catholic Free Press*. I told him about my book and how it started with my trip to Chimayo. When he left, I turned to find the husband and wife with the two adult daughters looking at me, their faces so open that I touched the mother's arm.

She motioned toward her daughter, the one who looked so sick. "She's got it," she says. "Like your father."

The family pressed together in the line. I recognized my own family in their good-natured teasing, and in their solidarity. The five of them came here together to save this woman. I remembered my family crowded together in hospitals and doctors' offices. Our faces had once been this open too. We had believed that the power of family could save my father. I realized I had not let go of the woman's arm. The sick daughter had religious medals, maybe six of them, hanging around her neck. She seemed already apart from the others, as if she had begun to leave them already.

"She's worried now," the woman said. "She heard you say about the chemo and she's scared."

"Oh," I said quickly, "but he wasn't in good health. He had emphysema."

"And he was old, right?" the mother asked, her eyes hopeful.

"Yes," I lied. My father was hardly old; these parents were probably older than he was.

Now the woman's father spoke. "For two months we've had a black cloud over our head," he said. His wife concurred. "Two car accidents. One with the baby right in the backseat. That one broke her foot," he said. "And now this."

They both looked at their daughter's drawn face.

"How do you feel about all this?" I asked her. "About coming here?"

She rolled her eyes and walked away, to stand back in the shade. Her husband and sister followed.

"But maybe this will change our luck," the woman said. "First we went to Boston to have both their auras changed. So they'd quit smoking. It's too late for that one, but still. This Indian man can get you to stop. So we went and she told him about her pain and that went away too. Plus they haven't smoked since Friday."

Hearing this, people in the crowd asked for the name of the man in Boston who changes auras.

The line began to move forward. We entered the church.

The first thing I noticed about Little Audrey was that she was not little. She was a teenager, with the face of a teenager. The second thing I noticed was that whether it was called a coma or akinetic mutism, she was not aware. Her eyes fluttered the way a person's in a coma might. They flitted around without ever landing anywhere. Then they closed, only to flutter open again. The tubes that crept out of the blanket discreetly pulled over her reinforced the fact that she was very ill. I had read descriptions of her, how saintly she looked, how like a Dresden doll. But I was struck only by how vulnerable she was, like the very ill people I saw all those months I sat by my father's bed in the hospital.

The sight of Audrey Santo, her mother at her side, behind a glass partition so people could view her, haunted me. Did her mother get the saint she had so desperately prayed for? Or did she simply have a child who would never recover from a tragic accident? The girl's uncle contended that whether her eyes were opened or closed she knew you were there. Did Audrey Santo know that thousands of people were walking past her, dropping to their knees, praying to her, not for her? I thought not. I thought she responded to the love and care her family showered on her, just as I believed my family's love kept my father alive when medicine said he should be dead.

Of course this did not answer the question of why and what those statues wept. Or how blood appeared on Communion wafers. There are some things, perhaps, for which there are no answers.

In the car on our way back home, I asked Sam and Grace what they thought when they looked through that glass at Little Audrey.

"I think she's very sick," Grace said somberly.

"Her hair is so beautiful," Sam said.

Her hair, a rich chestnut color, had never been cut, and it spread out on the stark white sheets, cascading by her feet.

Then Grace asked simply, "But, Mama, why did Little Audrey fall in the pool?"

"It was an accident," I said.

"But Mama," Grace asked again, "why?"

Finally I answered, "No one knows why."

IT WAS HARD NOT to notice the large inflatable rafts, of the type used in swimming pools, stacked on the side of the Santos' house. The irony of their presence seemed to go mostly unnoticed by the people who came to visit Audrey's Chapel. The chapel was a makeshift one in what was once the Santos' garage. On the day I arrived with Ariane and Grace, two white-haired men greeted us. They told us not to park on the street and where there were rest rooms for us to use. Finally we were ready to enter.

Despite the reminders posted everywhere to pray in silence and not to touch anything, the homemade altar at the front of the room, and the statues and crucifixes that occupy every surface, I couldn't stop feeling that I was in a garage. I had a morbid curiosity that embarrassed me in the reverent silence. These statues were supposed to weep and I had come to see them.

Little plastic cups taped under the Virgin Mary's chin and at Jesus' feet had liquid in them. Some were more than half full; others had a few drops in the bottom. On the altar was a Communion wafer in a gold display with a spot of what appeared to be dried blood on it.

This is the truth: I wanted to believe that the statues wept.

Believing it meant something important to me. Perhaps it gave me faith that there were things that we cannot understand, miraculous things. Perhaps it let me believe in a greater power, something like God. I would take comfort in the knowledge that things happened—fathers die even after they have had a miracle, statues weep mysterious oil— that we could not understand.

But I was in Audrey's Chapel in Worcester, Massachusetts, and I was cynical. The Virgin Mary was everywhere, in plastic and plaster, as the Virgin of Guadalupe with her golden rays around her and as the young innocent girl in a blue shawl. She was all around me and I knew that these statues of her could not weep.

Loss had made me bitter. Sometimes I found myself thinking terrible thoughts: that our acts were meaningless, that there was nothing after death but emptiness. I tried to remind myself that if this were true, then how did Mama Rose come to me that September night and warn me of my father's death? How did I explain the power of love, the miracles around me that I still believed until recently? Hadn't I still been willing to accept Augustine's "miracle of miracles," even right after my father's death? Now another quote from Augustine rang more true: "I became to myself a barren land."

I sat on the wooden bench in the chapel and tried to clear my mind. The room was an assault on my senses, an overload of images. There was Audrey as a healthy, normal little girl before the accident. And there she was in picture after picture in her coma, with priests and statues and a close-up blown up so large that I could see a tear in the corner of her eyes. There were collages of sayings and photographs. One had as its center: AUDREY: THE NAME MEANS GOLDEN. One collage referred to the bombing of Hiroshima on August 9, the day that over forty years later Audrey fell into the family pool. This place was not unlike all of the shrines to saints I had visited, except this shrine was to a living teenager who lay in a coma somewhere on the other side of the closed door.

As I sat trying to sort out what I saw and felt, people kept coming in. A steady stream arrived, grandmothers with their grandchildren, elderly women alone, a few young men. At times there were twenty of us inside, then it dropped to about a dozen. But people never stopped arriving, walking the few blocks from the main street, through the well-tended neighborhood, to this house at the end of a dead-end road.

Everything inside glistened. The neck on the tall statue of Jesus shines. The foot of the Virgin of Guadalupe. The tip of a crucifix, whose cup almost overflowed with oil. A framed picture of the shroud of Turin was so stained with moisture it was hard to see it clearly. Even the walls were tear-streaked. That was what it looked like: rivers of tears running down the walls, staining them.

I thought of the living room in an old house we had rented. A large, irregularly shaped damp spot appeared on the wall there and no one could determine its origin. Plumbers and carpenters and contractors remained stumped. Until finally, years after we moved out, someone found a leak above from a hole in a pipe and the mystery was solved.

I thought too of the way the lights that hung over the altar shone on the statues. Couldn't they be the source of Mary's glistening face? I understood the reason for the sign that said: DO NOT TOUCH, MARY AND JESUS WILL TOUCH YOU. There was nothing I wanted more than to sneak a touch, to run my fingers along one of the statues' cheeks and see if it was, as it appeared to be, wet.

From the house beyond the garage came the sounds of children laughing. I could hear small feet running, and then laughter and squeals of delight. When it grew quiet, one of the white-haired men appeared and gave the children in the chapel rosary beads. Then a priest led us in a prayer. I was struck by how easily the words of Catholic prayers came back to me, even though I had not said them regularly in three decades. The familiar words tumbled from my mouth, soothing me.

The priest began to recite the Our Father, and the voices around me joined in. Suddenly I was back in my father's hospital room on the Easter weekend when he almost died. A priest was called in to give the Sacrament of the Sick, what we used to call the Last Rites. Our family was around my father, all of us crying. The priest sprinkled him with holy water. Then he began to say the Our Father. Unbidden, we joined him, our voices coming together as these voices did today. That April morning, I was filled with a fear so large I could not imagine living with it. In his book *A Grief Observed*, C. S. Lewis wrote that grief feels like fear. Perhaps that day I took my first giant step into the grief that was about to take over my life.

Now, sitting among these strangers, the still face of Audrey Santo looking down upon me in black and white, beside tearstained walls, I said those words again for the first time since that day at my father's side. There was no fear now. It had been replaced by something else. I thought of Emily Dickinson's phrase, "quartz contentment." Although she referred to her own isolation, she meant it as something more, the settlement the soul makes in the face of the unfathomable.

My soul was beginning to settle. Now I had to understand how and where.

"Well," I asked Ariane and Grace as we walked up Audrey's street to our car, "what did you think?"

"I wanted to touch one of those statues," Ariane said.

"So did I," I agreed.

"I mean, they were wet. But what was that stuff?"

I frowned, remembering how willing I had been to blame a trick of light.

"Are you sure they were wet?" I asked her.

"Oh, yes," she said.

Grace touched her own cheeks. "Mama," she said, "they were crying."

We had reached the car and while I fumbled for my keys Ariane said, "That was amazing."

"You're right," I said. "It is amazing."

Amazing, but not enough to restore my faith. Odd that I could accept the possibility that something unexplainable was happening in Worcester but not have it open the door for me to find my way out of despair. We made the drive back to Rhode Island, and I continued my research.

One morning, I opened *The New York Times* and saw an ad for Air France Super Saver tickets to Paris during February, the very month in which school vacation fell. My old self would have read this as a good omen. The timing was right, the price affordable. My stack labelled "France" was one of the fattest; a country rich with miracles, from the obvious Lourdes to out-of-the-way places that boasted cures for everything from infertility to eczema. But my empty self saw it only for its practicality. I called Air France's 800 number and booked five seats for February 13, 1999. This was how modern American women began their pilgrimages in search of the hardest miracle of all.

france

WHEN I WORKED AS a flight attendant, I travelled frequently to Paris on layovers and short vacations. One summer I worked there enough to acquire a wardrobe from the department store Printemps and enough duty-free Chanel N°5 and Dom Perignon to last the year. But I never ventured outside the city. I never had the time on my forty-eight layovers or long weekend jaunts. Before I knew him, my husband biked through the Loire Valley. The children had never been to France at all. The entire country lay at our feet, undiscovered.

Our first stop after we picked up our rental car was the cathedral at Chartres. What most appealed to me about it was its history as a sacred site. Like Chimayo, which had been venerated by the Tewa Indians long before Don Bernardo Abeyta found the crucifix in the ground, the hilltop where the cathedral of Chartres now stands has a significant history over two thousand years old.

According to Jennifer Westwood's book *Sacred Journeys*, in ancient times "a rough stone dolmen covered a point where invigorating energy was believed to flow from the earth; beside it was a well." The elements of earth and water dominated much of my research. Miracle powers came from the earth at Chimayo and Plain du Nord, Haiti (to name just two), and the water at places like Lourdes, Winifred's Well in Wales, and Amristar, India, and here at Chartres.

Later, the Druids worshipped in this same spot. In a vision, they saw a child-bearing virgin and carved a statue of it to place beside the well. Third-century Christians built a church around the statue and dedicated it to Mary. Between 743 and 1194, five churches burned down in that spot.

The present cathedral stands as one of the finest examples of Gothic architecture in the world. Begun in 1020, the north and south towers, south steeple, crypt, and west portal survived the devastating fire of 1194. Peasants and royalty worked together to rebuild the cathedral, which took twenty-five years to complete. Legend has it that the Knights Templar brought back the secrets of divine number, weight, and measure from Solomon's Temple during the Crusades. These secrets were used to build the cathedral.

But there are two other features that convinced me we should visit Chartres. Like all churches, Chartres has relics. Its most significant relic is said to be the tunic of the Virgin Mary, called the veil of the Virgin. Miraculously it survived the 1194 fire. Some took its survival as a sign that an even finer church should be built. Somehow I felt that if I saw this relic, it had the ability to steer me onto the right path in my search. Here I was, disbelieving everything I once held true and dear. More than Brother Andre's heart or a statue dressed in finery, real evidence of the Virgin Mary might help me, just as its surviving the fire almost a thousand years ago reinforced belief for people then.

What I read about Chartres also reiterated its ancient sacredness. Some believed that its symbolism and proportions are so powerful that a visit there can actually affect consciousness. Others believed a visit realigned the spine. There was physical evidence of this too. A thirteenth-century labyrinth, common in most medieval churches, is inlaid on the floor of the nave. It consists of eleven circles around a six-petalled rose, and it represents the ways of the cross, which is the pilgrim's path to salvation. Pilgrims used to follow this path of 851 feet on their knees; it took one hour to complete.

But the labyrinth stands not just as a medieval Christian symbol. It is also said that, when done correctly, it indicates the very point where the Druids believed the currents of cosmic power were focused. In addition, an oddly angled flagstone at the entrance has what is called a solar nail, which catches the sun's rays on Midsummer Day at noon, another bow to the spot's ancient traditions.

The cathedral is close enough to Paris that on a clear day its steeples can be seen from the viewing gallery atop the Eiffel Tower. We left Charles de Gaulle Airport, squeezed into our rented Citroen, and drove southwest the forty-five miles to Chartres. The cathedral was easy to find; it dominates this small city.

As I had during other miracle trips we'd taken together, I told the children about the cathedral. In guidebook pictures, the labyrinth is a precise circle with eleven bands of broken concentric circles. They were eager to walk it on their knees. But they showed skepticism at the veil of the Virgin.

"It's too old!" one of them said dismissively.

"Well, you know how these things are," I explained. "It's probably a tiny speck of fabric under glass."

They nodded knowingly. The year before they had been disappointed many times in Italy, expecting to see dead bodies or large bones.

The cathedral, however, surprised us all right from the start. Despite all my reading, I was not prepared for the glory of its stained glass windows. Over 150 windows were donated by royalty, aristocracy, and merchant guilds between 1210 and 1240. They depict not only Bible stories, but also the daily life of the thirteenth century. During World Wars I and II, the windows were dismantled and hidden for safety. As a result, they remain intact and splendid.

Like many large stone cathedrals throughout Europe, the inside is cold and drafty, especially on a rainy February afternoon. But the magnificence of the light cast by the windows, in shafts of cobalt blue and rose red and amber, warmed us. We let out a collective gasp when we stood beneath them. Although its great rose window, with Christ seated in the center during the Last Judgment, is perhaps its most famous, it was the one called the tree of Jesse that captivated me. The tree rises up from Jesse, father of David, at the bottom, to Christ enthroned at the top, tracing the genealogy as it moves upward.

I stood beneath this window and considered the message I felt it gave. Although vague, I felt it spoke of the importance of family. Surely if that tree could grow in its stained glass glory, spreading out of the cathedral with its many branches, my family would eventually appear. I could trace my ancestors on both sides equally as far. Then my knowledge halted. But here at Chartres, an idea took root, an idea I could not yet begin to articulate.

The ancient name for Sri Lanka, I had read, was Serendip. And from this name came the word *serendipity*: to find something important while searching for something else. This definition would come to my mind often over the next month, until through more serendipity I finally understood it. For now, though, it only took seed, puzzling me in a way that was not at all unsatisfactory.

The children were disappointed when we saw that the labyrinth was so worn that we could barely make out the path. This too struck me as important somehow. While the children tried in vain to crawl along the circle on their knees, I thought instead of the path I was on. I could no longer see my way. But what did that mean? After so much emptiness, I found myself sobbing hard enough to wander away from the rest of my family. My consciousness was definitely being affected by this place, but it seemed to be going down an old path, the path of sadness and grief for my brother and father. A path I had hoped to leave behind.

Now I felt that grief in my gut, deep and powerful. Feeling something again was good, I told myself. Better than the dark numbness that kept me awake at night. But I could not really convince myself of the merits of my heartbreak. I stumbled through the church. In the distance I heard my husband taking videos of the kids, his voice echoing across the stone structure and vaulted ceilings.

"What are you doing?" he asked them.

"Crawling across the labyrinth," they shouted back. "We're pilgrims!"

I reached the back of the church and wandered into a small room with glass cases that held various religious garments and vessels. In here, I could not hear voices or see the colors from the windows. It was a dark, quiet place, just what I needed to collect myself. I roamed the room, and the ones behind it, paying little attention to what was in the cases. Finally I had stopped crying and could clear my mind.

Taking a breath, I stared into the case in front of me.

A fully intact beige-and-blue shawl stretched out for me to see. I pressed my face against the glass. Could this be the veil of the Virgin? I had imagined a veil to be gauzy, light. I had imagined a relic to be small, a corner of fabric, perhaps. But I remembered the relic being called a "sacred tunic" in one book. I was certainly looking at a tunic. With my rudimentary French, I translated a small card perched inside the case. This was it, the veil of the Virgin.

I found myself transfixed. For someone who had felt so emotionless lately, this short time in Chartres had raised many buried emotions. Where I had nothing but emptiness lodged in my chest and stomach, I now had the churning of feeling. In my grief, I had questioned my family's belief in a power larger than ourselves. I had cast aside hope that miracles exist at all. I had doubted my faith in Christianity or any religion. Nothing held the answers I so desperately needed. But here before me I saw what was believed to be the tunic of Mary. Without knowing any of the history of how it came to be here in Chartres, France, I found myself believing it was here.

I don't know how long I stood, awed, in front of the tunic. But eventually my family found me, bursting into the Apsidal Chapel amid Lorne's shushing them. Even after we all stared at this relic, complete and lovely and sacred, I still had trouble leaving this spot. When I finally did, I would later recall it as the place where I understood I could be saved.

SINCE WE DECIDED THAT France was our destination, Lorne had been eager to show me the châteaux and wineries of the Loire Valley. From Chartres, that is where we headed. Although ahead of us was the lure of the Château de Chenonceau, a magnificent Renaissance palace that was built out of fiery passion and dramatically spans the Loire, this journey was predominantly a miracle-seeking one. So we delayed our visit to Chenonceau by first going to Orléans, where Joan of Arc saved France from the English in 1429.

I thought of Saint Joan through the eyes of George Bernard Shaw or Otto Preminger. But I put those theatrical visions aside and hoped to find something here, where she was born. Responding to heavenly voices, Joan led the campaign to drive out the English during the Hundred Years' War. A champion of Charles VII, she convinced him of her holy mission, mustered the French troops, and led them to victory right here where my family, jet-lagged and cold, now stood.

At her birthplace was a replica of the original half-timbered house. The cathedral, with its stained glass tribute to Joan, was closed. And even the dramatic story of Joan's capture by the English, who accused her of witchcraft and burned her at the stake when she was nineteen, failed to move any of us spiritually. Sam asked a lot of questions about being burned at the stake, but otherwise we left Orléans uninspired.

One would suspect that a spiritual journey to France must include Lourdes. But after my impressions from my visit there in 1982, I did not feel compelled to go again. In fact, I had read about other interesting responses on pilgrimages, similar to my response to Lourdes. Jennifer Westwood puts them into the categories of distaste, disillusion, and disappointment. She points to the horror of witnessing penitents performing sadomasochistic rituals or confronting the poverty of India as we go there to seek spiritual enlightenment. In *Familiar Mysteries*, Shirley Park Lowry writes, "Most members of 'contemplative' Eastern societies are really too poor, sick and uneducated to know and enjoy the benefits of contemplation. These millions have no choice but to shuffle resignedly from day to day, their greatest hope not a better life but a final release from life."

But Westwood cites what I find the worst part of pilgrimage—its commercialization. What remains with me about Lourdes is my horror at witnessing illness and deformities in such a public manner, and in seeing kiosks hawking holy water and postcards. Similar kiosks line the entrance to the ruins of the city of Pompeii. But once inside the gate, you are allowed to go back in time, wandering the city privately, allowing your imagination to re-create what Vesuvius destroyed.

Lourdes's commercialization was relentless. Westwood calls this "religious kitsch," and it abounds in plastic and electric souvenirs. Her theory that these souvenirs give the pilgrim something tangible to take from the place is worthwhile to consider. But she also points out that they are part of our too-earthbound ego and are evidence that we have not yet grasped the transient nature that we seek. She mentions Assisi as one of the worst offenders. Among the simple relics of Saint Francis, one finds vulgar souvenirs that eclipse everything he stood for. Most vulgar of all, she says, is the monstrosity of a church, Santa Maria degli Angeli, which was built over the tiny chapel that became the birthplace of the Franciscan order; it is completely contrary to the humble chapel that it overshadows.

"Are you sure you don't want to go back to Lourdes?" Lorne asked me as we drove from the Loire Valley to Dordogne, a mere forty minutes from Lourdes.

"Positive," I said.

After all, I wanted a spiritual awakening, not a return to the deadened person I'd become. If Chartres had started a spiritual stirring, I did not want Lourdes to squelch it before I understood what it meant. This early spiritual stirring was a longing for renewal of faith in God and the optimism and confidence that had always sustained me. If faith is accepting things that cannot be proven, then my moving experience at Chartres had brought me closer to having faith again.

Something stuck in my mind long after we left Chartres and drove through the French countryside: the image of all the pilgrims who had gone there, traditionally barefoot, over the last thousand years. All of those people had found their way to that spot to walk the labyrinth on their knees and to mark a point in their own spiritual Odyssey. It is said that the labyrinth represents the pilgrim's path to salvation; was it possible, I wondered as we drove, that my visit had begun a path to my own salvation?

THE CAVES OF THE Dordogne region of France yield many treasures, including the astonishing Paleolithic paintings discovered by two young boys and their dog, Rocket, back in 1940. The cave paintings of Lascaux are not far from Rocamadour, where religious pilgrims have flocked since 1166, when an ancient grave and sepulcher containing an undecayed body was found in a cave high in the mountains near Souillac, east of Bordeaux.

The name *Rocamadour* has a double meaning: the langue d'oc expression *roc amator* means "he who likes the rock," and the undecayed body that was discovered in that cave is believed to be an early Christian hermit, Saint Amadour, who in folk tradition was the servant of the Mother of God.

Everything about Rocamadour seems to have two levels of meaning.

Although visitors can see the cave where Saint Amadour's body lay over eight hundred years ago, it is another attraction that draws pilgrims to this site. In a high-ceilinged stone chapel, standing above an altar, is a two-foot-high statue of a madonna. The statue is black, perhaps from centuries of candles burned at her feet. A child sits on the Virgin's lap. Both figures are elongated and thin, unlike the rounded curves of Michelangelo's Pieta.

The room dwarfs the black Virgin. Its walls are made of heavy stone engraved with thank-yous for various miracles attributed to her. In fact, the chapel is called the Chapel of Miracles and a bell above the statue is said to ring whenever a miracle occurs. It is unclear how the black Virgin and Saint Amadour are connected historically or miraculously. But there is yet another level of meaning at Rocamadour.

From the ceiling of the chapel hang dozens of models of ships, most of them covered with delicate cobwebs. Even though Rocamadour is miles from the sea, sailors believe that Saint Amadour is responsible for saving them from shipwrecks or storms, and they have made pilgrimages to this spot to leave models of their rescued ships as offerings. These seemingly unrelated stories have not stopped pilgrims from climbing the rocky site, some on their knees, to pay homage to the black Virgin.

WE ARRIVED IN THE Dordogne on a cold, rainy day. Our reservations were at a farmhouse in Pooch, run by a South African couple and their five-year-old son. Long before we made our own climb through the narrow streets and rocky steps of Rocamadour, a spell was cast on us. Here we had to pause for sheep to cross the street, their herder an old man with a knit cap and weathered face. Like a few other geographical areas in the world, I felt a settling inside me. There was something right about this place, something intangible.

Our hosts were talkative and friendly, even as they delivered bad news along with hot tea: The caves at Lascaux were closed this time of year, as was the Enchanted Railway that travelled through mountains, farms, and into caves. Closed too were many of the caves with displays of underground lakes and colorful stalagmites and stalactites.

"Is Rocamadour open?" I asked, almost afraid of the answer.

"Rocamadour," they said, "is always open."

There were newborn puppies in the house, a little boy who spoke English to play with, foie gras, and the region's black wine. We settled in happily for the night.

THE NEXT DAY, we drove through rich farmland and along cliffs to Rocamadour. The town is a maze, with little shops and cafés, most of them closed for the winter. The landscape, though beautiful, is harsh, and it is easy to understand why July through September is the busiest season. But we often travel off-season and have discovered that the disappointment of some attractions being closed is worth wandering streets empty of tourists and restaurants with tables always available.

In a sacred place like Rocamadour, that emptiness is even more stunning. Standing alone in the Chapel of Miracles, the power of that tiny black statue was palpable. She seemed to stare right at me as I knelt at her altar.

I said a silent prayer.

"I need a miracle," I told her. "But there are no words for the kind of miracle I need. Help me."

Even the children grew hushed when they entered the chapel. They ran their fingers over the walls with the words of thanks carved into them. They gasped as they pointed upward toward the cobweb-covered ships swaying ever so slightly above us.

"Is this a place for miracles?" Sam whispered in a little-boy stage whisper.

"What do you think?" I asked him.

"I think yes," he said, awed.

As in Chartres, it was difficult to leave. Lorne wanted to show me the cave outside the chapel door where Saint Amadour's body was discovered. But I was reluctant to leave. Something extraordinary existed here, something I could not name or even begin to understand. As I moved out of the dark chapel toward the gray light outside, I kept looking back at the black Virgin who sat calm and knowing before me.

As we drove north toward Cognac, I considered the importance of place in this journey. "The goal of the pilgrimage," according to Westwood, "is often described as a geographical location which attracts pilgrims because they deem it worthy of reverence as the scene of a divine manifestation or association with some holy person." In other words, there are places that seem to offer us a better chance of having our prayers answered. Even though we can pray at our local church or temple, we believe that going to Fatima or Lourdes or Medjugorje is a better opportunity.

Places where saints or prophets were born or lived have this aura. If we travel to Assisi or Siena, Mecca or India, and walk where these holy men and women walked, we will perhaps walk closer to them. This is not a strictly Christian belief: Hindus go to the places where deities have descended to earth; Buddhists visit the four sites in India that mark Buddha's life. There are even pilgrimages to places where the holy have left actual footprints. In fact, one such place in Sri Lanka attracts pilgrims of many faiths. Buddhists claim it as Buddha's, Hundus as Shiva's, Christians as Saint Thomas's, and Muslims as Adam's.

Shrines and tombs for the holy dead are other places for pilgrimages. Again, this is not a Christian tradition only. The *Lives of the Prophets* gives the location of tombs of Jewish "saints" from A.D. 50. Muslims also visit shrines and tombs of "saints" and pray to them for miracles. Buddha did not advocate such shrines; still, his relics are enshrined in many locations that pilgrims visit.

This idea of shrines and tombs as places of pilgrimage has translated into our modern culture to include rock stars, actors, and writers. In Paris, at the Cimètiere du Père-Lachaise, Jim Morrison's grave is not unlike the shrines I've seen to saints. It is decorated with notes and letters, votive candles, and offerings of beer and whiskey and cigarettes. Every year, people go to Elvis Presley's home, Graceland. There they tour not only his house but also his grave, where it is said that on the anniversary of his death people pray to him for miracles. Frida Kahlo's Blue House in Cuernevaca, Mexico City, draws pilgrims who get to see her art and her wheelchair and death mask. In the birthplace of James

Dean, thousands of fans arrive for the three-day celebration known as James Dean Days. They watch the three movies he made, have look-alike contests, and visit his childhood home.

I have made pilgrimages to the homes of many writers: Ernest Hemingway's in Key West, Louisa May Alcott's and Emily Dickinson's in Massachusetts, James Joyce's in Ireland, to name only a few. I have made pilgrimages to their graves as well, navigating snowy New Hampshire streets to find Willa Cather's grave, spending an afternoon in Rome at the cemetery where both Keats and Byron lie.

What did I expect to find at these places? What do any of the thousands who seek out the homes and graves of so many others, from John F. Kennedy to Jane Austen, seek? As with saints and their shrines and tombs and birthplaces, we expect to be closer to them when we pay homage at these sites. And by being closer to them, we are closer to God or their Muse or beliefs. Medieval Christian pilgrims went so far as to believe that if they slept at healing shrines they would be healed because the saint emitted energy there. Is this what the people who sleep in front of Graceland believe? Or those who run their fingers across the keys on Hemingway's typewriter or Herman Melville's desk?

Perhaps, I reasoned as we drove on, I was more affected by an actual place than the shrines and relics humans constructed. At Lourdes, the grotto had no meaning until Bernadette gave it one. But Chartres and Rocamadour and even Chimayo had transcended centuries and religions. The land upon which these shrines and churches stood had a history that was greater and deeper than its present one.

At the grotto of Saint Rosalia in Sicily, coins and other relics dating from prehistoric and Greek eras have been discovered. The water from an underground spring that feeds the grotto was sacred long before Rosalia's bones were found there. The grotto now forms the nave of a chapel, its roof crisscrossed by tin gutters that collect the rainwater and disperse it to the people who come to both honor Saint Rosalia and collect the sacred water with the miraculous powers.

With this in mind, we planned a visit to Mont Saint Michel in Normandy. Like Rocamadour, it has majestic and dramatic beauty. The site of pilgrimage since 708 when the archangel Michael appeared to a hermit there and ordered him to build a chapel on the summit of this island of rock, Mont Saint Michel has no relics or shrines or tombs. Instead, the place itself is believed to be a center of spirituality. I expected to arrive there and feel what I had experienced at Chartres and Rocamadour, a spiritual awakening, the beginnings of faith. Perhaps, I reasoned, each of these places would add a small piece to my spirit, until finally I would be whole again.

IN COGNAC WE STAYED at a château where the family grew the grapes for Rémy Martin's cognac. Two French schoolteachers and a French couple were also guests there, and no one's English was very good. But with the aperitif of homemade pineau served with rabbit pâté, a dinner of roast chicken and potatoes au gratin with plenty of local wine, and cognac after dessert, we managed to communicate and enjoy each other's company.

The teacher who spoke the best English asked us why we were there.

I explained I was writing a book about miracles. Despite the convivial atmosphere, I did not tell her about my personal searching.

She frowned. "What is this? Miracle?"

They all looked at each other and attempted to translate, but they were stumped.

"*La miraculeux?*" I ventured.

"Ahhh," they all said, nodding.

The teacher asked, "You went to Lourdes?"

Again, I avoided my personal visit and opinion. "A long time ago," I said.

"Because here . . . there . . . at Lourdes, there is a miracle," she said, pronouncing her new English word carefully.

"Yes," I said. I sipped my cognac.

"Today," she continued. "There is a miracle yesterday."

I put my glass down. "A miracle at Lourdes?" I asked her. "Now?"

She spoke in French to the others and they nodded and began to talk all at once.

Finally she translated, "A man went there three years ago to pray for this miracle to be cured from the disease . . . MS?"

"MS," I said. "Yes."

"And he was cured and the church investigated it all these years and yesterday they announced on the television that the church says it is a miracle. For certain. Yes." She smiled, pleased with her English.

Just a few weeks ago I might have scoffed at this news. After all, MS was known to go into lengthy remissions. Skeptics found it the easiest course to a phony miracle. Or I might have taken the fact that I did not go to Lourdes and therefore missed being there when the church made its announcement as further proof that God is not fair, or maybe does not exist at all. Wouldn't a merciful God lead me in my faithlessness to Lourdes to witness a miracle and renew my spirit?

But sitting at this large wooden table in a château in Cognac, I chose to take this as a good sign. A miracle, I thought. And my heart opened the slightest bit more toward that possibility.

EVERY YEAR PEOPLE IGNORE the warnings about the strong tides and die in the quicksand at Mont Saint Michel. The tides rise and fall up to speeds of eighteen miles an hour. The Celts believed the island was a sea-tomb for those who died in the tides. We arrived midmorning in a downpour. The island was surrounded by sand; when we left that afternoon it was surrounded by water. A causeway built in the nineteenth century has allowed two million pilgrims a year to visit safely.

The island on which the church stands is called Mont Tombe, "tomb on the hill." It is crowned by a fortified abbey that is almost as tall as the island and is topped by a Gothic spire that reaches 540 feet above sea level. Mont Saint Michel lies at the mouth of the Couesnon River, between Normandy and Brittany. The original eighth-century building is made of granite that was brought by boats from a nearby island and hauled up the steep hill with ropes. The Benedictine monastery that was added in the twelfth century is considered an architectural marvel. In fact, it is called La Merveille. The monastery was a famous center for medieval learning and during the French Revolution monks smuggled out precious manuscripts, some of which were saved.

Mont Saint Michel's history and geography made it rich with spiritual possibilities. I entered it hopeful. But those hopes were immediately dashed when, once through the entrance, we were swallowed up by throngs of tourists. Busloads of French schoolchildren, church groups, and families filled the maze of streets that wind up to the abbey, clogging them. We inched along, pushed from behind by the crowds who came after us, stuck in front of shops selling T-shirts—LA MERVEILLE they said above a picture of the rock and the church that sprung from it—and fisherman's hats and striped fisherman's shirts and souvenirs of every kind: plastic, bronze, wood.

"Let's go," I shouted to Lorne over the heads of strangers who stood trapped between us.

He had visited Mont Saint Michel before, and he had been struck by its austere beauty, the feat of its architecture, and its spiritual history.

"You've got to go inside," he said, pressing forward.

"I'm not going to get anything out of this," I muttered.

Head bent, I made my way slowly through the streets, bumping into postcard racks and creperie menus displayed on stands.

Then I heard Sam's voice, calling to me. I turned toward it. He, Ariane, and Lorne had broken free of the crowd and were climbing a set of steep stone stairs leading upward. Still disgruntled, I followed them. There were no crowds here and I could taste the salt in the air.

"This is a waste of time," I said, thinking of the other stops we wanted to make before we spent our final weekend in Paris: the cathedral at Rouen, Omaha Beach, a Brittany farmhouse where we were to stay the night among apple trees.

Lorne put his arm around me. "There are no crowds up here," he said. "Come on."

Slowly we climbed through deserted cobblestone streets winding their way to the abbey gates. Inside, an English tour was about to begin. Serendipity, I thought.

Another American family was among the group we joined. Sam smiled at their son, and the two became quick friends, playing hide-and-seek among the columns and hallways. Other than their footsteps and giggles, the monastery was quiet. A slow peace took hold of me, even as I listened to the guide's descriptions of Romanesque and Gothic architecture, of the history of this place. Her words lulled me, though she did not speak of miracles.

Lorne asked if people came here looking for a miracle and she smiled. "This place itself is a miracle, no?" she said.

WAS IT A MIRACLE that, lost in search of the American Museum and the American Cemetery in Normandy, I went into a small restaurant to ask directions and the owner was American? He gave me directions, then helped me find a place to stay.

"We've been staying at *chambres d'hôtes,*" I explained. "With three kids it's cheaper to stay where they give us dinner too."

"Tell me about it," he said with a hint of a long-ago New York accent. His own daughters chased each other through the restaurant while he made calls for me.

Finally, he found us rooms.

"She is too old to cook anymore. But her friend will have dinner for you at nine o'clock," he said, drawing me a map.

Was it a miracle that the friend cooked us the best meal we had during our entire stay in France? With miniature crème brûlées for each child, and crepes too?

And what of our visit to the American Cemetery, with its neat, endless rows of white crosses that stretched seemingly to the sea?

Was it a miracle that an old man walked there among the rows, searching for a particular name? "A pilgrimage," his wife said, shrugging.

AIR FRANCE LIFTED US into the sky, across the Atlantic Ocean, toward home. The children had souvenirs from the Eiffel Tower, puzzles from the flight attendants, small bottles of Orangina. Lorne had bought an ice cube tray with the shapes of the Eiffel Tower and the Arc de Triomphe. What was I bringing home?

I closed my eyes and tried to feel my father's presence. People had told me I was not opening myself up to that experience. But I felt nothing. He remained gone from me, distant and unattainable.

Certainly this trip had started something inside me, but I still could not see what that was. I thought of a Japanese saying I had scribbled in my research: The path is the goal in itself. I looked out at the fluffy white clouds and pale blue sky, the blue the color of my father's eyes. I had, I realized, started on the path again. Was this journey actually my goal? I could not yet say. When I closed my eyes and began to drift off to sleep, my mind was flooded with the jeweled colors from the stained glass windows in the cathedral at Chartres. The tree of Jesse came back to me in full and vivid detail. It had set me on this path. Could I understand why?

15

thanksgiving

IN A FAMILY OF so many rituals, somehow Thanksgiving got overlooked. Perhaps Nonna and Mama Rose, with their love and nostalgia for the Old Country, could never bring themselves to adopt this completely American custom. When I was seven, a cousin and I were playing at the house of a thoroughly American little girl by the name of Karen. It was the weekend before Thanksgiving, cold and blustery. Karen's mother leaned close to my cousin and me. "What do you eat on Thanksgiving?" she asked, speaking slowly and carefully, the way people do with foreigners. My cousin and I exchanged glances. "Uh, turkey?" one of us offered. Karen's mother straightened. "You do?" she said. "I thought you ate lasagna or something."

Thanksgiving is the one holiday that married cousins are forgiven for spending with their spouse's family, the one holiday that even I, the self-appointed carrier of our traditions, sometimes left early to visit friends or boyfriends. Even the food, so important in our household, does not stand out in my memory. Except for the soup. Oddly, it is the only thing I can remember Mama Rose ever buying rather than making herself.

West Warwick has a local place where everyone holds weddings and special banquets called the Club 400. A few years ago, the name was changed, but to me it is still the Club 400, named, I suppose, in an effort to conjure elegance among the town's mills and mill houses. As a child, it did seem elegant, with its maze of buildings and uniformed parking attendants. I could always glimpse a bride and groom, stiffly posed for pictures somewhere on the grounds. Inside, the dominant color was red, and I could almost always count on an elaborate fountain spilling whiskey sours into plastic glasses.

In a town bursting with Italian immigrants, the Club 400 served only Italian food. But unlike at home, where chicken marsala and ziti in red sauce often appeared on the table in the pan in which it was cooked, the Club 400 set dazzling platters of the very same food in front of us. Served family style, waitresses groaned under the overflowing platters they kept refilling. Mama Rose refused to eat macaroni unless she cooked it. Her disdain for anything in a red sauce other than her own made me equally as suspicious. But as a child I was content to study the food's presentation and pass on actually tasting it.

Some younger cousins would not even consider having a wedding at the Club 400, with its middle-aged waitresses and southern Italian food. Others selected it but chose some of the newer American touches the Club added to its menu when it changed its name. However, when I was a child, no one would think of holding a function anywhere else. Relatives streamed in, ready to be fed. We are not a family who enjoyed the small talk of cocktail hour, the delayed gratification of a five-course dinner served leisurely. When it's time to eat, we want to eat.

But the dinner chosen by the bride and groom was more important than just the quality and speed of service. Many things rested on it. The Club 400 offered appetizers to accompany those whiskey sours, a soup course and a salad course, and in the Italian tradition a pasta course followed by a meat course, dessert, wedding cake, and then plates of homemade cookies baked by each side's aunts and grandmothers. The more food, the more cost to the newlyweds. Many of my older cousins did not go to college and got married young. It was not uncommon for them to choose to serve the whiskey sours without hors d'oeuvres, or to eliminate the soup or salad course.

These decisions played into the intricate system of figuring out the size of the wedding gift. Our tradition is to give money as a wedding gift. But just how much money is determined by a formula. First, we consider how close a relative the bride or groom is. A godchild, for example, will automatically get more money. A niece or nephew who shows respect— visits dutifully every holiday, brings Mama Rose presents—will get more, as will the child of a favorite sister or brother, even if they don't show respect. The child of an aunt or uncle who died will also get more because of the pain they and everyone else has suffered.

The next consideration is how much the bride or groom's parents gave as a gift to us or anyone in our immediate family. Careful notes are kept on gift giving and we refer to them when determining the gift we are about to give. So if the bride's mother gave my mother a small gift when my mother got married twenty years earlier, the bride will now suffer. The question of how many family members attend the wedding is also considered. The gift is immediately lowered if no one actually comes; it is immediately raised if an entire family of five comes.

The final element is the meal itself. If there is no fountain at all, or no soup course, or a meat course that is considered unsatisfactory—a simple roast chicken rather than the chicken marsala, for example—the gift is less. As Mama Rose explained it to me, "Look at the food and pay for what you eat." So that is what we did. We entered the Club 400 and looked at what we got. We factored it into the formula and then slipped the appropriate amount into what we called "the envelope," although it was actually a card.

Discussion and persuasion are allowed. "Roast chicken," someone might snort. An aunt will nod but say, "She's a good girl. She comes every Christmas Eve to my house." "That's because she wants a good gift," another aunt might suggest. They look, they remember, they consider. Then the money goes into the envelope. A huge gift is one hundred dollars. But more likely it is somewhere between twenty-five and fifty. No one considers inflation. If you really want to send a message, a gift can be as low as five dollars.

EARLY EVERY THANKSGIVING MORNING, Mama Rose brought out her biggest pot and handed it to my father, who drove to the Club 400 to get it filled. With soup. If he didn't get there early enough, he had to wait in line for up to an hour behind other Italians getting their own huge pots filled with the Club 400's soup. It is the same soup they serve at weddings, if the bride and groom opt for soup. Unlike the soup we eat at Christmas, which is rich with escarole and eggs and tiny hand-rolled meatballs, this soup is not fancy. Chicken stock, bits of carrots, and tiny pasta. That's it. But in West Warwick, it is on most Italian Thanksgiving tables.

Even now, with the Club 400 renamed the West Valley Inn, and cousins dispersed across the country, that soup is a staple for Thanksgiving. Mama Rose used to serve it after the platter of celery, fennel, and olives accompanied by a small bowl of olive oil for dipping. She ladled it from the huge pot on the stove into bowls that we carried out to the table. A big bottle of cheap red wine sat, waiting. Everyone passed the bottle, pouring the wine not into wineglasses—we never drank wine with dinner—but into the soup. *"Salut!"* my father or Uncle Rum would say, toasting with his soup spoon.

Then dinner would follow, at a rapid pace. We always sat down at noon and finished in under an hour, as if to make sure we all understood it was not *our* holiday. Rather, it was something necessary but unimportant. There was the turkey, of course. Mashed potatoes, certainly. Then a forgettable lineup of American side dishes, the recipes culled from women's magazines or the Galloping Gourmet or the local newspaper. Various casseroles of sweet potatoes and canned vegetables baked with some form of Campbell's soup, maybe fresh brussel sprouts or cauliflower, Pillsbury biscuits. The centerpiece of this part of the meal was Mama Rose's stuffing, a combination of rice and sausage and turkey innards. Whenever one of us bit into something with a strange texture in the stuffing, she'd dismiss us. "Those are walnuts," she'd say as we ate turkey gizzards and livers and hearts.

Again we'd do our best at pumpkin and mincemeat pies. But the real end of Thanksgiving dinner was the roasted chestnuts. Still too hot for us to handle, Mama Rose would easily crack the shell and pluck the meat for us. My father, accustomed to something inedible back in Indiana called horse chestnuts, refused to even taste one. But for Mama Rose, this was part of the Old Country. She would lift the hot, slightly charred chestnut to her nose, close her eyes, and inhale deeply.

LIKE ALL FAMILIES, WE scattered. To New York and Boston. To California. To the American arms of in-laws. Until Thanksgiving found one aunt and uncle eating a roasted chicken alone, another with just one daughter, our own family dwindled through death—Nonna, Mama Rose, my own brother's death keeping his wife and daughter away too. One year, after our separate dinners, when everyone ended up at my parents' house as usual, the cousins hatched a scheme. Why not have Thanksgiving together, the way we did when we were very young, before everyone had a family and a house of their own? Cousin Gina grew dreamy. "Imagine a Thanksgiving dinner," she said, "that we actually enjoy." We all nodded. "A dinner that we eat slowly," she added. But more important, a combined Thanksgiving would bring our family together again, at least once a year. The cousins relished our memories of childhood holidays spent as one large family. Here was our chance to recapture that.

We worked on our parents and aunts and uncles for a year. Even though they too found our menu lackluster when compared to Easter or Christmas Eve and had complained at the amount of work required for so few people, they are not easily convinced to change even the simplest things. For instance, my mother will only stir her spaghetti sauce with the spoon her mother used—a half-burned, too-short plastic one. All of my aunts and uncles live in the first houses they moved to when they left Mama Rose's and got married. They did not like to vary menus, to tamper with traditions. For years I had suggested that my parents come to New York for Thanksgiving and they had responded by looking at me, horrified. It was not that they didn't visit me in New York; they did, frequently. But Thanksgiving was held at home.

By the time Thanksgiving of 1993 rolled around, we had several new bargaining tools. For one, I had my first baby, Sam. For my immediate generation of cousins, Sam was the first baby to arrive and everyone wanted to be with him. Also, I had moved from Manhattan to Providence, so no one had to travel far. Still, they weren't totally ready for the change, even without knowing that we were going to cook a meal full of our own specialties, a mix of gourmet Mexican and fresh vegtables.

"What about the Club 400 soup?" my mother asked me.

"Have Daddy get it early that morning and bring it." Mentally I eliminated the cream of pumpkin soup we had planned.

My mother looked down at Sam crawling around the same kitchen floor she had learned to crawl on. "We should all be together," she said. "But why not do it here?"

Each of the cousins had had the same discussion with their parents. The real answer was that in our mothers' kitchens, we would not be allowed to cook. But our standard reply had become, "Because we want you guys to relax."

She was almost won over. Sam's grin was irresistible.

Then my uncle appeared, unhappy. "Did you hear what they're trying to get us to do?" he grumbled.

"Let them do it if they want to do it," my mother said.

"But I don't like their food," he said. "I want the food we always have."

"What food?" I said, thinking of those canned green beans in some sort of condensed soup and sprinkled with canned fried onions. "We don't have special Thanksgiving food."

"The Club 400 soup," he said.

"Hood'll get it," my mother told him.

"Mama's stuffing!" my uncle said.

The two of them looked at me.

"Mama's stuffing," my mother said wistfully.

We had planned a poblano pepper and wild mushroom stuffing that leaped out at us from the pages of a cooking magazine. I thought of all those alleged walnuts in Mama Rose's stuffing, the earthy taste of the organs of animals that my grandmother so loved to eat. I thought too of those disjointed Thanksgivings of the recent past, the hurried dinners around nearly empty tables.

"Bring that too," I said. "Bring Mama Rose's stuffing."

Sam tugged at my uncle's pant leg and raised his arms to be lifted into my uncle's lap. "Fine," my uncle agreed. "Do it your way, you crazy kids."

FIVE THANKSGIVINGS LATER, IN November of 1998, the cousins and I were at my house cooking. Unlike Mama Rose, and all of her children, we like to share the labor. Everyone comes a day or two early and on Thanksgiving Eve, the cooking begins. The last to arrive gets the worst job: cleaning six pounds of fresh spinach for the creamed spinach we always serve. We have managed to spread out the dinner over four or five hours. Stragglers stay even longer to play a game or watch a video.

We serve cocktails and hors d'oeuvres, a four-course meal. There is always Club 400 soup and Mama Rose's stuffing. That first year, twelve of us crowded into my small two-bedroom apartment. This year, thirty-four people spent Thanksgiving in our house.

But in that way that holidays have, our Cousins' Thanksgivings have taken on their own bittersweet memories. My father's last time with us, he was undergoing chemotherapy. He showed up with the glazed carrots he always brought, and he managed to stay through dinner. I was leaving for Chimayo two weeks later. I watched him that day with a mixture of hope and sadness. He held court as always, telling off-color jokes, asking us for the recipe of something he especially liked. As I'd felt since his diagnosis, I couldn't believe that this might be his last Thanksgiving. There he was, tall and blond, with his hearty laugh and his true lust for life. How could he be taken from us? Having suffered other losses, I knew that it happened, usually without warning, that we lived through "lasts"—last birthday, last summer, last Thanksgiving—unaware of the importance of that particular day. Watching him leave, hurrying out the door in his tweed cap, suddenly overcome by exhaustion and nausea, my mother right behind him, I prayed. I prayed for a miracle to come into our lives. I prayed for another Thanksgiving with my father, one where he would stay until long after dessert and everyone sat, sleepy and sated, sipping wine and talking long into the night, the way he always had.

But prayers are answered or unanswered in ways we cannot begin to understand. Part of my spiritual crisis came from the mystery of prayers. I had replayed my first visit to El Santuario de Chimayo often: the small dark room, the hushed voices of praying people, the feel of the cool dirt in my hands as I dug in the pocito. I had prayed with more than words that day. I had prayed with my heart and my soul. I had felt my prayer, in a way that I never had before. For me, that ability to pray in that way marked a spiritual milestone. In the past my prayers were often deeply felt, but nothing close to the ones I uttered that December afternoon in 1996. If those prayers had been answered, if my father had received a miracle, then why did he die? His death made no sense if the other events were true.

In my despair, prayer became meaningless. At night I would close my eyes and try to summon the words that had put me to sleep through-out my lifetime, and they simply would not come. I knew that many people lived a life without faith, without God, without the comfort of prayer or a belief in miracles. And I knew that I did not want to be one of those people. My life, when it had a complex spiritual side, had been fuller and more hopeful. In my desire to regain that spiritual self, to forge a renewed faith without my father or brother in my physical life, the connection between family and spirituality took on a meaning that I had either taken for granted or had left unnoticed.

This marriage of spirituality and place and family is explored by the Japanese poet Basho, who set out on a pilgrimage to find his "everlast-ing self" in 1689. Although he had a physical destination of reaching the hermits in Japan's northern mountains, his six-month journey on foot included historical monuments and local wonders as well as tem-ples and shrines. Basho saw a link between his own cultural identity and enlightenment.

This was the link that I found in myself. To recover my faith, per-haps I needed to recover my history. Nonna had established a house-hold of saints and miracles, and that household was the source of my faith. If I found Nonna's village, I reasoned, maybe I would find my way out of my spiritual crisis.

At night I closed my eyes and saw myself climbing the arduous path Nonna had described. The village was built on a mountainside and the walk to the church was steep and difficult. But at the top stood the grand church of Maria della Libera with its mosaic facade. Perched at its high-est point stood the statue of the Virgin herself, her hands open and raised in prayer, her robe of blue and gold, a real gold-and-jeweled crown on her head. I would go to that church and find a nun. I would stand before her and say, "I am the great-granddaughter of Angelina Simone. Help me."

ANYONE WHO HAS TRIED to find immigrant ancestors knows how diffi-cult a task it is. Language barriers, miscommunications, harried customs officers, dialects, misspellings, and countless other obstacles are all thrown into our path for us to navigate. The information I had was conflicting. My grandmother always told us we were proud Neapolitans, although the town from which we hailed was sometimes referred to as Conga, sometimes as Campania. But Campania is the entire region in which Naples lies. Therefore I eliminated it as the name of our particular town, convinced that the name included the name of the region.

As for Conga, I discovered that it was a pronunciation of Conca. The only Conca I could find on the map was Conca de Marina, a small town high on the Amalfi Coast. A cousin trying to find the town several years ago went to Conca de Marina. "It's beautiful," he said when he returned. "But it can't be the place. No one would ever leave there." The story goes that my great-grandfather's family was from the same town originally but had acquired some wealth and moved to Sorrento. Sorrento starts the Amalfi Coast, so geographically that made sense. But the town Nonna and Mama Rose had so frequently described was not by the ocean at all. It was mountainous and in Campania. "We're Neapolitan," Mama Rose used to tell me whenever I acted in a way that made her feel less than proud. "We don't talk about family. We hold our heads high. We are Neapolitan." She pronounced it *"Nabolitan"* and that was how I pronounced it whenever asked where in Italy my family came from.

One aunt had made her own pilgrimage back to Nonna's village twenty years earlier. I had not communicated much with her, so I asked my mother to call her for details about the town. What was its name? How do I get there? Are there relatives to find?

My mother called me back with some spotty information. "You can't drive there," she said. "You have to park the car and walk and it's very steep. There was an old woman named Simone who lived above the grocery store. But she's probably dead by now."

Each detail made me more disheartened.

"What's the name of the town?" I asked. "Did she at least tell you that?"

"She said it's Conca de Campania."

"Well, she's wrong," I said. "Campania is a province."

My mother sighed, weary from my newfound interest in our ancestral past.

"It's Campania," an uncle insisted. "Mama always said it was Campania."

THEN AUNTIE JUNIE CALLED me.

"Do you know Al the Barber's brother Ugo?"

Uncertain where this was leading, I hedged. "I don't think so." The truth was, I had a vague image of him from my childhood, when distantly related men and women, most with Italian accents, visited Mama Rose. Their names and faces had blurred in my adulthood. There was the one we called the Man with No Fingers who showed up every Palm Sunday; the mother and daughter who came from the Farm with fresh eggs and loud voices; strangers from Jersey City and Connecticut; in-laws' relatives and the relatives of their in-laws. Somewhere among them was Ugo.

"He comes into the mall all the time," my aunt was saying. From her key location at the Hallmark card shop where she worked, my aunt saw everyone who passed through the mall.

"Uh-huh."

"And I told him you were trying to find Mama's town. He went there himself. He'll tell you all about it."

Suddenly, I was paying attention.

"Can I talk to him?"

"That's what I'm saying," she said. "Meet him at Al the Barber's any morning. Early. He has coffee there with Al."

"What's early?" I asked her.

"I don't know," she said. "Early."

The following morning at 7:30, I showed up at Al the Barber's. No Ugo.

"You have to come early," Al said.

I told him I'd be back the next morning. This time Ugo was there, getting his hair cut.

Al's barbershop sits on the one main street in my hometown. From it, you can watch the town go by. Although people go there for haircuts, it's an old-fashioned barbershop. You go there to find out what's going on around town, to talk to Al, to see old friends. You go there to find out about the Old Country. Al's smells of hair tonic and powder, the way my Uncle Joe's shop used to smell. The way, I suppose, my grandfather's smelled. It's comforting, that smell.

I introduced myself to Al and Ugo. Al knew who I was right away: Rose's daughter Gloria's girl, Ann-Marie. I still winced at that long-ago-discarded Marie.

Ugo was nodding. "I talked to your aunt at the mall," he said. "My people are from Torre."

"Torre?" I asked. "Is that where my grandmother came from?"

"No," Ugo said. He started to shuffle some papers he had in a big manila envelope. "*My* people are from Torre."

Ugo produced a road map of Italy, creased and faded from folding and refolding.

"Here," he said, pointing. "Look at this."

I followed his finger to a spot on the map, somewhere outside of Naples. "Muschiano! That's our name, Al and me. Look at that! A town with our name!"

Sure enough, underlined and marked with a double X, closer to Pompeii than Naples, was a town named Muschiano.

Ugo showed me another X, this one floating in the Bay of Naples.

"Here we go," he said.

I leaned closer, squinting at the spot where he pointed.

"Ischia?" I said.

"That's right," he said. "That's where Dr. Scotti had a house." Dr. Scotti, long dead, had treated most of the Italian population of West Warwick. "It was a beauty. Let me tell you."

I tried to hide my frustration. The map, full of strange towns dotting the mountainside out of Naples, held a link I was desperate to find. Ugo, I thought, was one more dead end.

"That's amazing," I said, watching the pleasure on his eighty-year-old face.

"But our people come from Torre," he said again.

He studied that map with something like love. I began to soften. At least this dead end was kind. And I was learning a little something.

"Everyone from around here came from Torre," Al added. "Torre or Conca."

"Conca?" I said, sitting upright. Despite the cool air in Al's barbershop, I started to sweat.

"That's where your people are from," Al said.

Ugo shuffled more papers.

"The thing is," I said, talking to Al the Barber now, "I went there. To Naples. And there's no such place as Conca."

Ugo thrusted a postcard at me. "Right here," he said. "Conca."

I took it from him gently. SALUTI DA CONCA CAMPANIA it said across the front. Ugo was talking about Rome now, how beautiful it was there, how delicious all the food tasted. But I was transported to the place on the postcard. Five pictures, bordered in red. A mountain with a town stretching out below it. A close-up of a church. A distant image of the same church. A statue of a soldier holding a gun. And an ordinary street, with stone houses and modern streetlights. My Shangri-la.

". . . the bus left me off right here," Ugo said, waving another postcard.

The church again. I turned this postcard over. CONCA CAMPANIA, PIAZZA IV NOVEMBRE E CASTELLO MEDIOEVALE. As far as I could tell, there wasn't a piazza or a castle in sight.

Ugo pulled more postcards from the envelope, different angles of the same three sites. But Conca Campania was a real town, large enough to sell postcards of, to have bus service to.

"Now these are your people," Ugo said. This time he took photographs from the envelope.

Old women dressed in black, women who could have sat around the kitchen table with my grandmother, stared back at me from a turquoise sofa.

Ugo smiled at me. "Yes," he said. "Here's more."

Could miracles come in the shape of eighty-year-old white-haired men?

"This is a Simone," Ugo said, showing me another picture—Ugo sitting way too close to a middle-age woman in a light blue dress. "She's a schoolteacher," he said, sadly. "I tried to get her to come to America with me. Who would want to live where they live? But she said no."

Where they lived looked fine to me, like any European small town. The fireplace had green and white tiles that would cost a small fortune here. The furniture was modern. In one photograph, a television sat right by the kitchen table.

I took a breath. "So this town is near Naples, right?"

Ugo shrugged. "Close," he said. "Maybe an hour."

"And a bus goes right into the town?"

"Sure," he said. "It's a nice town. Like this one."

"The reason I keep asking," I said, "is that I was just there, in Italy, a few months ago—"

"It's beautiful, isn't it?" Ugo said. He had the same relationship to the Old Country that my grandmother had: in love with it from a distance.

"Yes," I continued. "Of course. Beautiful. But my husband and I couldn't find Conca Campania anywhere. I want to be sure—"

"Well," Ugo said, grinning and tapping the stack of postcards on my lap, "there it is, eh?"

As I headed out the door, Ugo came after me.

"I have something else to give you," he said.

He led me to his car, parked right in front of Al the Barber's. I climbed in the passenger's side. It smelled new. From behind the steering wheel, Ugo searched for something. To fill the quiet, I told him again about my aborted attempt to find the town. I held on tight to the envelope he passed on to me.

"Here it is!" he said at last.

He held out two more postcards for me. They were larger, more colorful, than the others. They also looked very familiar. One was the Spanish Steps, the other the Colosseum.

I looked at Ugo.

He pressed the postcards from Rome into my hand. His eyes watered.

"Go," he told me. "Go to the Old Country. It's beautiful there."

AT HOME, I STUDIED page 20 of the road map Ugo had given me. There was Ischia, where Dr. Scotti had a villa. There was the town of Muschiano. There was Naples, a good twenty-five kilometers away, Torre del Greco, Torre Annunziata, but no plain Torre. And no Conca Campania. I looked in the index, in the section titled "Distanze Stradali," as far north on page 20 as Roma, as far south as the Amalfi Coast. The town was not there. But I had those postcards and the faces of those women dressed in black, beckoning me. I had the desire—no, the need—to find Conca Campania. So I looked at my son's school calendar and wrote, in big letters across the week of his spring vacation, ITALY.

IN HIS BOOK *THE Italians,* Luigi Barzini wrote: "Italy has been defined as nothing more than a mosaic of millions of families, sticking together by blind instinct, like colonies of insects, an organic formation rather than a rational construction of written statutes and moral imperatives. No Italian who has a family is ever alone. He finds in it a refuge . . . after a defeat, or an arsenal and a staff for his victories." That was why, late on the eve of Thanksgiving 1998, I told my cousins that I was going to find Nonna's town. Two sixteen-pound turkeys were soaking in large pots of salt water; that year all the magazines advocated brining for twenty-four hours. The spinach was washed. The tables were set. My cousin Chip, a late arrival from New York City, had decided to make pizza from scratch.

"But I looked for the town," he said, kneading the dough. "I told you. It doesn't exist."

I produced Ugo's postcards. For the first time all evening, everyone fell silent.

"Conca Campania," each of them muttered, as if saying it made it real.

Gina looked up from the postcard she held. "I'm coming," she said.

"Me too," Tony said.

"So am I," Chip said.

"We're going to find Nonna's town," Gina said.

Soon we were all teary-eyed, from wine and possibility. We had all begun to understand the fragility and fleetingness of love. We were separated by miles and death. But around our grandmother's old table we vowed to cross all of those miles. We vowed to go home together.

home

IN THE END, THERE were nine of us: Gina flew from Boston to Rome, taking the train to meet us in Naples; Tony went first to Venice, then on to Naples. I drove from Rhode Island to Kennedy Airport and a flight to Naples with everyone else: my mother, Tony's father (my mother's brother) and mother, and Sam and Grace. Since I last saw Ugo, senility hit him with a vengeance and he was put in a nursing home. Still, I had his envelope of postcards and maps and photographs tucked safely in my carry-on bag. I felt that I had not only Ugo's blessings for this journey, but Mama Rose's and Nonna's too.

The day we were supposed to leave, a spring blizzard blanketed the northeast. Roads closed, flights got cancelled or delayed. My aunt and uncle wanted to stay home instead of braving the storm. I watched the Weather Channel. A cloud of snow hung over Rhode Island, unmoving.

I called my mother. "Mom," I said. "We have to go."

She was reluctant about taking this trip in the first place. I was afraid she would side with my aunt and uncle and stay behind.

"I've already sent someone to pick up you and the kids," she said. "I'm ready."

Twenty minutes later, my niece and her boyfriend arrived. They loaded us and our bags into the car and drove us to West Warwick, where my mother waited. Then they picked up my aunt and uncle. My uncle was angry. We're crazy, he kept saying. But we managed to climb over the snowdrifts and squeeze into my mother's car.

"Move over," my mother told me. "I'm driving."

I sat in the middle of the front seat, pressed between my aunt and my mother. The smells of Chloe, my mother's perfume, and cigarette smoke were heavy, comforting in the blast of hot air from the heater. The snow hit the windshield at a dizzying rate. I glanced at my mother, her eyes focused on the road ahead. I realized that she, like me, was determined to get there. My hand rested on her leg.

"Don't worry," she told me, "we'll get there."

With her at the wheel, I knew we would. And a little part of me thought that when we did get there I might even find whatever it was I was looking for.

THERE IS AN ITALIAN tradition in which you celebrate the feast day of the saint for which you were named. Our family always celebrated March 19, Saint Joseph's Day: Joseph was the name of my great-grandfather and my mother's oldest brother, as well as his son, my cousin Joe.

Saint Joseph—San Giuseppuzzu—is the advocate of lost causes, the patron saint of the poor, the orphaned, and the needy. In some regions, his feast day is celebrated by eating lentils or dried beans, to finish off the remnants of the previous year's crop and call forth a similar generosity this year. Some villages prepare special bread, long loaves meant to symbolize a long beard. For Saint Joseph, the Father of Providence, everything must be big and spectacular. In Natick, we celebrated by bringing zeppoli, cream-filled pastries, to Uncle Joe.

When we discovered that we were to be in Naples over Saint Joseph's Day, we asked around for where to go for a feast. We heard stories about the parading of the statue of Saint Joseph, the slaughtering of a lamb, the zeppoli prepared and sold especially for that day. Sadly, these were old stories. No one could tell us it had stopped, but it had. On Saint Joseph's Day, we ordered some zeppoli from the hotel and ate them on our balcony staring out over the Bay of Naples, Vesuvius and Capri rising in the distance. Out there was our family, I thought, as I bit into the sweet pastry. Out there, I would find my way home.

COUSIN TONY GOT THE directions by phone from the police in Conca.

Everyone in Naples we asked gave us the same response I had

received a year earlier. They had never heard of Conca Campania. One thing was certain: We were not Neapolitan. The concierge in our hotel in Naples came up with the idea of calling the police. The town, we learned, was called Conca *della* Campania, part of Caserta. When Tony appeared in my doorway, he waved the paper with the directions written on it like a flag of victory. Like me, Tony had hope about this mission.

The next morning, the nine of us piled into the rented Mercedes van. The three cousins sat up front: Tony the driver, and Gina and I the navigators. The air in the van that day held excitement. I had notes written on scraps of paper, questions I wanted answered. Would I find a new generation of nuns at the church? Would they know the prayers and healing techniques Nonna had learned there? Would anyone know the name of Angelina Simone, even from old stories that had been passed down? What loomed largest for me was if this trip would help me with my struggle. So many pieces had to come together. The first one was getting there.

We travelled through unremarkable countryside, through small but modern towns. Soon we lost sight of Mount Vesuvius and the other landmarks that had grown familiar during our stay in Naples. It didn't take long for us to reach the exit off the highway and begin to climb up curvy mountain roads. The vineyards and gardens that covered the land there looked like the ones the old Italians kept in the neighborhood in West Warwick. It was hilly there too, and the immigrants from this part of Italy duplicated the landscape I watched unfold now. Every now and then the bent figure of a woman in black with a scarf tied around her head, working the soil, reminded me of Nonna. As a child I watched her from our back steps, hoeing and planting and watering, just as these women were doing.

A turnoff up ahead pointed toward Torre.

"That's Ugo's town," I said. I knew our own was nearby.

Then another sign appeared. In large letters: CONCA DELLA CAMPA-NIA. Tony slammed on the brakes. By now we were so excited we all shouted at once. Tony took all of our cameras and got out to snap pictures of the sign. Behind me, my mother and her brother stared, unbelieving. They had heard about this place their entire lives and had never expected to visit it. But here they were.

do not go gentle | 229

The road grew narrower, steeper, curvier.

"Nonna used to walk these roads with stones on her head when she was a little girl," Uncle Chuck said. "Look how hard her life was."

We drove and drove without reaching any town at all. A few stone houses lined the street, their shutters thrown open. Framed in one window sat an old woman, toothless. Her head wrapped with a scarf, dressed in black, she looked out at her world.

"Maybe we should ask if this is it," someone said, and Tony squealed to a stop across the street.

"My God," my mother said softly, "she looks like my grandmother." Unlike my little-girl fear of Nonna, with her missing teeth and foreign words and bad smell, my mother adored her. Nonna showed her a kindness that her own mother, with ten children, could not.

The Italian we spoke was in a dialect so thick that even the Neapolitans had trouble understanding. My mother started every dialogue by apologizing for speaking like a peasant. But now, as she walked from the van to the old woman, calling *"Senora!"* and explaining our purpose, the old woman's creased face brightened. She held out her arms and nodded enthusiastically. I heard the names, Angelina Simone and Giuseppe Urgolo, and then excited Italian. Another woman appeared at the window, this one middle-aged. There was pointing up the road, and more talk.

"They understand me," my mother said. "They understand me perfectly."

My uncle joined them. His Italian was not as good, but he too was grinning and nodding.

"Doesn't she remind you of Grandma?" my mother asked him. She took the old woman's face in her hands and kissed her on the cheek, as if that kiss could somehow reach Nonna.

We cousins snapped pictures, and then, after more kisses, we all got back in the van.

"Are they related to us?" we asked.

"No," my mother said.

"Do they know any Simones?"

She shook her head.

"Is this the town?"

Again she shook her head. "It's a few more kilometers up the road."

We had not found anything useful, but when I turned to look back at my mother she was staring out the window at the gnarled vines and careful gardens, smiling.

WHAT DID I EXPECT the town to look like? Even though I had the post-cards from Ugo, the stories I'd grown up with overtook them. I supposed my great-grandmother's family was poor, that their life was hard. Her father had died when she was a little girl from a fall out of a tree. She had gone to work for the nuns as a shepherdess when she was young. I didn't know much about how she and her mother and brother lived, but the stories I did know painted a rural picture of mountains and sheep that was far from bucolic. Ever since I got the postcards from Ugo, I had been unable to reconcile the modern stone buildings and World War II statue with the town I had painted from family legends.

The road climbed and curved until a small one-main-street town appeared at the top. No one said a word. It was the town from the post-cards. It was *our* town. Tony parked the van and gasped.

"Look," he said. "Look at the name on that house."

In blue and yellow tiles above the door of the house where we'd parked was the word SIMONE.

A trembling overtook me. I was certain I could not get out of the van.

"Why don't you and Gina go in that bar and see if you can find out anything," I said.

Across the street was the type of bar that served as the centerpiece for every small town in Italy. Mostly it served espresso and small things to eat. But there was also soda and grappa and anisette, candy, and maybe a pool table or place for cards in the back. Tony and Gina went inside and we waited. We did not talk much, each of us lost in our own thoughts and feelings about finally arriving at this place.

When the door to the bar opened, Gina and Tony spilled out in a burst of laughter and excitement. They motioned us inside.

"You're not going to believe this," Tony finally managed to say. "But the guy who owns this place is an Urgolo."

We had been in Conca della Campania for less than ten minutes and we had already found Simones and Urgolos. Something inside me shifted, as if to make room for an unknown thing. I stepped from the van and stood for a moment right there on that road. Above me loomed mountains, below me the roofs of houses and the tops of vineyards. I watched as my small children walked the street where perhaps my own great-grandmother had walked, and I knew I should be there.

LIKE ALL ITALIANS, OUR perhaps distant cousin Giampaolo did not rush. Even though nine American relatives had landed in his tiny bar in the mountainside of Italy, he first had to make us all espresso. He spoke fluent English from years spent living outside of Italy. He was probably in his midthirties, tall, with longish dark hair and large green eyes.

"A hunk," Gina whispered to me.

"Sssshhhh," I said. "Remember we're related."

"Distantly," she said.

Giampaolo gave the children the chocolate eggs they loved and consumed in large quantities whenever we travelled in Europe. Inside the egg was a small toy or puzzle. In our American desire to get things done, we kept asking him questions. Did he have records or papers we could see? Was his mother, the Urgolo, available?

But Giampaolo waved away our persistent interrogating. Instead, he worked the espresso machine slowly and lovingly.

"Yes, yes," he said. "We'll get to that."

He made the dark, strong coffee favored by southern Italians weaker for us. Still, we winced when we sipped it.

The children occupied themselves with the treasures hidden inside the eggs. The rest of us lined up at the bar, eager.

Finally, Giampaolo talked. He had an uncle in London, his mother's brother, who was tracing the family tree.

"Wait until he hears you came," he said sadly. "He's the one you need to talk to. He has all the information."

Giampaolo gave us spotty details, a few unfamiliar names. He was frustrated too with his lack of knowledge. "If only my uncle was here," he kept saying.

My mother's impatience was growing.

"What about the Simones?" she asked at every opportunity.

"Ah! The Simones," Giampaolo finally said. "They're tall people."

My great-grandmother stood at five feet nine inches tall. My mother grinned. "Yes! That's right!"

"There are Simones here," Giampaolo said. "I will call someone who may know. But first, it is time to eat, yes?"

We agreed we were all hungry.

"I will take you to my friend's restaurant. It is good food."

We pulled lire from our pockets but Giampaolo pushed them away, insulted.

"But all the eggs," my mother said. "And the coffees."

"You'll eat lunch and then come back and we will take care of everything," he said.

"I don't want to come back," my mother whispered to me. "We have to find Nonna's church. You want to hear about the healing."

"Church?" Giampaolo asked. "We have many churches here."

My mother faced him squarely. She had not inherited the Italian way of seduction, of taking one's time to eat or talk or learn. She liked to get things done quickly and move on.

"My grandmother worked for the nuns at a church," she said. "On top of the church was a statue of the Virgin Mary with her arms held out—"

"Yes! That's the old church!" Giampaolo said, excited. "Maria della Libera!"

"Della Libera! Yes!" my mother said. Now she was willing to listen. "Where is that church?"

"It is in the old part of town," Giampaolo said. "Since your grandmother Angelina Simone left, the town has been damaged. Three earthquakes. The war. As the buildings fell and crumbled, the townspeople built higher. You are in the new part of town. Where your grandmother lived you have to walk. You drive just twenty meters and park and then walk down the street. You will find the church and the old houses. Young people live in this new part."

It was just as my aunt had told us: You have to walk.

The door opened and a group of teenagers came in. In the center, holding court, was a tall, red-haired beauty.

"That girl," Giampaolo exclaimed. "She's a Simone!"

Nonna had been tall like that, and fair. The girl took my breath away. How was it possible to be in a strange place and feel so connected? There was a kind of geographic memory getting triggered. Looking at my cousins, I saw that it was in each of us.

"See," Giampaolo said, "tall, huh?"

He called her over and she came right away. She was beautiful and flirty. Stephanie.

"These people are from America," he said. "Your cousins."

"Simones?" she said, delighted.

Stephanie's father had left Italy and moved the family to Montreal, where she'd grown up. They'd spent summers in Conca della Campania. A few years ago, her father decided to move back. Living here full-time was not as fun or romantic as those summers had been.

"I can't wait to get out," she told us. She was eighteen years old, and thinking of moving to Naples.

Her friends playing pool at the back of the bar called to her. "Stephanie! It's your turn."

She rolled her eyes and rejoined them, moving gracefully across the bar.

I was not the only one who imagined her as a modern version of Nonna as a young girl.

"She's beautiful," we told Giampaolo.

"Yes. The Simones are beautiful people. That is why she must leave here. This place will turn her ugly. It's dead. There is nothing here."

Giampaolo gathered his keys and wallet to take us for lunch.

"You know, many Urgolos left town and went to America," he said. He named some relatives but they did not sound familiar. "If only my uncle was here," he said again. "There was one family he told me about that had some money and moved first to Sorrento."

My mother and uncle grew excited. "That's Tata!" they said. "His family left here and went to Sorrento. Then he moved with Grandma to America!"

Giampaolo grinned too, happy that he had finally given us a piece of our history.

"So we'll go to eat," he said, "and then I will call Giovanni Simone."

By the time I arrived in Conca della Campania that day, I understood some of what had brought me there. Since my father had died, I had gone over and over what had led me to Chimayo. Why had I so firmly believed that I could get him a miracle? The easy answer, of course, was that I'd grown up in a superstitious family who believed people could throw curses and cures in the path of others.

The rules in our household were dominated by superstition: Don't put shoes on a bed. Don't put shoes on a table. Always leave from the same door through which you entered. Don't tell your dreams until you've eaten something. To dream of a baby means news is coming. To dream of losing teeth foretells a death. Cross your fingers when someone talks about a witch. Deaths always happen in threes. A howling dog is announcing a death. Never leave something in a glass you've drunk from; it can be used to put a spell on you. There is a spell for making someone fall in love with you, a spell so bad that if you use it your soul will be lost to the devil. If you are pregnant and see someone deformed or terribly ugly, you must make a sign of the cross on your belly or your baby will be deformed or ugly. If you are pregnant and crave a certain food you must eat it or your child will look like that food; how did you think people got noses shaped like bananas or eggplants? eyes that looked like fried eggs? cauliflower ears?

A magazine editor reprimanded me for writing about these things. She told me I was insulting Italians. She told me it was clear I had never travelled around Italy. If I had, I would understand that Italian culture is about beauty in art and landscape. She herself had spent time in Florence and saw nothing like what I described. "Admit it," she said of my family, of the generations who came here and the ones who stayed on, "your family is a bunch of ignorant peasants."

I do not know this woman's ethnic background but her naivete astonished me. I was not insulting Italians at all. I love being Italian, and I love that I was raised as an Italian-American. It is true that I cannot speak for all Italians when I describe the combination of superstition and religion that pervaded my family. But I can say that the neighborhood in which

I grew up was also ruled by this order. A mix of immigrants from all over southern Italy, the town knew where the witch lived, which houses were shared with ghosts, the signs people received to warn of deaths and betrayals. We were all taught to cross the street when certain women came by and to fold our fingers, extending just the pinky and pointer, to ward off evil. And it was these Italian immigrants who lined the street in front of our house, believing my great-grandmother could cure them.

For much of my adult life, I hid behind my Wasp last name, my blond hair and light eyes. When a friend or lover glimpsed my Italian heritage on trips back to my childhood home, I presented the stories of Uncle Brownie's ghost wandering our hallways or Mama Rose doing the prayer in the bathroom as quaint fairy tales. I laughed when I told them, weaving these stories the way I wove the stories I invented—an opening that grabs you, dramatic tension, a strong climax. In my fiction I created families with last names like Porter and Nash and Handy. Although my characters were idiosyncratic and quirky, they were not Italian. They did not believe that if you heard knocking at your door when no one was there, Death had called upon your house. They did not have great-grandmothers who healed people or grandmothers who lit votive candles at the feet of statues of saints.

For five books I kept my life and my fiction nonethnic. Then I wrote a novel in which the setting was a town like my own hometown. I gave it a different name—East Essex—because it was very much the hometown I remembered as a child rather than the way that town is today. But I populated it with different immigrant groups (in fact, my editor asked me to change the neutral names to more of those interesting ethnic ones) and even allowed my main characters to be Italian. Still, I only told one cultural secret: Mama Rose's code for deciphering dreams. I wrote that book after the birth of my son, when I had returned to live in Rhode Island after fifteen years away. Without realizing—or admitting—it, I had begun my first tentative steps into exploring my cultural past. It is, I suppose, no coincidence that the protagonist of my seventh novel, *Ruby*, is an Italian-American whose family hides in the world of New England Wasps.

The editor who reprimanded me for my portrayal of my Italian family must have never read Amy Tan, who shares with us the superstitions of Chinese immigrants, or Maxine Hong Kingston, whose book *Woman Warrior* begins: " 'You must not tell anyone,' my mother said, 'what I am about to tell you.' " Writing about her culture, Kingston explains, is betraying her culture. Julia Alvarez, a Latina writer, uses the phrase *entre la familia*. Everything, she says, is *entre la familia*. Her Dominican mother compared her writing to the *gringas*. "They get on the late-night TV and they tell their secrets to all America." Like me, Alvarez cites Kingston with freeing her to write about her culture. "Something about her writing about her culture, and making sense of it, gave me permission to write about mine," Alvarez explains.

For Italians, this secrecy may be even more deeply rooted. The nineteenth-century poet Giacomo Leopardi wrote: "Italians do not write or think about their customs, as if they thought such studies were not useful." And so no one writes about being Italian-American.

As much as I live in the modern world, get my yearly mammograms and Pap smears, take Advil and TheraFlu and cough medicine when I need them, I believe still in this other powerful thing. I still call my aunt to say the prayer for me when relationships or work are precarious or uncertain. I have been known to consult psychics and tarot cards. I believe that Mama Rose stopped my bloody noses when I was a child, got rid of my mal occhio, cured my earaches and sore throats.

Before my father died, I believed in miracles enough to think that I could find one for him and save his life. As I stood in a bar on a street in Conca della Campania, I had lost that faith in powers greater than me. I had lost my father. In many ways, I had lost so many important things that I could find nothing to believe in anymore. By going back to Nonna's hometown, I realized, there was a chance that something greater than me would enter my world again. I did not know what that thing was. But I felt that I had to be open to it, despite my emptiness and faithlessness. And I felt too, that day, that Nonna had led me back.

AFTER LUNCH, ONCE AGAIN gathered in Giampaolo's bar, we tried to link our tenuous family ties.

"My uncle knows everything," Giampaolo said again, washing the espresso cups.

"Maybe we could go to the town hall," I suggested.

"What day is today? Thursday?" He shook his mane of dark wavy hair. "It's closed. Why didn't you say this earlier? They were open when you were here this morning. Now, no."

What I felt at that moment was dread. This was it. I had come this far and found these glimpses of my ancestral past, but nothing more. A large part of me was smug, as if I had proven that my faithlessness was founded. We are born and we die and all that happens in between is only fleetingly meaningless. There is nothing before and nothing after. That was why my father and my brother could so easily disappear from my life. If I had come here hoping to find a spiritual reawakening through family, the message I was getting seemed to shut out this path.

Giampaolo was looking through a thin telephone book now.

My mother rolled her eyes at me. This dead end had the same effect on her, no doubt.

"Forget the Urgolos," she said. "We want the Simones."

"That's who I'm calling," Giampaolo told us. "Giovanni Simone. He lives in the old part of town."

As Giampaolo dialled and began a conversation in rapid Italian, my mother tugged at my arm. "Let's go," she said. "We're not going to find anything out."

Giampaolo took the phone from his ear and said in English, "Do you have a relative named Rosindo? In Connecticut?"

"No," my mother said. She tugged my arm harder. "Come on."

My aunt was on her feet. "You do have a cousin Rosindo in Connecticut," she said.

"Rosindo!" my mother said. "That's right." Now she was nodding her head and shouting at Giampaolo. "Yes!" She looked at her brother. "He was run over, remember?"

"That's his cousin too," Giampaolo said. "Giovanni Simone has some papers, some records."

My mother put on her coat and began to hustle the children out the door. "Let's go see him then," she said.

More Italian, then *ciao*, and Giampaolo hung up. "Sadly, he has business today. I caught him just as he was leaving."

"You mean we can't talk to him?" I said. Suddenly, talking to Giovanni Simone was the most important thing I could imagine.

Giampaolo shrugged.

The nine of us stood, ready to leave, to go back into the bitter March cold.

My mother walked back to the counter behind which our very distant cousin stood. "How do we find the church?" she asked.

Giampaolo pointed. "Just here. Twenty meters or so. You'll see a turn on the right. You can go a little ways with the car. Then you have to walk."

"Then we'll walk," she said.

We all followed her outside.

the miracle

OUR LARGE VAN MADE the sharp turn and began down the steep road. Here the houses had shrines in the front, with saints inside and candles and flowers at their feet. The road grew narrower. Dogs chased us, barking.

"Whoa," Tony said. "This is tight."

"Get as close as you can," we directed him.

Uncle Chuck was fed up. "Let's get the hell out of here," he said. "This is stupid."

Old stone walls loomed closer and closer. We folded in the side view mirrors and squeezed down the cobblestone road. A man shouted at us in Italian. My uncle shouted back, in English, cursing.

"Sssshhhh," we all told him.

The man began to chase us too, still shouting, the dogs nipping the tires.

I shrank in the seat, embarrassed. "This is terrible," I moaned.

"The hell with him," Uncle Chuck said.

The van could go no farther. The man caught up to us easily.

Tony rolled down the window. I imagined getting shot or arrested. But the man was smiling.

In broken English he said, "You Americans?"

We nodded.

"Giampaolo from the bar called Giovanni Simone?"

"Yes," we told him.

He pounded his chest like Tarzan. "I am Giovanni Simone!"

We broke into excited shouts, my mother apologizing in Italian for her brother's behavior, explaining he was crazy. Giovanni liked that and laughed. He told us cars did not travel this road. He told us that we were stuck. But, he added, he would get us out. With Giovanni and the dogs motioning from behind, Tony slowly backed up the van, until we were almost back where we started.

"*Basta!*" Giovanni shouted, and relieved we all climbed out and fell into his arms.

My mother gave her usual explanation. "My grandmother," she began, "was Angelina Simone. . . ." She told him what we knew, about her life here and the church.

Giovanni listened, nodding.

"Do you want to go into the church?" he asked.

"Oh, yes," my mother said, and I saw her soften. She turned to me. "The church is locked," she said. "He's going to get the key."

Giovanni motioned for us to follow him. As we walked, my mother translated for us what he was telling her. The church had been badly damaged in several earthquakes. During World War II, the Germans had stolen the gold inside, the chalice and pieces of the altar. Then, in 1983, a final big earthquake struck the town. Here, Giovanni paused. We were standing at the church now, a small, crumbling building with the shadows of a now-missing mosaic, and half-broken steps leading to a gated door. But Giovanni was looking upward, at the steeple. He continued his story. During this earthquake, my mother translated, the statue of the Virgin that had stood there for over a century was shaken. She turned around so that she faced the mountain instead of the town. They say she held the mountain back with her raised hands, and saved the town from total destruction. To thank her, they took her down and put her safely away in a vault. The church, Giovanni said, is empty.

We all stood in front of it, silent.

"I get the key," he said, walking away hurriedly.

It was not the church I had imagined. No gold glistened in the sunlight. No Virgin stood on top. But it was Nonna's church. She had walked these steep hills to come here and work for the nuns. She had brought her sick daughter here and prayed for her recovery. And she had left her daughter's hair here at the feet of the Virgin as a thank-you for saving her life.

Uncle Chuck gripped my mother's hand.

"This was Grandma's church," he said.

They held on to each other tight and stared up at what was left.

"She walked right here," he said, his voice filled with awe.

I looked into each of their faces. Tears streamed down them all. We had made it.

THE LOCK WAS SO rusted that the key wouldn't work and we could only press our faces against the gate and stare in at the empty church, with its cracked walls and strong smell of mold and neglect. But I didn't care. None of us did. When Giovanni pressed prayer cards into our hands, the statue of the Virgin in bright colors on the front and a glimpse of the valley behind her, I felt my heart lifting. What I had found here I couldn't say. But it was filling me, taking hold.

We went home with Giovanni. His wife and daughters gave us homemade wine and cookies. He showed us his papers, a death certificate of a young man in New Jersey who had died from strangulation in a mill accident. Yes, we had relatives there, in Jersey City. And yes, Rosindo from Connecticut. The name Angelina Simone meant nothing to him. But, he told us, she left one hundred years ago. He shrugged. Everyone who knew her was dead. He told us about a very old woman, the oldest woman in the town, who lay sick and dying in a nearby house. Maybe she would know something, but she could not speak any longer.

Had I known beforehand that really, in the end, I would not find out anything new about Nonna, I might have thought the trip was futile. But sitting in the kitchen of my distant cousin Giovanni Simone, in the shadow of Maria della Libera Church, I felt a peacefulness that had eluded me for too long now. I didn't want to leave. I wanted to sit and drink the homemade wine and find comfort in the familiar language that I did not understand but that filled my ears and my heart.

But we had to drive back to Naples down these mountain roads and it had grown dark. With much kissing and hugging and promises to write, we left Giovanni's house. Right out his front door, beside his garden and grapevines, stood a shrine to Saint Anthony, like the one my grandmother and great-grandmother kept. Saint Anthony, Giovanni told us, was the patron saint of Conca della Campania. He seemed to look right at me when he added, "He helps you find what you have lost."

As my mother talked in Italian with Giovanni, I studied the familiar face of the saint who had sat in my childhood home. Dressed in the brown robe of a friar, his face appeared almost childlike.

"Ann," my mother said. In the candlelight from the shrine I could see her cheeks were wet with tears. Giovanni had his arm around her. "I told him that you were writing a book. I told him about Nonna and the nuns. How they taught her to cure things, sciatica and the evil eye. I told him about the prayer." Beside her, Giovanni nodded. "Do you know what he said?"

"What?"

"He said they all knew those things here. He said everyone believed in them and they always worked. But the young people today, they laugh at it. They don't believe anymore."

I was crying too. I had stopped believing in everything, in anything.

"He said those prayers and healing worked because of faith," my mother continued.

I was crying hard now. I don't know what kept me from dropping to my knees.

"He said you have to have faith for things to work."

The tears seemed to come from someplace deep inside of me. I could not stop them.

Giovanni kissed his fingertips, then pressed them to Saint Anthony's lips. "He will help you find your way home," he said.

ON THE RIDE BACK to Naples, no one could stop talking. We traced our relationship to Giampaolo, to Giovanni. We reviewed all the stories we had heard, filling in what some had missed, trying to put it all together. Our spirits were high as we entered the chaos of the city where we dodged cars passing red lights and pushed our way through corners without stop signs.

Half turned to see everyone in the back, I talked excitedly about what Giovanni had said. In true Italian fashion, my hands flew about the air, adding emphasis. Our hotel and the Bay of Naples with the imposing Mount Vesuvius appeared. I made my final point, poked myself in the eye, and sent my contact lens flying out.

Just as I announced, "I lost my contact lens," my cousin and I watched it tumble in the space between us and we all heard it land with a small clink on the floor.

"Don't move!" I ordered.

The van pulled up to the hotel and Tony turned on all the interior lights.

"I've seen these things bounce farther than you can imagine," I said, squeezing my nearsighted eye shut and carefully running my fingers up and down my leather jacket.

"Don't bother there," everyone said as they climbed past me from behind. "We heard it fall."

Still I checked my jacket and pants. I combed my fingers through my hair and looked at my boots. I ran my hands along the seat and frisked Gina. But we were all certain it had fallen to the floor. Tony got a large lamp from inside the hotel and shone it on the floor of the van. One of the good things about still wearing out-of-date, hard plastic lenses is they reflect light if it catches them. But tonight no glint came back in the bright light. I dropped to my knees and covered every inch of the floor at my feet with my fingertips. Nothing.

"It must have gone under the seat," I grumbled.

I glided my hand back and bump!—hit a piece of metal. The front seat was fastened to a metal base, and there was no way to penetrate it. The metal ran the full length of the seat, front and back. Surely my contact lens had fallen down the crack between Gina and me and now lay somewhere in that base. The seat was immovable. I reached my arm as deep as I could into the crack but only felt crumbs and dirt down there.

"Maybe when we bring the van back they can take the seat off," Tony suggested.

"Sure," I said. "It's only a contact lens."

The next day we were leaving Naples for the Amalfi Coast and a swanky hotel in Positano. I had never gotten over my family's rejection of glasses and only wore them if I absolutely had to. Eating in great restaurants and scouring the beach at Positano for sea glass didn't rate as times when I wanted to wear my glasses. But I guessed I had no choice.

I emerged from the van, able to see perfectly with one eye, discouraged. A cold spell had arrived the day after we did and I shivered in the brisk sea air. Thrusting my hands into my jacket pockets, I pulled out my gloves and put them on.

"No big deal," I lied, and joined the part of our group headed out for pizza.

ALL OF US WERE in high spirits when we left Naples the next morning and headed down the Amalfi Coast, fueled by the fried balls of rice that we agreed ranked as our favorite food on our trip, despite all of the excellent pizza, pasta with seafood, and buffalo mozzarella we'd eaten. Anyone travelling in Italy eats well and often, but a family of Italian-Americans travelling around their own region of Italy has to eat even more to compare and contrast with how they cook the same food. My uncle refused to admit that anything we ate surpassed his own or his mother's cooking. But everyone else began each course by taking a bite and pronouncing it the best ever.

Our stomachs full of rice balls, we navigated the curves of the Amalfi Coast to Positano. I began my daily ritual of asking if anyone found my contact lens every time we got in or out of the van. It became a running joke. The weather stayed cold and overcast. Silently I was glad since I couldn't wear sunglasses when I wore my regular glasses. I found myself reverting to my childhood habit of taking off my glasses whenever someone snapped a picture.

We settled into a routine in Positano. Everyone met for the lavish breakfast overlooking our hotel's garden, where giant lemons hung from drooping branches and small, pale orange kumquats dotted the trees. Like chestnuts and pomegranates, kumquats always remind me of Mama Rose. On the rare times she found them in a supermarket at home, she filled her apron with them and sat outside to eat them alone. I can see her there, her face tilted toward the sun, as if to catch a piece of the Old Country in its warmth. Had I never travelled to Italy, I would not have known the sensual power of these, for New Englanders, treats. But now I saw how plentiful kumquats were here, and how every time Mama Rose ate one at home, she was transported back.

My uncle sensed this too. One morning he asked my mother to join him for a walk. We watched as the two of them strolled through the garden, arm in arm. My uncle plucked some kumquats from a tree and, heads bent, they turned them over in their hands, checking for ripeness. They bit in. Then they both tilted their faces upward, transported too, I suppose.

After breakfast we separated, to our balconies overlooking the beach, or treasure hunting on the beach, or shopping for Vietri pottery. At one we all met up again at Bucca de Bocca for pizza or *panini* overlooking the ocean. And then it was time for a siesta until cocktails and dinner. Every day, I stuffed my jacket pockets with the sea glass and shards of broken pottery that Sam and Grace had discovered, colorful lire, and my gloves that I had to take on and off all day as the clouds hid behind the sun and then emerged again and again.

For four days we basked in the beauty of Positano, with its houses clinging precariously, impossibly, to cliffs and its winding streets. But there was more to our good spirits than our setting. Our journey to Conca della Campania had reaffirmed our familial bonds. Each of us went there and saw our past, a piece of our history that had existed only in old stories. Until now. The fact that there were three generations of us on this trip made that connection even stronger. We had always been a tight family; Mama Rose's warnings of trusting only each other, depending only on each other, had worked on all of us. But time and geography had made it easy for my generation to grow lazy in matters such as this. Now that would change; we all knew it.

For me, of course, Giovanni Simone gave me even a greater gift. He had reminded me of the power of faith. Although at its heart, my faith had been a faith in God, it had translated into the everyday life of my family and me through the lives of saints, the power of prayer, and the faith that comes from strong family bonds. Faith gave us hope and possibility; without it, we could not believe that Saint Anthony would help us find lost things, that a handful of dirt could save a father's life. My faith had its roots in a small village in southern Italy, but like most faith, it depended on God, on giving ourselves over to what could not be seen or proven.

On our final night in Positano, as we prepared for a celebration dinner in a fancy restaurant, I tried to imagine how, back at home, I could continue on this path toward the comfort of faith. I could not come up with answers that evening, but that did not propel me back to the dark place where my father's death had sent me. I felt content as I dressed in the bright blue dress I had brought for a big night out. I took the time to apply makeup, mascara and lispstick. And I wore the coral necklace I'd bought on the street near the beach.

When I put on my glasses and looked in the mirror, my heart sank. I remembered another evening over twenty-five years ago. I was fourteen years old and on my way to my first dance. My dress was a soft shade of lilac, and my mother helped me apply rouge and lipstick for the first time. I stepped back, startled by my transformation. But when I put on my thick round John Lennon glasses I started to cry. No one would see what I could be; they would only see my glasses. Foolish to have that same feeling now, all these years later, when I knew better. Still, I longed for my contact lenses. Vanity aside, I saw better when I wore them.

Sighing, I told myself that when I got home and replaced my lost lens, I would see anew. I would take my frustration and turn it into a metaphor that worked for me. The night I lost that contact lens, I reasoned, I had been given a gift. But I was not yet able to use it. I would see that when I regained my vision again. This satisfied me. I picked up my jacket and headed to my mother's room down the hall.

"You look pretty," she said, admiring the necklace.

"I wish I hadn't lost my contact lens," I told her.

In that instant, something came over me. I *was* ready to see the world again through a vision of hope and faith. I don't know why I thought it, but I did, and I believed it with absolute certainty.

"Isn't it Saint Anthony who helps us find what we've lost?" I asked my mother. In the past, he had helped me find insignificant items, a few misplaced dollars, a set of keys. But now I knew that I had lost something much more meaningful.

"Saint Anthony, Saint Anthony, look around," she recited, "let what is lost, now be found."

I reached my hand into my jacket pocket. "I think my contact lens is in here," I said.

My mother laughed. "You've put in and pulled out more things from that pocket. If your contact lens was in there, it isn't going to be now, four days later."

My hand was trembling as I slowly pulled out my gloves and shook them. Sea glass, purple, green, and amber. Lire. Wrinkled receipts. Then nothing. I reached into one pocket and found it empty.

"I thought," I began, but it was too difficult to put into words what I had thought.

I put my hand into the other pocket. Empty. Saint Anthony, Saint Anthony, I said to myself, look around. Let what is lost, now be found.

My fingertip touched something as small as sea glass. I pulled it out and held it in the palm of my hand. My contact lens.

"Mom," I said.

Shaking, I licked the tiny green lens and put it in my eye. It was unharmed, perfect. I could see again.

THIS JOURNEY BEGAN with dirt. In December of 1996, I took my ten-week-old daughter, Grace, an hour north of Santa Fe, New Mexico, up into the Sangre de Christo Mountains, to the little town of Chimayo and the El Santuario there. In that small chapel, I dropped to my knees and dug dirt from the pocito, praying with everything I had for a miracle to save my father.

I have told this story many times by now. I have written about it and talked about it. I have relived it again and again in my own mind, replaying the way the light fell on that winter afternoon, how the dirt got under my nails, the smell of the old church and candles burning, and the breast milk on Grace's lips. In those replayings, I can still conjure that feeling of desperate hope I had then, my faith that this pilgrimage would result in a miracle. I can still remember the resolve I had that my father would live.

But despite all the writing and retelling, this story has two parts that I have not ever told. The first one happened months after that trip to Chimayo, when my father lay dying in the hospital. Four years later, the time I spent at that hospital watching him die, believing that he would keep surprising us all by pulling through, by coming home, by living, has blurred. When I think of it, I remember strange pieces of it perfectly and other pieces only vaguely, almost as if they happened to someone else.

I remember all the hours spent in the lounge at the end of the hall, a few doors away from my father's room, doing jigsaw puzzles. We would sit and work on them while the nurses worked on my father. I have always liked puzzles, and took comfort in those weeks and months in sorting the pieces, placing all of the borders together, the pale blue ones that made up the sky. There was a comfort too in finding pieces that fit together and watching the puzzle take shape, watching it make sense. Although many of us spent time doing those jigsaw puzzles—an aunt adding just a piece or two, a friend making a pile of pale pink pieces—I remember mostly doing them with my niece Melissa, the two of us sitting across from each other, silently making a puzzle.

I remember waiting, anxiously, for the doctor to come and give us news. There were several doctors and they came any time—after midnight, before breakfast; we never knew when one would show up. So we waited, jumping up and peering out of my father's door whenever we heard the firm footsteps of a doctor. It was almost never one of ours. Or so it seemed. And when one of ours finally did come, we would have talks in the hall outside my father's room, speaking in low voices. These were serious talks, talks about how he was dying and the things that could no longer be done to save him.

Sometimes a moment comes to me, a snatch of memory that is almost pleasant. Perhaps I am sitting in the chair beside my father's bed, holding Grace. She is wearing her pale green flowered dress, the matching floppy hat, her tiny purple shoes. The sun is bright outside. My father is sitting up in bed, and we are talking. What we are talking about doesn't matter. The memory is only a good one because, despite the IVs, the monitors, the smell of institutional disinfectant and cafeteria food that permeates this place, despite all of that, there is something ordinary about the moment: I am sitting and talking with my father.

One day I drove to a bakery not far from my parents' house to bring my father a surprise. One of our favorite treats to share when we had coffee together was danish pastries from this bakery. My father would get there early so that when he arrived at my house in Providence they would still be warm. On the day I went there, it was not as early, and there were not as many choices. I stared at the case, aware of the woman waiting for me, the wax paper already in her hands.

Then I looked up at her and began to cry. "My father always brought these to me," I explained, "and now he's in the hospital and they say he's not going to get better."

I couldn't stop crying, even as she cooed words of comfort to me, things like, "What do the doctors know anyway?" and "These pastries will make him feel better, you'll see," and "You're a good daughter."

I cried while I selected the danish, the cherry ones he liked, the cheese-filled kind, the lemon that he always got for me. I cried when I walked out the door, the small bell over it jingling.

"Honey," the woman said, "God bless you and your family."

I cried as I drove to the hospital, the white bakery box tied with white string safely on the floor beside me. But when I parked the car and walked through those hospital doors, swinging the box in an almost carefree manner, I stopped crying. A little cart set up in the lobby sold what they referred as "gourmet" coffee. It was terrible, really, but better than the kind sold in the cafeteria downstairs. I stopped and bought two large coffees, adding extra cream and two sugars in my father's because that was how he liked his coffee. Then I rode the elevator up to the third floor and smiled at the nurses and walked down the hallway to my father's room.

"Surprise!" I said from the doorway, holding up the box for him to see.

"Oh," he said, grinning at me, "look what you brought for us."

Carefully I pulled the string from the box and opened it for my father to admire the danish.

"Cherry," he said. "My favorite. I can't believe you got lemon." He made a face. My father did not like anything with lemons or peaches. "You can have that one," he said.

I took a lemon danish and sat in the chair beside his bed, placing a cherry one on his tray. I ate mine, complaining that when he got them for me, they were still warm and tasted better.

"Well," he said, "you've got to get there early for that."

His pastry remained untouched. He had stopped eating by then. But that too is part of the blur of those days. I remember how one nutritionist used to make him a special "milk shake": the high-caloric drink that came in a can mixed with ice cream. Eventually he stopped drinking those too.

Sometime—it must have been shortly after that morning, because it was when he was growing worse each day—I remember hours alone with him, me sitting by his bed and him asleep, breathing oxygen through both a mask over his nose and mouth and tubes directly into his nostrils. In those lonely hours—and I can't say where everyone else was—watching my father, I used to pray, prayers without words, silent prayers.

One night, late, the oncologist came in during a time like that, with me alone there with my father, praying.

"Do you know what I did?" I asked him.

He shook his head.

"I went to a place in New Mexico where they say the dirt has healing powers and I brought it back for him." There were so many details that I left out, but that was all I could manage.

"That is what you need now," he said. "A miracle. That's the only thing that will help him now." He looked over at my father and shook his head sadly.

This is all part of one of the stories I have never told. Later that night, or maybe early the next morning, when other people came and sat by my father, I left the hospital and drove home. There, I went up the stairs and into my bedroom and opened my closet. In that closet, on a shelf in the back, sat the Ziploc bag of dirt I'd brought home from Chimayo. I put the bag in my coat pocket and went back to the hospital.

I remember that it was daylight when I found myself alone again with my father. Until then, I kept fingering the bag of dirt in my pocket, like a talisman. Once we were alone, I went to my father's side and stroked his head and face. Being such a big man to begin with, even after he lost so much weight in the hospital, he never looked haggard. His face, pink from the steroids, was as handsome as ever to me.

"Daddy," I whispered, "I brought more dirt."

I stuck my hand in the bag and took out a handful. "Do you want some of it?" I asked him, but what I meant was, "Should we keep trying to save you?" What I meant was, "Do you want to live?"

My father nodded at me. He nodded and whispered, "Yes." He squeezed my hand.

I took the dirt in my hand and placed it on his chest, where I calculated his failing lungs lay. I rubbed the dirt into his skin, and my body screamed one of those prayers without words.

I have not told this story before because until I took this journey over these past four years, I did not know what to make of it. But now I do. It is an example of the strength of our faith, mine and my father's. It is an example of the strength of our love. At times, when I thought of this story, I felt pathetic, desperate, even embarrassed. But no longer. Now I understand it.

The second story actually happened first. During my life, memories of my father are often of arrivals and leave-takings. He left often, on the destroyers on which he worked in the navy. I can see him waving hello to us as his ship came into port, and waving good-bye as it took him away. Later, I was the one always going and coming. I can seen both of my parents at airports, train stations, bus terminals, waiting for me to leave or waiting for me to come home.

When I went to Chimayo that December of 1996, I took the bus to Logan Airport alone with Grace. Travelling with a newborn is difficult. There is the car seat, the diaper bag, the luggage, even the baby herself. But that morning we left, my father had a doctor's appointment, and because my mother wanted to be with him, Grace and I went alone by bus to the airport, which is an hour from home. Our flight back arrived in Boston late, and my husband was home with Sam, who was long asleep by then.

I remember how long it took after the plane landed to gather Grace and buckle her into the cradle of her car seat, to place a blanket over her and get my own coat on, and to gather all of our things. I remember how I kept touching the dirt that rested in that bag in my pocket, the hope I had then, as I walked slowly off the plane, through the terminal. The bus from Logan Airport to Providence leaves every hour, and I calculated that we had just missed one. It would be a long hour in the cold December night waiting for the next bus to come.

Just as I thought this, I happened to look up. A crowd waited by the security area; they were not allowed to wait at the gates. I looked up, and there in the crowd, towering above everyone else, I saw my father.

He and my mother had driven the sixty miles to the airport to bring me home. I saw my father, smiling, waving at me, calling to Grace and me. And despite all of the things I carried with me, I began to run toward him. I pushed through the crowd and into my father's arms.

Beside him, my mother was saying, "We weren't going to let you and Grace go all that way home this late on the bus."

I breathed in his smell: Old Spice, Vitalis, and winter air.

I was crying when I looked up. "I got the dirt," I said. "It's going to work, Dad."

"You bet it is," he said. "I'm not going anywhere."

In the months after he died, whenever I thought of him, the image that came to me was of him in that hospital. I thought of him with that oxygen mask and the tubes in his nose. I could not, no matter how hard I tried, think of all the other ways I had known my father.

Eventually though, another image took the place of those horrible ones. That image is from that December night when I returned from Chimayo with the healing dirt for my father. It is of me walking slowly through the terminal late at night and looking up to find him waiting for me. He is smiling and happy. He is calling my name.

Just a few nights ago at a dinner, I was telling some people about my journey these past four years, about my father and the dirt from Chimayo and how his tumor disappeared that Christmas. "His doctor," I told them, "said it was a miracle." I told them what had happened after that, how he had died cancer-free, and about all of the miracle sites I had visited in the months that followed. I told them about my pilgrimage to Conca della Campania and about my prayer to Saint Anthony.

When I was done, we all grew silent.

Then one of the women looked at me and asked, "Do you believe you got a miracle?"

There were times over this journey when my answer would have been different. But my journey has come to an end, and my answer came easily, without hesitation.

I looked back at her and said, "Yes. I believe I got a miracle. Yes."

And when I looked away, I saw for an instant my father waiting for me that night. I saw him alive and hopeful. I saw him smiling. And I knew that if I listened hard enough, I would hear him calling my name.

acknowledgments

THIS BOOK HAS TAKEN years to write, and it would not have been possible without the help, support, inspiration, and love of many people. I give my most heartfelt thanks to them all: My family—Gloria Hood, Lorne Adrain, Sam Adrain, Grace Adrain, Ariane Adrain, and Melissa Hood; my fellow pilgrims—Matthew Davies, Gina Caycedo, Tony Masciarotte, Alfred Masciarotte, Dorothy Masciarotte, and Gloria-Jean Masciarotte; the aunties—June Caycedo, Angie Padula, Rose Solitro, and Julia Masciarotte; my cousins—Chip Soucy, Judy Hood-Yandle, Keith Hood, and Penny Martin, Giovanni Simone, and Giampaolo Urgolo; my fabulous baby-sitters—Hillary Day, Jessi Hempel, Eryn Simon, Paul Anglin, Heather Watkins, Leah Carroll, Marielle Henry, and Elizabeth Gregory; the incredible women who have helped me with more support than they can imagine—Jennifer Becker, Barbara Bejoian, Cate Gilbane, Amy Green, Sharon Ingendahl, Devin McShane, Lila Neel, Sarah Thacher, Pam Young, and especially my friend, the amazing Tracey Minkin; my children's teachers, who have been inspiring and kind and loving—Pat Endreny and Janet Estes; Maryjane Heymann and Kristen Feeley; Elizabeth Bakst and Kristin Fraza; Suzanne Toothaker; Stuart MacGregor; all of the people who have fed me and housed me while I was away from home, including the Corporation of Yaddo and the MacDowell Colony, and those who listened and exchanged ideas with me—Mollie Falvey, Father Roca, Karen Gadbois, Polly Handy, John Searles, Fred Dolan, the women at the Women's Resource Center of South County, Leslie Snow and Jim Allen, Jan and David McClain; the people of Natick, especially Julia Muratore, Al Muschiano, Ugo Muschiano, and the research librarians at the Champlin Library; all of the magazine editors who saw parts of this and thought it special—Barbara Fairchild, Alison Humes, Valerie Monroe, Rob Odom, Dawn Raffel, David Rowell, and Kristen von Ogstrop; friends in need—Rand Cooper, Helen Schulman, Nancy Laboissoniere, and Joshua Ziff; the amazing Marianne Merola; the best agent anyone could have, Gail Hochman; the hardworking and incredible Patricia Fernandez; my editor, Diane Higgins, who believed.

And to Nonna, Mama Rose, Skip, and my father, whose spirits touched every page.

about the photographs

frontispiece

Skip, my father, and me in the kitchen, around 1967.

prologue

The shrine to Saint Anthony in the front yard of Giovanni Simone's house in Conca della Campania.

chapter 1

My father in front of the family house at 40 Fiume Street, around 1963.

chapter 2

My parents' wedding picture, November 11, 1950.

chapter 3

My father and me, summer 1989.

chapter 4

El Santuario de Chimayo, Chimayo, New Mexico. *Courtesy of El Santuario de Chimayo.*

chapter 5

My brother, Skip, in our backyard, around 1962.

chapter 15

My father's last Thanksgiving, at my house, 1996.

chapter 16

The road outside my great-grandmother's house in Conca della Campania. She walked this road to reach the convent.

chapter 17

The statue of Virgin Mary that used to be on top of Santa Maria della Libera, my great-grandmother's church.

acknowledgments

My father dancing with me at my wedding.